FALLEN NOW FORGOTTEN

The Anzacs that are now just a name on a memorial

PATRICIA KENNEDY

Fallen Now Forgotten
The Anzacs that are now just a name on a memorial

First published in Australia by Patricia Kennedy 2024

Copyright © Patricia Kennedy 2024
All Rights Reserved

*A catalogue record for this
book is available from the
National Library of Australia*

ISBN: 978-1-7635913-0-1 (pbk)
ISBN: 978-1-7635913-1-8 (ebk)

Cover images: Silhouette of Australian ANZAC soldiers against the sky. Keith Tarrier © (shutterstock)
Red poppy field over sunset, Brittany.
Kochneva Tetyana © (shutterstock)

Typesetting and design by Publicious Book Publishing
Published in collaboration with Publicious Book Publishing
www.publicious.com.au

No part of this book may be reproduced in any form, by photocopying or by any electronic or mechanical means, including information storage or retrieval systems, without permission in writing from both the copyright owner and the publisher of this book.

Contents

INTRODUCTION i

CHAPTER ONE	GALLIPOLI 1915	1
CHAPTER TWO	FROMELLES 1916	38
CHAPTER THREE	POZIERES AND MOUQUET FARM 1916	61
CHAPTER FOUR	FLERS 1916	94
CHAPTER FIVE	BAPAUME TO BULLECOURT 1917	113
CHAPTER SIX	MESSINES 1917	141
CHAPTER SEVEN	THIRD BATTLE OF YPRES 1917	155
CHAPTER EIGHT	VILLERS – BRETONNEUX 1918	172
CHAPTER NINE	AMIENS TO MONT ST QUENTIN 1918	191

ACKNOWLEDGEMENTS 213
ENDNOTES 215
BIBLIOGRAPHY 239
INDEX 245

INTRODUCTION

On the 11 November 1993, the 75th anniversary of the end of the First World War, the Tomb of the Unknown Australian Soldier was installed in the Hall of Memory at the Australian War Memorial. On that day visitors queued to lay a poppy on the Tomb, then some also placed a poppy alongside a name of a soldier on the Roll of Honour to commemorate a family member. That tradition has continued to this day when visitors to the Memorial seek out the name of a grandfather or a great uncle they wish to remember.

At the end of the First World War many households in Australia had on their mantelpiece a photo of a young man in uniform, his face was that of someone who died far too young, his resting place was far away in a land that his mother, father, brother or sister would never visit. Through the years each Anzac Day these young men would be remembered by their families who marched every year either carrying a photo of their soldier or by proudly wearing their medals.

Now that the centenary of Gallipoli, the various battles in France and Belgium and the Armistice have passed, many descendants of these soldiers are still seeking out their stories to remember and honour the great sacrifice that these young men paid so that this country can live in peace. There are soldiers who don't have anyone to remember them over a hundred years later, these soldiers have no family to mourn them. This book offers just a small selection of these forgotten soldiers as my search has resulted in to numbers I never envisaged.

INTRODUCTION

The idea for this book came about when I was researching a soldier from the 16th Battalion by the name of Charles Pennells. Charles was born in England to an unmarried mother, was abandoned by her and placed in a Workhouse. He came to Australia aged 22 to start a new life and when war was declared he enlisted. Charles landed on Gallipoli 25 April 1915 and was killed two days later; he named a friend back in England as next of kin who received his war medals. I then wondered how many young men like Charles Pennells enlisted, was killed and now over one hundred years later they are just a name on a memorial.

Searching for these forgotten soldiers has been a slow and time-consuming process, by using as a primary source, the website of the Australian War Memorial Roll of Honour Database I located the names of soldiers who were killed. There are soldiers who were brought up as a Ward of State and soldiers who named a foster parent as next of kin, or they may have been an only child, not to mention soldiers who enlisted under assumed names and many who today have no descendants to remember that they ever existed.

Several years before 1914 the Australian Government encouraged migrants from Britain to settle in Australia, many took up the offer. Now Britain was at war these men were among the first to join up. There was no system in place to prove who anyone was or their age, many put up their age and just as many lowered their age to suit.

The Army created the Base Records at Victoria Barracks, Melbourne under the command of Major James Lean and his staff of just two clerks. Every enlisted soldier had a file with an attestation form which held his name, age, religion and next of kin, also details of his enlistment, embarkation, promotion, any injuries, death or if he was missing. It very soon became the link between the men and their relatives back home.

The Attestation Officer would ensure that the soldier named his next of kin although on some files this was not done, making it impossible to notify anyone of the soldier's death. These files were marked Untraceable after extensive searches by the staff of Base Records to find any possible blood relative. By the end of the war Major Lean had a staff of nearly 400 to deal with the escalating paperwork. Major Lean left no stone unturned trying to locate anybody who knew the soldier in order to pass on his effects and medals.

Now these soldiers over time have been forgotten and I hope that anyone, who reads this book, just may place a poppy next to their name at the Australian War Memorial Roll of Honour.

CHAPTER 1
GALLIPOLI 1915

Early in December 1914 the Australian Imperial Force arrived in Alexandria Egypt, from there the troops travelled by train to Cairo then marched to Mena Camp where they would undertake their training. Mena Camp was situated on the edge of the desert where they saw for the first time the Pyramids. The 1st Australian Division plunged at once into the work of training, the first month was devoted to training of companies or squadrons, then training as a battalion. This took place for at least eight hours a day six days a week with Sunday a rest day. Late in January the 4th Brigade arrived.

The battalions would march out every morning and then would split into companies. All day long, in every valley around the Pyramids were lines of men advancing, retiring, drilling or in groups listening to their officers. At first, in order to harden the troops, they wore as a rule full kit with heavy packs on their routine marches through soft sand. For nearly four months training continued with the men of the AIF eager to go into battle.[1]

Slowly the men begun to feel like soldiers, when they left Australia, they were a mixed bag of men consisting of accountants, teachers, shearers, miners, labourers, bushmen, timber workers and railway men etc. After months of training and drills they considered themselves soldiers and were eager to get amongst the fighting. Now that they were part of a team, strong friendships formed within the squads and companies.

The 3rd Brigade, which included the 9th 10th, 11th, & 12th Battalions, were the first to leave Egypt late in February for an unspecified destination. Even though most of the troops had a dislike of Mena and Egypt it was noted that *all men turned round and had a good stare at the Pyramids as they swung into the El Harem Road*.[2] From Mena the 3rd Brigade made their way to Alexandria where the 9th and 10th Battalions embarked onto *Ioniam*, the 11th Battalion on *Suffolk* and the 12th Battalion on the *Devanha*. Destination was to be the island of Lemnos although the troops were not aware of the impending landing on the Gallipoli Peninsula. The rest of the 1st Division sailed into Mudros Harbour on Lemnos Island one month later joining hundreds of other ships, transports, warships, torpedo craft, trawlers and white hospital ships with green bands around them.

More training was now in store for the troops, this time they had to practise disembarking from a ship, getting ashore and charging forward. This they did time and time again, becoming practised in climbing down the ships' side in full kit on swinging rope ladders, in rowing and landing themselves.

The scheme that was worked out by General Hamilton (Commander of the Mediterranean Expeditionary Force), was that the Australians should land on Gallipoli at daybreak after a heavy bombardment of the hills and shore by the navy. This plan was refused by General Birdwood (Commander of the Anzac Corps), as his great desire was to make the Australian attack a simple surprise. Instead, it was agreed the Australians would land before daylight and without any preliminary bombardment.[3]

On the morning of the 24th April the troops of the 3rd Brigade were issued with 200 rounds of .303 ammunition, rifle and bayonet; an entrenching tool with two empty sandbags wrapped around it, a heavy backpack with two white bags containing two day's extra rations which included a can of bully beef, biscuits, tea and sugar. After midday the destroyers came alongside the transports of the 3rd Brigade and transferred half of the 9th

Battalion onto the *Queen,* half of the 10th Battalion to the *Prince of Wales* and half of the 11th Battalion to the *London.*[4] These were to be the first wave. The landing scheme seemed simple, after the first wave, the rest of the 3rd Brigade would go ashore as the second wave. Once ashore the rest of the 1st Division would arrive on their transports, grouped in fours and coming in at regular intervals.[5]

As the tows approached the cove, Lieutenant Colonel Sefik Aker of the Turkish 27th Regiment was looking out to sea from the Ari Burnu headland at the northern end of Anzac Cove.[6] They had been spotted. At 4 a.m. the first glow of dawn allowed men to distinguish between hills and sky which meant that the Turks could also see them. Single shots first then two or three, before it began very fast, war had now started for the Australian Imperial Force. The 9th Battalion landed first closely followed by the 10th and the 11th. In their rush to get out of the boats many slipped on the stony sea bed, getting wet in the process.

Once ashore confusion was starting to set in, the men had been told that they would have to run across ten or fifteen yards of sand, take cover under a low cliff four or five feet high, drop their packs, form up and then rush across 200 yards of open to the first hill.[7]

Something was not right; it didn't take long to realise they were in the wrong place and started taking whatever cover they could. Their clothes were heavy with water, and rifles blocked with sand and gravel. The bank in front of them was so high and steep that anyone who tried to clamber up slipped back.

On the beach where the 11th Battalion had landed, a machine-gun in the foothills 500 yards to their left had started shooting into the men behind the bank. *What do we do next sir,* somebody asked a senior officer. *I don't know, I'm sure,* was the reply. *Everything is in a terrible muddle.*[8]

The troops remembered what they were told and that was to advance no matter what. This they did, dropping their packs, they managed to claw their way up the steep and stony cliff face. The cliffs being quite high, nearly 300 feet and almost perpendicular, sandy and covered with low, thick scrub and that the air above seemed full of a swarm of angry bees.[9] Climb they did making their way inland under intense fire.

For the rest of the day confusion reigned, all the battalions, the companies, the officers and men were hopelessly intermingled but they pressed on storming inland shooting and being shot. Officers trying to find their units, instead would come across a soldier and attached him to the rest of the men they found. Battalion and brigade commanders were unaware of the position of many of their troops and the true number of casualties. By the afternoon most of the 1st Division was ashore however, all units, companies and battalions were still intermingled.

By nightfall the men found whatever cover they could, a few were able to dig in and get some sleep while others kept defending their line. With night also came the cold and as their clothes were soaked with sea water, moisture invaded all that they were wearing. Leaving their kits behind on the beach also meant that they had no food or water. A very uncomfortable night was had by all although some managed to sleep due to the fact they were so exhausted.

At the end of the day a legend was born, 25 April 1915 is now enshrined in Australia's history. On that day and every day for the next eight months' men died and are still being remembered by their descendants every year on 25 April. The rest of this chapter remembers just a few of the men who never left the shores of Gallipoli and over 100 years later don't have anyone to remember them.

Charlotte Maria Adcock, a widow from England, gave her two young sons to King and Country and at no time did she think that they would never come home to her. They left to fight for what they believed was the right thing to do, both enlisting within a few weeks of each other. The eldest son, **Frank Henry Burton Adcock [394]**, was born in 1889, his younger brother,

Frederick Brenchley Adcock [1044], was born in 1893. The family lived in Melton, Mowbray, Leicestershire, England, their father, John Henry Adcock had died in 1907,[10] after John Henry's death Charlotte and her boys made the move to Western Australia. Charlotte and her eldest son, Frank arrived first in during 1911, Fred arrived two years later in 1913.[11]

Within days of Britain declaring war on Germany Frank enlisted at Helena Vale 17 August 1914, Fred followed on 9 September enlisting at Blackboy Hill. Both were assigned to 'B' Company of the 11th Battalion.[12]

The 11th Battalion was one of the first battalions ashore in the early hours of 25 April 1915. By the end of the day both brothers had died, probably side by side. Due to the confusion and uncertainty of the initial landing there was no roll call of the troops for some days after 25 April. As a result, there was no list of killed or wounded available that could be sent back to next of kin. If a soldier did not answer a roll call, he was inevitably marked as wounded or missing. On 22 June 1915 their mother received an official telegram reporting that both sons were wounded, but 'not seriously, no other particulars available, will immediately advise anything further received'.

On Friday 23 July 1915 the Western Mail published photos of the two brothers stating that they had been wounded in action. With no further news Charlotte contacted the authorities in September asking for information in regard to her two sons, the nature of their wounds and the hospital they were in. The Army then sent a cable to Egypt for news on their condition. Reports came in from soldiers belonging to their battalion stating that yes, they had been wounded and in hospital some two months after 25 April. This would have been very distressing for Charlotte as she was trying to get any information she could on her two sons.

Sunday, 31 October 1915 The Sunday Times printed an article on the missing two brothers. *In June last Mrs Adcock, of South Fremantle received news that her two sons, Privates F. H. B.*

Frank Henry Adcock

and F. B Adcock had been wounded in Gallipoli. Since then, though every inquiry has been made, she has heard nothing further either from her boys or through the official channels. Some three weeks ago she communicated with the authorities in Melbourne, asking them to make further inquiries, and though she was subsequently informed that the Base Records Office was despatching a cable of inquiry to Egypt and would let her know on receipt of a reply, she is still without news. We publish this in the hope that someone who has relatives at the front may have seen any mention of the Adcock boys in letters from Gallipoli. If so, we shall be glad if they will get in touch with us, so that we may inform Mrs Adcock, and so relieve the anxiety, which is becoming tenser with every week.[13] Charlotte was indeed getting anxious and becoming distraught with every week. Finally, in April 1916 a Court of Enquiry, held in France, pronounced both Frank and Fred as officially killed in action on 25 April 1915. Charlotte found this

Fredrick Adcock

hard to believe but had to accept that her only boys were dead and now she was alone.

Frank's body was found after the war and buried in the cemetery at Baby 700, Row D.24. The area had been occupied early in the morning of the 25 April 1915 by parties of the 11th and 12th Battalions. His younger brother, Fred has no known grave and is commemorated on Panel 33 on the Lone Pine Memorial. On 3 June 1920 Charlotte Maria Adcock moved back to London perhaps to be closer to family as she had lost her only children.

George Willcox [39] was aged 23 years and 3 months old when, on 29 August 1914 he enlisted in the AIF at Maryborough Queensland. George stated he had been born at Kentish Town, London Middlesex, giving his occupation as Barman. George was 5 feet and 6 ½ inches tall with dark complexion, black eyes and black hair. His previous military was 2 ½ years with the Royal West Kents (Territorials) then 6 months with the 19th County of London (Territorials), he was assigned to the 9th Battalion.[14]

After considerable searching there are no birth or census records for George other than an admission to the Southwark Hospital and Infirmary. The records show a George Willcox entered, aged 5 on 10 January 1895 and discharged 20 April 1895.[15]

George was killed on 25 April 1915 during the landing on Gallipoli, however as his body was not found, he was listed as missing. A Court of Enquiry held on 5 June 1916 concluded that he had been killed in action on the 25 April 1915.

On his enlistment record George named as next of kin Joseph Ming, Ellis Street, Maryborough, Queensland who was not notified of his death until 27 October 1916. Base Records in Melbourne wrote to Mr Ming 19 May 1920 asking for any blood relative of George. He replied 27 May 1920 that George had none and was alone in the world.

He also stated that George had been adopted by a Mrs Willcox, her address was C/- Mrs A Cook, North Cottage, Limpsfield, Surry England. His medals, Memorial Scroll and Circular were sent to England to be forwarded to Mrs Willcox. There is no evidence to show that anything was received by her. George Willcox is remembered on the Lone Pine Memorial on Gallipoli.

Charles Llewellyn Williams [554] was born in Bristol England in 1878, he enlisted in Maryborough, Queensland 29 August 1914. He gave his father William Williams, who lived in England, as next of kin. Charles stood 5 feet and 6 inches tall, his complexion was fresh with grey eyes and brown hair, his occupation was Sailor. He was assigned to 'E' Company in the 9th Battalion.[16] Prior to his arrival in Australia, Charles had served for 12 years in the Royal Navy signing up 19 March 1896 when he was 18 years old and was discharged 31 May 1908 aged 30.[17] The photo of Charles appeared in the supplement to the Queenslander Pictorial 24 October 1914.

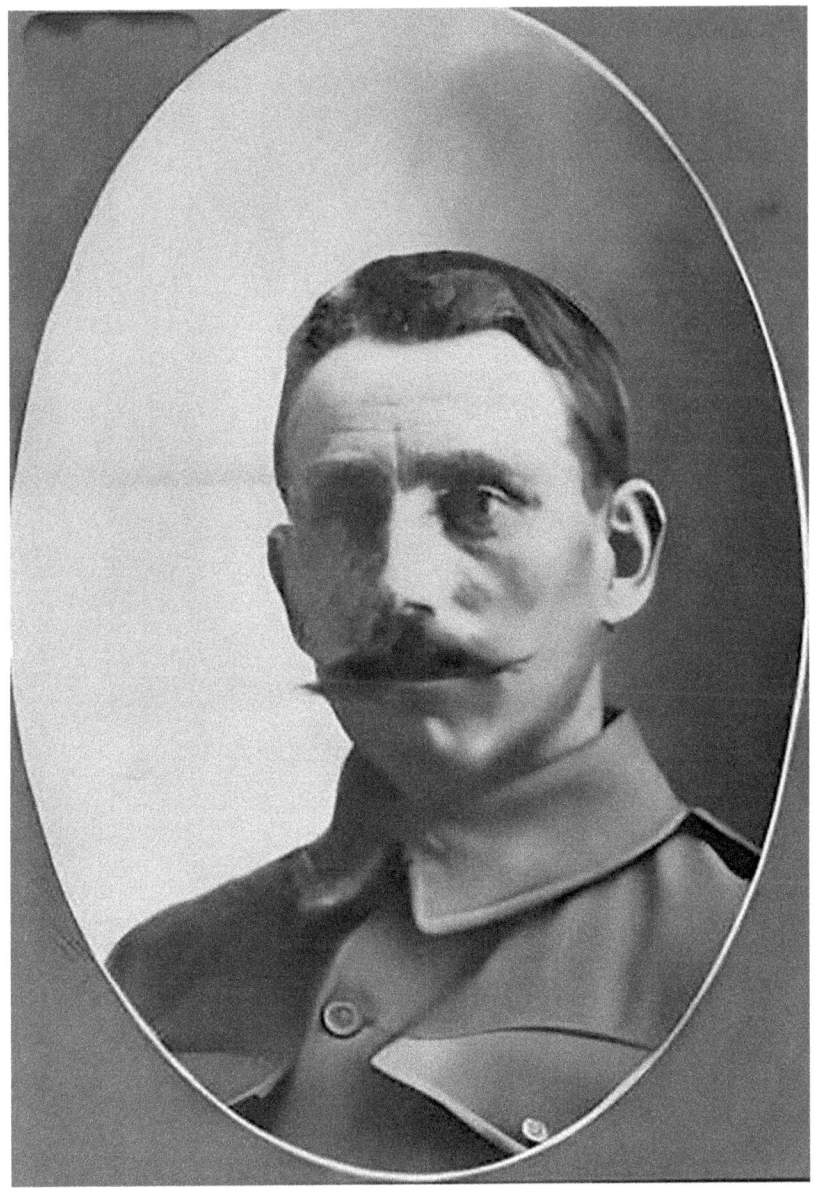

Charles Llewellyn Williams

Charles took part in the landing at Gallipoli along with the rest of the 9th Battalion and on 2 May 1915 when the battalion commander was able to conduct a roll call Charles was reported as missing. A telegram was sent to his father at West Ealing, London

23 June 1915 notifying him of his son's fate but the telegram was returned stating that the address given was insufficient A Court of Enquiry, held in France 5 June 1916, concluded that Charles Llewellyn Williams was killed in action on 25th April 1915. Major Lean from Base Records in Melbourne endeavoured to locate any relation of Charles but was unsuccessful. After extensive advertising in newspapers throughout England during March, April and May 1920 Major Lean was forced to mark Charles' war medals as Untraceable.

Charles Joshua Sussex [310] was born 1881 in the mining district of Stawell, Victoria to Joshua and Maria Sussex. His younger brother, **Joshua David Sussex [996]** was born in 1883 also at Stawell but by the time of his birth Maria's husband Joshua had been killed in a mining accident.[18]

Maria raised her two boys in Richmond, Victoria where they attended school at King Street, West Melbourne State School. Maria's youngest son Joshua David travelled to South Africa, where he joined the South African Light Horse for eight months during the Boer War. He returned to Australia to enlist with the Contingent for Service in South Africa on 7 January 1902 with the Service Number of 501.[19]

Maria's eldest son, Charles Joshua, meanwhile had joined the Royal Australian Artillery at Queenscliffe, Victoria as a Gunner. This did not last long as the Victoria Police Gazette on 10 April 1902 listed Charles as a deserter.[20]

In 1907, Joshua David was now living in Sydney, New South Wales where he was a Gunner with the Royal Australian Artillery. The New South Wales Police Gazette 25 July 1907 has him listed as a deserter from the Artillery, the notice was repeated 7 August 1907 and 11 December 1907.[21]

When war was declared the Sussex brothers were among the first to enlist, Joshua David enlisted 17 August 1914 at Melbourne naming his mother, Maria as next of kin. Joshua David was 5 feet 8 ½ inches tall with fair complexion, blue eyes and fair hair. He was attached to 'D' Company of the 6th Battalion. His older brother, Charles Joshua enlisted 25 August 1914 in Brisbane, Charles also gave his mother Maria as next of kin. He stood 5 feet 10 ½ inches tall, his complexion was dark, eyes brown with black hair. Charles Joshua was assigned to the 9th Battalion.[22] Neither of the brothers were married.

The 9th Battalion was one of the first ashore on the morning of the 25 April, the 6th Battalion was in the second wave that landed during the morning. Both Charles Joshua and Joshua David were killed on the same day, 25 April 1915. Charles Joshua was first listed as missing 2 May 1915 when the battalion had its first roll call. A Court of Enquiry, held in France 5 June 1916 found that he had been killed on the day of landing.

On 1 August 1916 a Private McDonald was interviewed where he stated *I saw him in the afternoon of the 25 April coming back from the Turkish trenches towards our line. I spoke to him but he did not seem to know me and he seemed dazed. I never saw him again after that.*[23]

On 10 June 1915 it was reported in the Service Record of Joshua David that he was killed in action on 25 April 1915. His disc was returned to his mother but there is no grave for either son. Both Charles Joshua and Joshua David are remembered on the Lone Pine Memorial.

By Tuesday 27 April the Anzacs were in desperate need of reinforcement or relief, but neither was forthcoming, the need for water, food and ammunition remained vital. Supplies were coming ashore on the beach which was already packed with the wounded, but these supplies had to be carried up those steep cliffs. That day saw some of the fiercest battles of the campaign, Turkish reinforcements had arrived and Lieutenant-Colonel Mustafa Kemal strived to throw the enemy back to the sea. The chances of doing so were never better as the Anzacs trenches were only dug to knee height or a little deeper.[24] The Turks threw everything at the Anzacs, their attacks were brutal often close-up and hand to hand. The tired and weary Anzacs pushed back the Turkish counter attack of thousands of men around 2.30 in the afternoon.

That day more Australians died, one of them was **Alexander Henry Osborne [159]** a young man just 22 years of age. Alexander was born 17 May 1893 at Carlton, Victoria, his mother was Amy Osborne, the birth index states that the father was unknown.[25] Alexander was committed as a deserted child 31 May 1893, at just two weeks old, to the Victorian Ward of State. Alexander's father was stated to be Alexander Sweetman but the State could not locate him, or his mother Amy. He was fostered out to many homes, but after about the age of 10, he repeatedly absconded until he was discharged from care 17 May 1911 aged 18.[26]

Alexander enlisted at Melbourne 20 August 1914, he was assigned to 'B' Company 5th Battalion, his next of kin was Mr J M Young (best friend) Dandenong Road, Oakleigh, Victoria. Alexander stood 5 feet 4 inches tall with a florid complexion, grey eyes and brown hair. His previous military experience was 2 years in the State School Cadets. The 5th Battalion trained at Broadmeadows in Melbourne but on 11 September Alexander was absent without leave and was fined one day's pay. On 21 October 1914 Alexander with his battalion embarked on the troopship *Orviete* leaving Melbourne the same day for Albany in Western Australia.

Alexander was listed as wounded 2 May 1915, later on 15 October 1915 Base Records notified Mr Young to say that Alexander was now listed as wounded and missing. Mr Young was eventually informed by Base Records that Alexander was killed in action 27 April 1915. Alexander's personal effects were returned to Mr Young, consisting of 2 Soap boxes, Tin pocket knife, Cigarette holder and Photos. Major Lean wrote to Mr Young 16 April 1920 asking if he knew of any blood relations of Alexander.

A reply was sent back to Major Lean by Mrs Young stating that her husband was now deceased. She also believed that Alexander had no relations at all and that he considered the Young family as his own. Mrs Young had written to the Victorian Child Welfare to enquire if the Department knew of any of his relations. They did not, his papers at the Child Welfare Department have been marked killed in action 27/4/1915.[27] Major Lean made the decision that Alexander's medals could go to Mrs Young along with the Memorial Scroll. Alexander's body was never found; he is remembered on the Lone Pine Memorial.[28]

Another soldier to die on 27 April was **Charles Percy Pennells** [83] he was born 16 October 1889 in the rural village of Burwash, East Sussex, England.[29] His unmarried mother was Harriett Selina Pennells, a domestic servant who was previously employed in the household of George and Elizabeth Hayward.[30] In the English Census for 1891, Charles was living with his mother Harriett and her parents, James and Mary Pennells in Burwash.

Just one year later life changed dramatically for young Charles, his grandfather James had died in 1892, his grandmother Mary then went to live with a married daughter, which left Harriett and her young son in a difficult situation. Harriett clearly could not bring up her son as in the 1901 Census, at the age of 12, Charles was an inmate in The Union of Workhouse of the Guardians of the Poor at Flimwell, East Sussex.[31] There is no trace of Harriett in the 1901 Census however, in 1905 she married William Diprose, by then Charles was sixteen years of age and there is no evidence to show that he had been re-united with his mother.

In the 1911 English Census Harriett was listed living with her husband William Diprose at Hunters Farm Cottage, Brightling, Sussex, on the census form Harriett stated that she had no children.[32] The census does not list Charles at all as he had embarked on the ship *Bremen* in Germany arriving in Freemantle, Western Australia in November 1911 leaving England behind to start a new life aged 22.[33] When war was declared Charles Percy Pennells enlisted on 8 September 1914 taking his oath on 15 October, he gave his occupation as Labourer; his address was the Duke of York Coffee Palace, Perth. Charles was 5 feet 7 ¾ inches tall and weighed 135lbs, his complexion was fair with blue eyes and brown hair. Even though his mother was still alive he gave as his next of kin a friend, Thomas Roff, from Mount Pleasant, Etchingham, Sussex.

Charles Percy Pennells

Charles was assigned to the 16th Battalion, 'B' Company, three-quarters of the battalion were recruited in Western Australia with the remainder coming from South Australia, their commander was Lieutenant Colonel Harold Pope. They initially trained at Blackboy Hill before moving to Melbourne on 21 November 1914 where the 16th joined three battalions (13th, 14th and 15th) which formed the 4th Brigade under the command of Colonel John Monash. Charles left Australia on 22 December 1914 on the transport ship *Ceramic* from Port Melbourne sailing for Egypt stopping briefly at Albany. He arrived at Alexandria then travelled by train to a camp at Heliopolis. On the 11 April 1915 the 16th Battalion left by train for Alexandria where they boarded the troopship *Hyda Pasha* for Lemnos Island.

On 25 April 1915 the 16th Battalion went ashore on Gallipoli late in the afternoon and by the next morning the entire 4th Brigade had landed. When Colonel John Monash went ashore, he realised that his whole brigade was scattered from Russell's Top to 400 Plateau under heavy fire from the Turkish troops. The 26 April proved to be a difficult day for Charles and the 16th Battalion, completely separated from their platoons and companies they took what shelter they could find. Many now found that leaving their kits behind was an error as they spent the night hungry, cold, thirsty, tired and endeavouring to keep alive.

The 27 April Private Charles Percy Pennells was killed, his war now over, there is no record to say how he died. Charles was buried in the Shrapnel Valley Cemetery (Plot 1V, Row C, Grave No.9). Thomas Roff was notified of his friend's death and received his medals, Memorial Plaque and Scroll. The Roll of Honour Circular that Thomas Roff filled out stated that his friend had attended Elementary Church of England School.

The information provided to the Commonwealth Graves Commission by Thomas Roff for Charles' headstone has his Service Number as 85 instead of 83. The demise of Charles was reported in the Western Mail (Perth) Friday 25 June 1915, along with his photo. His name is also listed in the UK, De Ruvigney's Roll of Honour, 1914-1919 however his Service Number is stated to be 85 and the date of his death given is 27 May 1915.

Within the Service Record for Charles there is a letter written by Major Lean from Base Records to the Office Secretary (Military) of Australia House, Strand London. Major Lean noticed that Charles medals had been sent to his friend Thomas Roff without first attempting to find any blood relations. The Major went on to state that this is not the usual practice however considering Charles' background it may have been the right decision.[34]

Lieutenant-Colonel Mustafa Kemal on 1 May decided now was the time to drive this stubborn invader back to the sea.[35] All day long the fighting raged but the Anzacs were undefeatable. The 1st Battalion received orders to relieve portions of the firing line and report to General Trotman. On 2 May while in the firing line **Sydney Thomas Smith [786]** was killed in action. Sydney was born in Wilcannia, New South Wales, there is a birth record for a Sydney Smith born in Wilcannia in 1894 to a John and Alice Smith, there is no definite proof this is Sydney Thomas although the age does match his Service Record.[36] By the age of six Sydney Thomas was a Ward of State and was placed into the foster home of Mrs & Mrs Hayward, Wilberforce, Via Windsor. Within days of war being declared Sydney travelled to Randwick where he enlisted on 18 August 1914 aged 19 years and 3 months. Sydney stood 5 feet 5 inches tall with fair complexion, blue eyes and fair hair. He gave his next of kin as Mr J Hayward, who had raised Sydney, he also stated that he had 3 years of Senior Cadets and 1 year with the 34th Infantry. Sydney was assigned to 'B' Company of the 1st Battalion and by 17 October 1914 was promoted to Corporal. He gave his occupation as Motor Chauffeur.

The Commanding Officer of the 1st Battalion listed Sydney as missing on 2 May 1915, then a Court of Enquiry held at Tel-El-Kebir on 11 January 1916 found that Sydney had been killed 2 May 1915. The Sydney Morning Herald on Tuesday 2nd May 1916 contained a memorial notice from Mrs Gertrude Hayward for her foster son. It included the words *A young life nobly ended*. Major Lean on 26 November 1920 made the decision that Mrs Hayward should receive Sydney's medals. He is remembered on the Lone Pine Memorial.[37]

A week has now passed from the initial landing with no further advance. General Birdwood, General Sir William and General Godley make the decision that Baby 700 must be captured using the 4th Brigade and the New Zealand Brigade. On 2 May 1915 Colonel John Monash was informed what is expected of his brigade. Monash did not like the plan at all and suggested that a staffer from General Godley come up and look at the problems faced. General Godley refused which left Monash most unhappy, he had to obey orders and put aside his doubts.[38]

Colonel John Monash thought that you didn't go into battle unless you had a pretty fair chance of victory.[39] He believed that the plan he was given would not be a success and many of his troops would be killed. The 4th Brigade did what they were ordered during nightfall on 2 May. On the morning of 3 May 1915 Colonel Monash started doing the calculations on the losses. By his count he believed his whole brigade may number fewer than 1800 men. By mid-morning Colonel Monash ordered the 16th, and 13th Battalions to withdraw and if needed to do so under the cover of nightfall.[40]

One soldier killed in action on that day was **Alfred Mayne** **[67]** of the 13th Battalion. Alfred enlisted 28 September at Rosehill in New South Wales stating that he was born in Sydney and was 42 years old. None of this can be proven and it may be possible Alfred Mayne enlisted under an assumed name. When the Attesting Officer asked for next of kin Alfred gave the name of S Mayne, South Africa. Alfred stood 5 feet and 10 inches tall with fair complexion, blue eyes and brown hair – turning grey. His occupation was Shearer, he also stated that he served in the South African War with the 1st Australian Bushman, again this cannot be confirmed. Major Lean from the Base Records in Melbourne knew there was no chance of contacting his next of kin. After attempts to locate any blood relations Major Lean was forced to stamp his record as Untraceable.[41] Alfred Mayne is remembered on the Lone Pine Memorial.

That same day **John George Robb [908]** also from the 13th Battalion was killed in action at the age of 28. John enlisted 7 September 1914 at the Roseberry Park Camp in Sydney, he stood 5 feet and 11 inches tall with dark complexion, grey eyes and black hair.[42] John stated he was born on Boobra Station, Goondiwindi, Queensland, occupation was Bushman, his next of kin was given as William Knulla also residing at Boobra Station. There is no record of John's birth that can be found in either the Queensland or New South Wales Indexes. There is also no trace at all of a William Knulla.

A cable was sent to William Knulla 20 June 1915 informing him of John's death. A letter from Base Records was sent again 6 April 1916, but there does not appear to be any reply. Major Lean from Base Records wrote again to William Knulla asking if he knew of any blood relations, again no reply. Base Records kept up the search but eventually had to mark his medals as Untraceable. Private John George Robb is remembered on the Goondiwindi War Memorial, at the Australian War Memorial and on the Lone Pine Memorial.

John George Robb lasted eight days on Gallipoli, a young man in his prime at the age of 28. There are no records at all on John, it may be possible he enlisted under an assumed name. It is possible that he may be of aboriginal descent as nearby Boobra Station is the Boobra Lagoon, a culturally significate site to the Bigambul and Kamilaroi people.

Following the failure of the First Battle of Krithia, by the British, down at Cape Helles a second attempt was initiated on 6 May. The four battalions of the AIF 2nd Brigade with the New Zealand Infantry Brigade left Anzac Cove in the early hours on 6 May arriving at Cape Helles 5.30am. Under the command of General Aylmer Hunter-Weston another attack would be made on Krithia. This time he believes he will be successful, now the Anzacs have arrived his force has increased to 25,000.[43] At 10.30am an assault by the Wellington, Canterbury and Auckland Infantry Battalions failed. Troops advanced in broad daylight across an open valley into gunfire from unseen Ottoman positions, they were decimated.

General Hunter-Weston ordered another attack late in the afternoon, after all he still had troops left. Using the 2nd Brigade with the Otago Battalion they to advance into a hail of bullets to within 400 metres of Turkish lines. They were slaughtered, of 2,500 soldiers, 182 are dead, 539 wounded and 335 missing – over 1,000 casualties in less than an hour.[44] In the course of three days, Hunter-Weston's forces have suffered 6,200 casualties, three times more than the Turks. There was some ground won but was the price too high to pay?[45]

A soldier who died that day was **George Jones [757]** born in Edinburgh, Scotland during 1879. George stated his occupation was Soldier when he enlisted at Bendigo, Victoria 18 August 1914. He listed his mother Mrs M Jones as his next of kin, giving her address as 42 Princes Street, Edinburgh. George was assigned to

'D' Company 7th Battalion. George stood 5 feet 5 inches tall, with dark complexion, brown eyes and black hair. He also stated that he served for 16 years with the 75th Royal Field Artillery and left when his time had been served. It was obvious that his previous military experience was taken into account when he was promoted to sergeant the day after enlisting.

After arriving in Egypt, George decided he did not want to be a sergeant anymore and at his own request reverted back to private on 19 February. Five days after landing on the shores of Gallipoli George was promoted from private to corporal 30 April 1915. Mrs M Jones was advised of her son's death however the cablegram was returned marked Not Known. Base Records kept sending George's mother letters regarding her son but all were returned. Eventually Major Lean was faced with the fact that blood relations of George could not be found, as a result his medals etc. were marked as Untraceable. Corporal George Jones is remembered on the Cape Helles Memorial.[46]

Another soldier to die during the Second Battle for Krithia was **Arthur Frederick Kitson [116]**. Arthur enlisted at Melbourne 17 August 1914, claiming he was 27 years and 4 months; his place of birth was Melbourne and occupation was Electrical Wireman. On his Service Record Arthur claimed he had been in the Royal Navy for 7 years in Signals. The next of kin was Miss Fanny Day who lived at 38 Hawke Street, West Melbourne, he also had made a will naming her as his beneficiary.

Arthur was killed on 8 May 1915; Miss Day was informed of his demise. The Weekly Times 10 July 1915 on page 52 printed a photo of the young man stating he had been killed in action. On 26 February 1918 a Mr J Williams, from Portsmouth in England, wrote to Base Records claiming that he had read in the English papers that Arthur Frederick Kitson had been killed in May 1915. He stated he believed this soldier was his son, his real name was Arthur Frederick Williams and asked why he had not been notified of his death. Major Lean replied that Lance Corporal Kitson had stated he had been born in Melbourne and that the next of kin

Arthur Frederick Kitson

was Miss Day, Mr Williams did not reply. Further investigation has shown that there is no birth record for Arthur Frederick Kitson anywhere in Australia.

Research in England has revealed there was an Arthur Frederick Williams born in Portsmouth 15 March 1889 who joined the Royal Navy in 1904 for 12 years.[47] He advanced to Signals in the Navy but while his ship H.M.S. *Powerful* was in Sydney 4 April 1911 he deserted along with two other sailors. His description was given as 22 years of age, English, 5 feet 5 inches high, black hair, blue eyes, fair complexion.[48]

The description on Arthur Frederick Kitson's Service Record has a difference of two years for birth, his height is 5 feet 7 inches, a difference of 2 inches in ten years. His complexion was noted as dark with grey eyes and black hair, while Arthur Frederick Williams had fair complexion blue eyes and black hair. The mystery here is that Mr Williams knew his son had enlisted with the surname of Kitson. Are they the same man, we will never know?

Base Records contacted Miss Day asking if she knew of any blood relations, Miss Day replied that she had known Arthur Frederick Kitson for four years and that he had told her all of his relations were dead. Major Lean then wrote to the Authorities in London 27 July 1920 requesting that they attempt to locate this Mr Williams. The reply was he had left the address in 1919 and could not be located. Arthur's medals etc. were then marked Untraceable. Lance Corporal Arthur Frederick Kitson is remembered on the Cape Helles Memorial.[49]

The 16 May 1915 there was one soldier from the 1st Battalion who was wounded while manning the firing line at Anzac Cove. This soldier was **Frederick Fergus [344]**, who suffered a basilar skull fracture. Frederick enlisted into the AIF on 21 August 1914 at Randwick, Sydney stating that he was born in 1876 at Newcastle-On-Tyne, England. An extensive search of birth records in England has failed to locate any birth for him, and there are no census records that relate at all to Frederick Fergus. There is a possibility he may have been born about 1870 as later in his Service Record his age is recorded as 45 years old in 1915.

Frederick was 5 feet and 9 inches tall, weighed 12 stone 3 lbs, his complexion dark with blue eyes and black hair. His occupation was Bootmaker serving a 5-year apprenticeship with Howlett and White at Norwich, England. His next of kin given as Mrs C Harwood, friend, at Pumping Station, Meeks Road, Marrickville. Frederick was assigned to 'A' Company, 1st Battalion, firstly as a private, then on 23 September 1914 he was made Lance Corporal. It is believed that about four days after the landing of the 1st Battalion Frederick was promoted to Sergeant, although there is no mention of this on his Service Record or within the 1st Battalion or the 1st Brigade War Diary.

The day of Frederick's injury, the 1st Battalion was subjected to 8-inch-high explosive enemy shelling, although the Battalion War Diary noted that there was 'no damage done'.[50] Frederick's injury caused a break of a bone in the base of the skull which causes severe bruising behind the ears and eyes. Sergeant Fergus was transferred to a hospital ship and taken to the Military Hospital at Valetta, Malta on 24 May. From there he was transferred to England 20 June where he was admitted to the Royal Victoria Hospital at Netley. He was again transferred to the 1st Australian Auxiliary Hospital at Harefield where it was confirmed that he had lost the sight of his left eye due to explosive shell concussion and optic atrophy. Discharged as unfit for active service he was returned to Australia leaving England on H M T *Seuvic* 8 October 1915.

On 23 November, one day after his ship arrived in Melbourne Frederick took a walk through the city. He stopped for a rest in McKillop Street taking a seat on a ledge outside a printer where he was killed by an unfortunate accident. The Age (Melbourne) reported the accident the next day.

A SOLDIER'S DEATH

After having come through all the dangers and horrors of modern warfare with a loss of an eye, a returned Australian soldier, whose name is believed to be Frederick Fergus, a sergeant in 'A' Company 1st Battalion AIF, met his death yesterday in a lift accident. Although nobody witnessed the accident, it appears that deceased was sitting on a ledge near the bottom of a lift well on the premises of G A Green, printer, M'Killop-st, when a descending lift caught him and crushed his chest in, apparently killing him instantly. He was taken to the Melbourne Hospital, and subsequently removed to the Morgue. In his pockets were found several letters addressed to 'Sergeant Fergus'. They were posted in Marrickville, Sydney. Documents in his possession indicated that same man had served at Gallipoli, where he had lost the sight of one eye. He had been an inmate of the Monto Video Camp Hospital, Weymouth, and had only recently returned to Australia. Deceased was a man of splendid physique.[51]

An inquest was held by the Coroner's Office, at Melbourne on 6 December 1915 into the death of Frederick where it was determined that he had died by misadventure.[52] The Army was officially informed on the cause of death 17 December 1915. All correspondence on Frederick's Service Records states his rank as Sergeant after his initial injury in May 1915.

Sergeant Fergus' next of kin was Mrs C Harwood from Marrickville but there was also a Miss Adeline Agnes Isabel Paterson, 13 Challis Street, Marrickville who claimed Frederick's body and, at her own expense had the body returned to Sydney where she laid him to rest in the Waverly Cemetery with full military honours. She had previously contacted the Army to inquire about Frederick, which hospital he was in and when he was to return to Australia.

When it became time to dispose of Frederick's medals Base Records wrote to Mrs Harwood to enquire if she knew of any blood relations, she replied that she did not know as he was only a boarder. Major Lean wrote next to Miss Paterson, she wrote back telling Base Records that she was to marry Frederick on his return and as she had brought his body back to Sydney and arranged his burial she asked if she could claim his medals. Miss Paterson also informed Major Lean that Frederick's parents had died when he was only a baby and he was raised by grandparents, he had no brothers or sisters and that she was the only person he had.[53] The Army agreed that Miss Paterson should have his medals, Miss Paterson also filled in his Circular for the Roll of Honour Database, she never married and died a spinster in 1951.

The 18 May was a strangely quiet day at Anzac Cove, there was hardly any firing from the Ottoman troops. Unbeknown to the Allies, the Turks were planning an enormous attack on the Anzac front line, still confident of driving the invaders back into the sea. During a reconnaissance flight by the Allies, it was found that the Turkish had amassed thousands of troops in readiness for an attack. Being alerted to the build-up of the Turkish forces the soldiers made themselves ready for an attack on the 19 May.

The 15th Battalion relieved the 16th Battalion at noon on 18 May at Quinn's Post with the 16th acting as the reserve battalion. Shortly after 3.00am attacks began all along the Anzac line, from Russell's Top in the north to Bolton's Ridge in the south. By 5.00am large bodies of Turkish troops began massing in front of Quinn's and Courtney's, the attacks then began to surge heavily against Quinn's. The 15th rose from the trenches and firing rapidly blew the attack away. Two or three times the Turks attempted to take the trenches. They failed hopelessly out flanked by machine-gun posts at Popes and Plugge's Plateau. They may have been outnumbered by the Turks who had about 40,000 troops compared to 12,500 Anzacs but they stood their ground.

The Turks just ran towards the trenches on mass, the men of the 15th could not miss, again and again the Turks charged each time into a barrage of rifle fire and machine-guns. The soldiers said it was like going rabbit hunting, they could not miss. Numbers of the 15th were exposing themselves in order to shoot at the enemy retreating from Courtney's but a Turkish machine-gun from the Chessboard killed three Australians and wounded seven with a single burst. At the end of the day the Australians had 160 killed and 468 wounded while the Turks suffered about 3,400 dead in No-Man's Land and 6,700 wounded.[54]

A soldier killed that day was 20-year-old **Frederick Cecil Swain [201]** from the 15th Battalion. Frederick was born in 1895 at Ashfield in Sydney, his unmarried mother, Eliza Swain registered his birth as Cecil Swain.[55] While still a newborn, Eliza, deserted her son, leaving him with the Kilburn Sisters at Waverley. When war was declared Frederick was in the Cairns district working as a Farm Worker. By the 8 August his Service Record states that he was aboard the *SS Kanowna* heading to Thursday Island for Garrison Duty. After his arrival on Thursday Island Frederick enlisted, while still aboard *SS Kanowna*, for service outside of Australia on 14 August.

He was taken on strength to the Australian Navy and Military Expeditionary Force, 2nd Infantry Regiment with the Service Number of 1803. The *SS Kanowna* with Frederick on board sailed for Port Moresby, then in convoy with other vessels from Sydney headed for German New Guinea for the capture of Rabaul from German control. Shortly after leaving Port Moresby the *SS Kanowna* signalled 'lost control', the firemen on-board had mutinied and refused to stoke the ship, objecting to proceeding any further. Frederick's ship was ordered to return to Townsville where Frederick was discharged on 18th September.

Just 10 days later Frederick enlisted again this time at Enoggera, Queensland on 28 August 1914 into the AIF. Obviously, he was determined to join up. Frederick stated that he was born at Ashfield, Sydney and named as his next of kin his guardian, Mr A W Green, Richmond Terrace, Domain, Sydney. Mr. Green had previously given permission for Frederick to join when he enlisted in early August.[56]

Frederick stood 5 feet and 4 ½ inches tall, his complexion was medium with dark brown eyes and fair hair. He also stated that he was a member of the Yungaburra Rifle Club (near Cairns) from 2 July 1915 until he left for Thursday Island. He was given another Service Number [201] and assigned to the 15th Battalion.

As Mr Green was named next of kin he was informed of Frederick's death, shortly after a Mr Whitburn from Wingham, in New South Wales, wrote to the Army on 28 June 1915 asking after Frederick. He had read in a newspaper of Frederick's death and asked why he had not been informed. Base Records replied that Mr Green was nominated as next of kin, but after correspondence it was revealed that after Frederick was abandoned, the Kilburn Sisters asked Mrs Whitburn, who lived nearby, to raise him. Mrs Whitburn took care of Frederick until the age of five when the Sisters took him back.

In 1904 the Kilburn Sisters' School was sold and Frederick's care was transferred to the State, with Mr Green becoming

Frederick Cecil Swain – AWM P08624.114

his guardian. It is thought that when this happened Frederick was sent back to the Whitburn Family who were now living in Wingham. When it came time to locate any blood relations Mr Green told Base Records that Frederick was very close to the Whitburn Family and always referred to them as Mum and Dad. His foster family gladly accepted his medals and filled out the Circular for the Roll of Honour. Frederick was buried at Shrapnel Gully by the Rev. F W Wray on 20 May 1915; although it appears after the war his grave was never found. Frederick is remembered on the Lone Pine Memorial.

In early May the 1st, 2nd and 3rd Light Horse Regiments joined the Anzacs leaving their horses behind in Egypt, as reinforcements were badly needed at Gallipoli. Among the 1st Light Horse Regiment was **Alfred James Clark [638]** who enlisted at Roseberry Park 7 September 1914. Alfred claimed on his Attestation papers that he had been born in Melbourne in 1895 but no trace can be found of his birth anywhere in Australia. He gave his next of kin as Gaston Cook (guardian) who lived at Pittwater Road, Manly. Alfred stood 5 feet 8 ½ inches tall, his complexion was noted as fresh with brown eyes and dark brown hair, his occupation was Labourer. Alfred left Sydney onboard *Boorara* for Egypt where more training was undertaken. After arriving on Gallipoli 12 May, the 1st Light Horse Regiment, without their horses, took over the trenches at Pope's Post the next day.

Alfred's war ended 27 May 1915 while manning Pope's Post when he received a gunshot wound to the head. On that day there was only one from the 1st Light Horse Regiment wounded.[57] Alfred was evacuated immediately to the H M S *Newmarket* but died from a 'herniation of brain' and buried at sea the same day, he was only 19 years of age.

When it came time to pass his medals on, Base Records contacted Gaston Cook asking the whereabouts of any blood relations. Mr Cook replied stating that he did not have any and as far as he knew his father was presumed dead, his mother, Alice Clark became demented and was placed in a Lunatic Asylum. When this happened Mr Cook was given guardianship and Alfred had stayed with him and Mrs Cook until his enlistment.[58] On 27 July 1920 Major Lean from Base Records made the decision to pass on Alfred's medals, the Memorial Scroll and Memorial Plaque to Mr Gaston Cook. The Circular for the Roll of Honour was never filled out by Mr Cook, instead this was compiled by Official Historian Staff. Trooper Alfred James Clark is remembered on the Lone Pine Memorial.

As June and July arrived so did summer, with it came the heat and the flies, now dysentery was raging amongst the troops. The strength of the men was declining, faces became lined, cheeks sunken and now many were starting to die from sickness. Gallipoli was practically a prison, the Anzacs held just a small portion of the Peninsular, fresh water was scarce, the diet of the men was limited and what bathing they did was back on the beach in sea water.

As in the past the Commanders had a plan of attack, with fresh reinforcements arriving they have even more troops, amongst the attackers are the 8th Light Horse Regiment with Lieutenant Colonel Alexander Henry White in command. The 8th was to attack the Nek after a naval bombardment which started at precisely at 4.00am on 7 August. When the bombardment stops at 4.30am four successive waves of the Australian Light Horse, consisting of 150 men in each wave, immediately charged across open ground.

Well, that was the plan, the only problem here is that the bombardment stopped at 4.23am, Colonel White looked at his watch, he had hoped the Turks will get a final blast. No there is just silence, even the Turks are confused. Colonel White had previously made the decision to go over the top with his men but now they just wait. Their orders were to have no ammunition in their rifles, they had to use bayonets and bombs.

At 4.30am the first wave of the 8th Light Horse Regiment, led by Colonel White left the trenches running into a dense hail of machine-gun and rifle fire, many are killed, some before they get to clear the parapet including Colonel White. Because the Nek was so narrow only 150 men could go forward in one rush, they were easy prey to the Turkish machine-guns and rifles. The second wave followed without hesitation two minutes after the first, they were cut down like the first.

The third wave, from the 10th Light Horse Regiment probably knew they too were going to die. Again, more of Australian's youth were cut down but only part of the fourth wave charged before their commander called the attack off. The 8th had 234 casualties, including 154 dead. The 10th had 138 casualties, including 80 dead with no ground gained.

Second Lieutenant Cyril Godfrey Marsh [187] from the 8th Light Horse Regiment died on 7 August 1915 as he went over the top, he was 22 years of age. Born in South Melbourne in 1893 he was the second son of John Garrett and Clara Marsh, his elder brother, John Charles, was born in 1891 but died at the age of 15 in 1907.[59] Cyril enlisted 15 September 1914 at Broadmeadows,

Victoria where he was assigned to the 8th Light Horse Regiment. He stated that his previous military experience was 2 years as a cadet and 4 years with the 29th Light Horse Regiment. Cyril stood 5 feet 9 ½ inches tall, his complexion was medium with blue eyes and dark brown hair, he gave his occupation as Clerk, naming his mother, Clara as next of kin.

Shortly after his enlistment Cyril was promoted to Squadron Sergeant Major 28 October 1914, leaving Melbourne aboard *Star of Victoria* 25 February 1915. The 8th Light Horse Regiment arrived at Anzac Cove on 21 May 1915, one month later Cyril was promoted to Second Lieutenant 28 June 1915.

The Army informed Cyril's parents of his death; his picture appeared in The Argus on Tuesday 14th September 1915[60] stating that he had been killed in action. When it came time to pass on

Cyril Godrey Marsh

his medals etc. his father wrote to say that his wife had died in 1919 and as Cyril was his only child could everything be sent to him. Cyril's body was never recovered; he is remembered on the Lone Pine Memorial.[61]

In August 1915 more troops started arriving to boost the declining numbers of the Australians, one battalion was the 18th attached to the 5th Brigade which was part of the newly created 2nd Division. The 18th was formed in Liverpool, New South Wales during March 1915, following training the battalion moved to Egypt, arriving on Gallipoli 19 August, it had not been ashore a day when it was committed to the attack on Hill 60. The hill was a low rise in the foothills on the north-western end of Anzac Cove, the battalion was to be in reserve to General Godley but when a request came in for more troops the 18th was ordered to move to Damakjelik Bair.

A soldier attached to the 18th Battalion was **Frank Bardon [166],** when Frank enlisted at Liverpool 26 February 1915, he stated he was 23 years old and was born in Wagga Wagga, New South Wales. A search of birth indexes does not find any such birth for Frank. He gave his next of kin as a cousin, John Smith who lived at 6 Rose Street, Richmond, Melbourne, Victoria. Frank stood 5 feet 4 inches tall, his complexion was fair with blue eyes and brown hair, his occupation was Labourer. [62]

Lieutenant Colonel A E Chapman, the Commander of the 18th Battalion said the battalion had no bombs but the reply was to make do with what they had. The attempt to round off the capture of Hill 60 by sending a raw battalion, without reconnaissance, to rush the main part of a position on which the experienced troops had only succeeded in obtaining a slight foothold, ended in failure.

Within a few hours the 18th Battalion which marched out with 750 strong had lost 11 officers and 372 men, of whom half were killed. On that day Private Frank Bardon was killed. When the army sent a telegram to his cousin, John Smith, it was returned as unknown. Attempts were made to find this cousin but after extensive advertising in all newspapers for any relation, Base Records were forced to mark his file as Untraceable. Frank Bardon is remembered on the Lone Pine Memorial

Another Untraceable soldier was **James Field [1752]** who enlisted 30 November 1914. James stated he was born 1887 at Mudgee, New South Wales, there are no birth records to confirm this. Enlisting at Liverpool, New South Wales James was aged 28 year and 4 months, giving his occupation as Butcher he did not name anyone as his next of kin. James was 5 feet 6 inches tall, his complexion was dark, with blue eyes and dark hair.[63]

Assigned to the 4th reinforcements of the 4th Battalion, James embarked from Sydney on the troopship *Shropshire* 17 March 1915. After he was taken on strength at Gallipoli 31 May 1915, James was promoted to Acting Sergeant. The 4th Battalion took part in the attack at Lone Pine which was launched at 5.30pm 6 August, their objectives were gained but the battalion suffered heavy casualties. James Field received several gunshot wounds to the torso and was taken to the General Hospital in Alexandria where he died from his wounds 5 September 1915. As he had not named any next of kin his file was marked Untraceable after attempts to locate any relatives by Base Records had failed. James is buried at the Alexandria (Chatby) Military and War Memorial Cemetery.

After the battles of August, a stalemate was starting to take place with so many of the troops now becoming ill and the battalions diminishing in their numbers. On 4 August 1915 the 9th Battalion received 125 reinforcements, amongst them was **Second Lieutenant Cecil Claude Oliver.** Cecil had joined the 9th on 23 April 1915 leaving Australia aboard *Karoola* 12 June 1915.

There are no birth records for Cecil as he was adopted by Edward Charles and Elizabeth Oliver from Goulburn and was given their surname. Cecil had a troubled upbringing as at the tender age of 10 he decided to run away from home on 1 April 1902. His disappearance was reported in the local paper.

Grave of James Field – National Archives of Australia

A Boy Missing

A little boy named Cecil Claude Oliver, adopted son of Mr Oliver, cabinet maker, of Eastgrove, has been missing since Tuesday last. On that day, the boy, who is about 10 years old, left home with other boys to go to the bush near Governor's Hill. The boys in playing with young Oliver ran after him into the bush, and Oliver ran away from them. After a time, the boys desisted. Oliver was then about half a mile away, and that was the last they saw of him. The boy had a tomahawk with him, and said he was going to join the blacks. A search has been made, Oliver's companions have pointed out to Senior-constable Frazer where the boy was last seen, and two mounted police are now engaged in the search. A black-tracker has been sent for, and one from Parramatta is coming. The boy's parents are distracted at his loss. It may be mentioned that the missing child has red hair, was dressed in a knickerbocker suit, with straw sailor hat and lace-up boots, but was wearing no socks. Later – Word has been received that the boy called at a house at Towrang to obtain food. The police expect to be soon on his tracks. The black tracker was to arrive this afternoon.[64]

The Missing Boy

The missing boy Oliver was recovered at Marulan on Thursday. It seems that he called at a place and was detained. Mr Oliver proceeded to Marulan and brought the boy back with him by the mail train.[65]

It seems that Cecil could not stay out of trouble as on 25 January 1906 he was charged with the unlawful use of a firearm in High Street, Eastgrove. He fired the gun across the street, and on Mrs Goodwin remonstrating with him he went to her place and shot four fowls. The loss had been made good by the adopted parents. He was fined £1 with Court costs of 8/-, in default 14 days Goulburn Gaol, the fine was paid. The Magistrate then suggested to Cecil's father that the boy should be kept away from any firearms.[66]

It didn't take long for Cecil to find himself in trouble again, this time the consequences would affect his way of life. On 2 May 1906 aged just 15, he stole the sum of four pounds and fifteen shillings, the property of William Henry Bye and William Bye, produce dealers in Goulburn. Cecil was employed as a carter by the produce firm and when left in charge of the shop his saw his opportunity to break into the till and steal the money.

At the hearing, when asked by the bench if he would return to his adopted parents if given another chance, he was most emphatic in his refusal to do so. Cecil was immediately sentenced to the naval training vessel *Sobraon*.[67] The *Sobraon* was a ship, moored off Cockatoo Island in Sydney Harbour, that served as an all-boy public industrial school. Cecil would not be released until he reached the age of 18. His admission took place 22 May 1906. The paperwork for his admission stated that he had been born in Sydney November 1891 and had attended Eastgrove Public School, Goulburn. It was noted that his adopted parents, Edward and Elizabeth, were very old residents of Goulburn and of good character and that Cecil was the only child in the family.[68]

Shortly after Cecil was sentenced his parents decided to move to New Zealand. The townspeople of Goulburn gave the Olivers a send-off which was reported in the local paper, where it stated that a change of air and scenery being necessary for the health of both of them.[69]

It is possible Cecil travelled to New Zealand to visit his parents after his discharge from *Sobraon,* but it is understood he may have been living in Queensland when he enlisted receiving his commission as Second Lieutenant 23 April 1915. Cecil's postal address on enlistment was 2 Chilka Street, Berhampore Wellington, NZ giving his father's address as 30 Sydney Street Petone Wellington, NZ, but by 1919 Cecil's parents had moved permanently to their son's address. Cecil gave his occupation as Wireless Expert.[70] Cecil and the other reinforcements were needed to boost the numbers as throughout August and September sickness was decimating the battalion, the 6th reinforcements arrived at Anzac Cove 4 August 1915.

On 16 September the Battalion Commanding Officer noted that 'considerable volume of fire delivered by the enemy especially from Snipers Ridge'. Just five days later on 22 September the War Diary noted that a 2nd Lieutenant was killed at 17.00 whilst sniping from 'C' Coy. Cecil was buried by Chaplain M E Dexter at Shell Green Cemetery, Plot 1, Row D, Grave 23. Cecil's adopted parents wrote many letters from their home in New Zealand, to Major Lean at Base Records, telling him how devastated they were at the loss of their only child, but at the same time how proud they were of their son.

Winter was now descending onto Gallipoli, night after night the cold was creeping into the trenches and the bones of the battle-weary troops, low morale was taking a toll on the despondent men. Then, to add to the misery of troops on both sides, a notorious flood started on 26 November. The rain started in the afternoon and increased after dark. Both Turkish and Allied trenches filled with water and a number of troops, on both sides, were drowned. The next day the wind turned into a cold north-eastly then a severe snow storm hit the Peninsula. Knowing it would be impossible to stay on Gallipoli during the winter months a decision was made to evacuate the Peninsula. By 20 December the last of the troops had left but most of them were in a very poor condition due to sickness.

One soldier who was suffering from Influenza was **Otto Lessing Evers [1785 & 1544]** who was admitted to the 27th General Hospital, Mudros on 5 January 1916. Otto was born in Marrickville, Sydney in 1890, the only child to Frederick Ferdinand Evers and Emilie W Lessing.[71] It is believed that both parents were German, and were married in 1888 at Sydney.[72] Otto's father, Frederick, was a sea captain on the schooner *Vailele*, Emilie's father, Carl Gotthold Lessing was also a Master Mariner.

Otto grew up never knowing his father as he had died from malaria 17 July 1891 while on a voyage to the Solomon Islands.[73] Even though Otto was from a seafaring background his mother enrolled him into the Fort Street Model Public School in Sydney, and then at the age of sixteen he attended the Hawkesbury Agricultural College, New South Wales where he undertook the Piggery and Dairy Certificates. In 1907 he also received a Certificate in Cheese Making leaving the College January 1908.[74]

Shortly after leaving the College, Otto was in the Illawarra district engaged in dairy herd testing before starting a business in 1914 at Yungaburra west of Cairns, Queensland as an Auctioneer and Commission Agent.[75]

Within days of war being declared Otto, as part of the Yungaburra Rifle Club and the Kennedy Regiment, sailed from Cairns aboard *SS Kanowna* for Garrison Duty on Thursday Island. While at Thursday Island volunteers had been called for service outside the Commonwealth, half the Regiment had responded, Otto included, his Service No was 1785. Re-embarking on board the *Kanowna* the 500 new recruits then sailed on 16 August for Port Moresby where they waited for other vessels to arrive from Sydney before sailing in convoy to German New Guinea for the capture of Rabaul from German control.

Shortly after the convoy had left Port Moresby the *Kanowna* had hoisted the signal 'lost control', the firemen onboard had mutinied and refused to stoke the ship, objecting to proceeding any further. The troops had volunteered for overseas service, however the *Kanowna's* crew had not. Otto's ship was ordered to return to Townsville and the detachment on board was disbanded 18 September 1914. It had been noted that supplies of clothing and boots for the 500 men were non-existent, there were no tents, no mosquito nets and no hammocks issued to the men.

Otto again enlisted at Atherton, Queensland 5 June 1915, this time he was attached to the 1st reinforcements of the 26th Battalion with the Service No 1544. Otto was 6 feet and 1 inch tall, with fair complexion, blue eyes and fair hair.[76] The battalion embarked from Brisbane on board *Aeneas* on 29 June 1915. After training in Egypt Otto's battalion embarked for Alexandria arriving at Anzac Cove 11 September 1915.

The 26th played a purely defensive role on Gallipoli and at various times was responsible for the defence of Courtney's and Steele Posts and at Russell Top. On the 12 December the 26th was withdrawn from Gallipoli but Otto had already succumbed to influenza. He only spent a short time in the hospital at Mudros before he was transferred to the No 3 Auxiliary Hospital at Heliopolis on 14 January then onto a Convalescent Camp at Helouan. Otto was discharged back to duty 29 January 1916 however; within days he was back in the Convalescent Camp again suffering from Influenza.

During his time on Gallipoli, he became interested in the workings of the periscope rifle which was invented May 1915 by Lance Corporal William Beech. After they were shown to be effective the rifles were produced in a makeshift workshop on the beach at Anzac Cove. It proved to be a useful weapon where the closeness of the opposing trenches had earlier made it virtually impossible to fire a shot by day.[77]

While recovering from his illness Otto was granted special permission, at the request of General White and on the recommendation of Brig. General Sellheim, to carry out construction of a model of two periscopic sights for two machine guns. Otto had invented the machine gun sights while on duty as a machine gun driver on Gallipoli. He was to carry out this work in the Egyptian State Railway Workshops at Boulac, Cairo.[78]

Sadly, before completing this work he became ill again and was admitted to No 3 Australian General Hospital at Abbassia on 3 May 1916, within two days he was listed as dangerously ill and was transferred to the Government Hospital, Abbassia 12 May 1916 with smallpox. Private Otto Lessing Evers died 15 May 1916; he was buried in the Cairo War Memorial Cemetery, Cairo, Egypt, Row F, Grave No 62.

On 15 February 1918 a wooden box was delivered to Otto's widowed mother, Emilie (Emily) Evers inside was one Patent Periscopic Sight in two parts and plans for same. Mrs Evers wrote to the Army 6 December 1920 stating that 'Otto was my only child, with my son's death his father's family has died out.' She went on to inform the Army that she did not want any of her son's medals as she would have no one who would value the medals after her death. Otto's medals were posted to Mrs Evers 23 December 1921. Otto's mother, Mrs Emilie Evers died at Rydalmere Mental Hospital in 1952.[79]

CHAPTER 2
FROMELLES - 1916

Following the evacuation of Gallipoli back to Egypt, and the success of recruitment campaigns in Australia, there was a large accumulation of Australian and New Zealand reinforcements in Egypt. The decision was made to reorganise the existing battalions with the intention of doubling the size of the Australian Imperial Force on the Western Front. Reinforcement numbers had been sufficient to allow the 1st and 2nd Divisions to be split to form the new 4th and 5th Divisions, a new 3rd Division was to be formed and trained back in Australia before moving to England for further training.

The news of the splitting of veteran battalions that had served in Gallipoli came as a shock to the men, not wanting to see mates lost to the new battalions or for that matter have their units divided. After some time, the veterans understood the reasons behind the plan. The splitting of each battalion in half and transferring these veterans to the new battalions meant that experienced soldiers would work with the new arrivals.

By the second week of February 1916 the separation had started, the sight of half the old battalions marching away was distressing to their former comrades who were left behind. An Officer of the 12th Battalion felt as though he was having a limb amputated without any anaesthetic.[1] By 13 March the 2nd Division left for Alexandria where they embarked for France, the 1st Division followed on 21 March.

Early in April 1916 the 9th Battalion, from the 1st Division, had arrived in Marseilles then travelled by train through the countryside of France before finally arriving at their billets in the vicinity of Strazeele. Training for the battalion began almost immediately, after two weeks the Battalion moved to Rue du Bois about a mile from the front line where again they were housed in billets.

On 20 April 1916 many in the 9th Battalion were to have their first taste of war when at 13.15 hours the billets occupied by 'C' Company received a heavy bombardment. Early in the bombardment a shell landed in one of the canvas huts wounding four men, some men ran to the assistance of the wounded and another shell caught these. A subsequent shell struck the wall of a billet which also caused many casualties.[2]

There were 75 soldiers from 'C' Company killed or wounded, amongst the wounded was **William Wilson [1626]**. William claimed on his Attestation paper that he was born in 1878 at Ballarat, Victoria. Shortly after war was declared William was living in Rockhampton where he enlisted. His address was C/- Post Office Rockhampton, occupation given as Labourer, initially he gave next of kin as Nil then gave the name of Mrs Mackey, Federal Hotel, Rockhampton.[3]

William stood 5 feet 9 ¾ inches tall, his complexion was dark, had brown eyes and black hair. William was assigned to the 3rd reinforcements of the 9th Battalion, after some initial training William left Brisbane 13 February 1915 on the troopship *Seang Choon*, he did not join his unit on Gallipoli until 6 May 1915.

On the 18 July 1915 William had succumbed to the ravages of Gallipoli and was taken off the Peninsula suffering from dysentery and diarrhoea and sent to a hospital at Malta. By 28 August 1915 he still had not improved and as a result was sent to England on 11 September 1915 where he was admitted to the Military Hospital Bethnal Green, London. William did not re-join his Battalion until 6 March 1916. It is most likely that during his stay in London he met and married his wife, Nora. There is no copy of the marriage certificate on his file, however, he named his wife as his next of kin. Her address at that time was C/- Mrs Winks, 6 Tolmers Square, Hampstead Road, London.

William Wilson had survived Gallipoli and sickness but was one of the badly wounded members of 'C' Company, dying from his severe headwound 22 April 1916. His personal effects were returned to Major Lean at Base Records, there is no indication that they were forwarded to his widow. His effects contained a Marriage Certificate, Clasp Knife, Purse, Mirror, Crucifix, Prayer Book, Postcard, Shaving Brush and Tobacco Pouch. William is buried in the Merville Communal Cemetery in France, sadly there is no epitaph on his tombstone, there is also no Roll of Honour Circular filled out for him by his wife. Nora Wilson did apply for her widow's pension which was granted, her address then was 14 Ossington Street, Notting Hill Gate, London.

The 11th Battalion of the AIF had moved into the Sailly Sur-La-Lys area by 20 May 1916 taking over front-line trenches in the nursery section. The nursery section was used to prepare the troops before engaging in major operations on the Western Front as this was the quieter section. Here they learnt about battle conditions and experienced new weapons of modern warfare such as gas. The extra training was needed for the raw troops who had not experienced battle before even though some were veterans from Gallipoli.

Nearly every evening the 11th experienced artillery attacks by the Germans which caused damage to the trenches especially the communication trenches, some troops were either killed or wounded. Then on 30 May at 20.10 the enemy commenced a fierce bombardment on a section of front and support lines. The bombardment raged with unabated and awful fury until 21.30 when it slackened and then ceased at 21.40.[4] Charles Bean wrote of the attack: *The great bombs dug huge craters in the soft agricultural soil and the flimsy breastworks (of the trenches) and shelters were flung up into the air in shredded and splintered fragments.*[5]

One Gallipoli veteran, from the 11th Battalion, killed during the bombardment was **Albert Owen Hart [440]**. Albert enlisted 14 August 1914 at Blackboy Hill in Western Australia naming his mother, Esther Hart as his next of kin.[6] Albert stated that his occupation was Boundary Rider, however the 1915 Electoral Roll records his occupation as Baggage Man,[7] perhaps he was trying to get into a mounted regiment. Albert stood 5 feet 6 inches tall, his complexion was fair with blue eyes and fair hair. Albert's address at enlistment was 50 Douro Road, South Fremantle however prior to that he lived with his mother, at 186 Sewell Street, East Fremantle.

The 11th Battalion left Australia 31 October 1914 aboard the troopship *Ascanius*, after more training in Egypt Albert took part in the landing at Gallipoli. Albert, and the 11th Battalion were heavily involved in defending the front line of the Anzac beachhead.

In July 1915 Albert succumbed to the various sickness that was afflicting many of the soldiers, as a result he was sent back to Lemnos on 24 July, then back to Egypt where he was admitted to the 2nd Australian General Hospital at Ghezirth Palace. Albert finally re-joined his unit 3 October but was back in hospital on Lemnos by 16 December with Jaundice. Albert was promoted to Lance Corporal 1 March 1916 before moving to France with his unit on 3 April. Over a month later Albert was killed in action during the bombing raid by the Germans on 30 May 1916. He is buried at the Military Cemetery Rue Petillon, 4 miles south west of Armentieres. His effects were sent back to his mother, they consisted of a Gift Tin, Letters, Turkish Beads and a damaged Cigarette Case.

When it was time to dispose of Albert's medals a letter was sent to Esther Hart asking what blood relations he had. Esther replied that he had no one except her and that she had adopted him and named herself as his foster mother. When Albert enlisted, he stated his age in 1914 to be 23 years but when Esther filled out the Circular for the Roll of Honour, she gave his age as 22 when he was killed. She also stated his occupation as Carrier and that he was educated at State School and Christian Brothers in Fremantle.

The 5th Division, formed in 1916 at Egypt consisted of three infantry brigades: the 8th, 14th and 15th. Upon formation, each brigade consisted of around 4,000 personals organised into four infantry battalions. James McCay assumed command of the division on 21 March 1916. The 5th was allocated to the defence of the canal around Ferry Post with the 8th Brigade moving part of the way by train to Moascar then by foot to Ferry Post. The 14th and 15th Brigades were to complete the march on foot, a journey of 57 kilometres from the camp at Tel El Kebir. James McCay initially showed some apprehensions about the march but followed the orders. The troops felt the terrible heat, which topped 100 degrees Fahrenheit marching over deep sand. Taking three days the men in the two brigades suffered severely with many distressed from the extreme heat. Their Commander did not seem to care and after that march they didn't care much for him after his rant to them when they arrived.[8]

The 5th Division finally arrived in France in late June 1916, landing in Marseilles, the last of the four divisions, the 3rd was still in Australia. The 5th was to replace the divisions of 1st Anzac Corps, which had been in the quiet sector near Armentieres since April 1916, but was now needed in the Somme as reinforcements. Little did anyone know that the 5th Division, the most inexperienced of the Australian divisions in France, would be the first to see major action a week after going into the trenches.

The 8th and 15th Brigades arrived on the night of 10/11 July, while the 14th moved into position on 12 July. Unbeknown to the 5th Division, on 29 June, Lieutenant-General Richard Haking had sent two British battalions to attack a German salient, Boar's Head, two miles south-west of the Sugar Loaf. The Sugar Loaf was a heavily fortified elevated concrete stronghold bristling with machine-guns. This new attack was to be a feint to stop the Germans sending reserves to the Somme. The two British battalions attacked and even briefly held parts of the German frontline but when it was over the two battalions had lost 1,153 men, a shocking casualty rate.[9]

As the 17,800 men took over the front lines Lieutenant-General Haking was at it again, this time the attack was to be towards Fromelles which was over the very ground where the British, and

Haking, had failed in the battle of Aubers Ridge the previous year. Aubers Ridge in the German rear area was, at 40 metres high, the highest feature on the landscape. The attack was to take place 17 July but was put back to 19 July due to the weather.

The 57th Battalion had been in the front-line trenches ready for the attack but was relieved by the 59th Battalion at 4.00pm on 18 July. A guide from the 59th took the 57th back to their billets, the man chosen to be the guide was **William O'Sullivan [3867]**. On his Attestation paper William stated he was aged 27 years and 3 months when he enlisted 9 June 1915. He was born in Melbourne, a Farmer, residing at 46 Capel Street, West Melbourne.

William stated that both parents were deceased and named a cousin, Maud Maynard (nee Robinson), as his next of kin. Maud's mother Ellen Robinson (nee O'Sullivan) also resided at 46 Capel Street, West Melbourne. There are no birth records for William, although it may be possible, he was the son of William and Emily O'Sullivan, William Snr., was an older brother to Ellen Robinson (nee O'Sullivan). William stood 5 feet and 2 ½ inches tall with fresh complexion, brown eyes and brown hair. Initially he was assigned to the 7th Battalion.[10]

William left Melbourne 23 November 1915 onboard the troopship *Ceramic* and after his arrival in Egypt he was transferred to the newly created 59th Battalion. In April 1916 William came down with Influenza which landed him in hospital at Ferry Post, after a few days he had recovered enough to re-join his unit.

After the 57th Battalion arrived at the billets which had been vacated by the 59th they settled down for the night, William O'Sullivan included. Private John Ingram from the 57th Battalion was sentry over the billet of No. 13 Platoon, 'D' Company, from 0400 to 0600 on the morning of July 19th. At about 0415 he heard the report of a rifle. He looked into the shed where the men were billeted, but could find no reason for the cause of the report. He reported the incident to Lieut. Morgan, who came in the billet about 5 minutes afterwards.

Lieut. Morgan investigated Private Ingram's report, immediately looking round but could find no cause for the report. Acting Sergeant Allan Potter also heard the shot fired, looking into the yard he could see no cause for the report. At about 06.10 he was told by a French boy who lived at the billet that there was a dead soldier in the cow-shed, going into the shed he saw a 59th Battalion soldier lying on some hay with blood on his face. He felt his pulse and could detect no signs of life. Acting Sergeant Potter reported the matter to Lieut. Morgan he then examined the deceased soldier's rifle and found a discharged cartridge in the chamber, but no cartridge in the magazine.

Two soldiers from the 57th Battalion were able to identify the soldier as Private William O'Sullivan who had been their guide to the billets the night before. At 10.05 Captain Hugh Rayson, Medical Officer of the 57th Battalion, examined William's body and in his opinion the wound could have easily been self-inflicted. A Court of Enquiry was hurriedly convened, and sat just prior to the departure of the battalion to the firing line for the attack on the 19 July. The outcome of the enquiry stated that he must have committed suicide while of unsound mind.[11]

Private William O'Sullivan was buried 5 miles south west of Armentieres, at No. 2 Military Cemetery, Sailly-Sur-La-Lys, Grave IB6, by Rev F P Williams. Just why William decided to end his life there in a cow-shed instead of returning to his battalion will never be known. William's cousin, Maud Maynard, was notified of William's death, Maud wrote back to the Army asking for a death certificate but then did not answer any more mail sent to her by Base Records in Melbourne. In 1923 Base Records wrote, first, to Maud Maynard then to Mrs Ellen Robinson, William's aunt, enquiring the whereabouts of any blood relation in order to dispose of his medals. There was no reply from either his cousin or aunt and as a result his file was marked Untraceable.

Preparation for the attack by the 5th Division was now underway, the idea was to prevent the Germans from moving southward to take part in the battle of the Somme. Lieutenant-

General Haking in his wisdom would use a bombardment that will be continued with increasing intensity up to the moment of the assault. After all he now had a whole Australian Division plus the 61st British Division, he could not fail this time.

There was to be a seven-hour bombardment starting at 11am on Wednesday 19 July, the infantry would attack at 6pm. Brigadier General Elliott of the 15th Brigade was horrified and believed that the plan would cause more casualties. He thought the bombardment would take away any hint of a surprise but General McCay was pleased his 5th Division was at last going into action.

The allied bombardment sounded better than it was, the barrage was working in some places but was failing where it was needed most. Of the seventy-five concrete shelters in front of the 16th Bavarian Regiment, sixty still remained intact. The German gunners waited several hours until the British and Australian front-line trenches were full of troops. Then, they began to bombard the front and support lines, killing and wounding many soldiers while still in the trenches, blowing up piles of ammunition, cutting telephone wires and starting small fires.[12]

From Aubers Ridge where the Germans were entrenched, they could see everything the Allies did. They knew an attack was coming and set out to destroy the attack before it had a chance to begin. The attacking battalion from the 15th Brigade had to cover up to 400 yards across No-Man's Land to reach the German line and was exposed to flanking fire from the Sugar Loaf.

At 5.45pm, the 59th and 60th Battalions climbed over the parapet into No-Man's Land and charged, many would not return, the Australians fell all along the line. The two-assaulting battalions of the 14th Brigade only had to cover 250 yards but it was still a long way over open ground in daylight. The German guns that fired on the battalions from the 15th Brigade also opened up on the battalions from the 14th Brigade. Unbelievably some of the men got through and even captured some German prisoners.

By dusk the Australian attack at Fromelles was becoming a disaster, the men who got through to the German lines were now coming under attack, all waves of the Allied forces were now in the battle, so no reinforcements. By dark the Germans had regrouped and were now attacking from behind. By 11pm the brigade commanders were aware that the whole battle plan just did not work, instead the wounded were now coming back, some crawled while others were dragged in.

The next morning the scene in No-Man's Land was one of devastation, the wounded could be seen raising their limbs in pain or turning hopelessly, hour after hour, from one side to the other.[13] The sums were done that morning, the 60th Battalion had been wiped out as a fighting force, only sixty-one answered roll call from 877 men. Brigadier General (Pompey) Elliott's 15th Brigade had gone into battle with about 3,750 now it was down to about 2,000. The memory of losing so many of his men stayed with the brigade commander for the rest of his life.

The night of 19th and 20th July was the greatest loss of Australian soldiers in a single 24-hour period, sadly the British put out an official dispatch, 'yesterday evening south of Armentieres, we carried out some important raids on a front of two miles in which Australian troops took part. About 140 German prisoners were captured.' They failed to mention the Australian casualties, 5,533 dead, wounded, missing and prisoners of war, the British at 1,547.[14] The 5th Division effectiveness was greatly undermined and it would take many months to recover.

One young man who lost his life that night was **Henry Wilson [421]** a member of 'B' Company 32nd Battalion. When Henry enlisted 7 July 1915, at Adelaide, his age was 32 years and 2 months. Born in Sydney, New South Wales he gave his address as Glebe Point, Sydney, Henry stated his occupation as Clerk. He named an uncle, Mr Arthur M Solly, Glebe Point, Sydney as his next of kin. Henry stood 5 feet and 7 inches tall, his complexion was fresh, with blue eyes and fair hair.[15] After some initial training Henry was made a Lance Corporal before his battalion left

Adelaide 18 November 1915, onboard the troopship *Geelong*, arriving at Suez 18 December 1915. While at Tel-El-Kebir Henry came down with a case of Mumps 6 March 1916 but was back with his unit 22 March 1916.

Henry was promoted to Sergeant while at Ferry Post 26 May 1916 before the 32nd Battalion left for France. After only a couple of days in the front-line trenches Henry was finally at war, as part of the 8th Brigade, Henry and his mates occupied the left of the front line. It is not known when Henry was killed and his Service Record indicates that his body was never recovered. His name appeared in the newspapers as missing which resulted in a Miss Ruby Kastberg, Cross Road, Unley, South Australia to write to Base Records regarding his wellbeing. When she had been informed that Private Wilson had been killed, she asked if she could have any of his belongings. Base Records replied stating the uncle was next of kin and had the only right to his possessions. Miss Kastberg replied stating she had never heard of this uncle.

Base Records left no stone unturned in trying to track down Arthur M Solly but was unsuccessful. Henry had named as an allottee Reverend W G Murphy, All Souls Rectory, St Peters but the Reverend had no knowledge of any next of kin. As a result, Henry Wilson's file was marked Untraceable. Henry's name appears on the VC Corner Cemetery and Memorial, Fromelles, Panel 4.

Private Walter Smith Arnold [2329] was another soldier to go missing 19 July, 1916. Walter's birth was registered as Walter Arnold Smith, born 1888, his mother was noted as Ellen Smith, father unknown.[16] It is possible that Walter's father was William Arnold who married Annie Ellen Smith in 1894.[17] Walter enlisted at Melbourne 9 July 1915, naming his mother, Annie Arnold as his next of kin, he also stated that he was his mother's sole support.[18] Walter stood 5 feet 5 ½ inches tall, his complexion was sallow with grey eyes and black hair, his occupation was Painter. Initially he was assigned to the 21st Battalion, leaving Melbourne on the troopship *Osterley* 7 October 1915.

Walter Smith Arnold – AWM DA10726

While at Tel-El-Kebir Walter was taken on strength to 21st Battalion on 7 January 1916 and at Ferry Post on 1 April he was transferred to the 57th Battalion then finally the 60th Battalion 4 April 1916. Walter and the 60th Battalion embarked on *Kinfauns Castle* for France 18 June 1916 arriving at Marseilles 29 June 1916. Walter's mother was notified that her son was missing after the battle at Fromelles although it took until 4 August 1917 before an enquiry was held that he was officially killed in action 19 July 1916.

Annie's husband, William Arnold had died in 1903, her youngest son, William Watkin Arnold, had also died, aged 19, in 1915[19] now her remaining son, Walter had been killed in action. Walter's body was never found and this was a concern to Annie, she had written a letter to General Birdwood General Sir William regarding Walter, he did reply to her. Annie sent a copy of the reply to Base Records.

> *This is a few words which might be of use in the fighting on the nineteenth July. Your son's Battalion fought their way most gallantly into the German position but later it was decided to return to their original line. In such operations a certain number of men are invariably posted as missing. In the absence of any news of your son I fear there can be no doubt that he was killed in the fighting on that day and buried by the enemy.*
>
> *1st Anzac Corps France*
> *2nd Aug 1917.*[20]

Walter Smith Arnold is remembered on the VC Corner Cemetery Memorial.

The whole of the 5th Division suffered terribly on the night of 19 July with many soldiers posted as missing, their bodies never recovered. The families left behind in Australia always had the hope that their soldier may be a prisoner of war and will return home. The family of **Herbert Evan Jones [194]** still hoped, at the end of the war, that perhaps their son will return to them.

Herbert enlisted at Melbourne on 18 January 1915, naming his mother Clara Ann Jones as next of kin. Herbert had been born in 1893 at Benella, Victoria, his father was David John Jones, 64 Park Road, Middle Park, Melbourne. Herbert, a Tailor was 5 feet 7 ½ inches tall, his complexion was fair with blue eyes and fair hair. He allocated three-fifths of his pay for the support of his mother.[21] Herbert was one of five children born to David and Clara, four boys and one girl, sadly two of the boys, John Wembridge and Robert David died young.[22] Herbert had an older brother; Maurice Theodore Jones and his sister was Alice Maud May Jones (known as May). Initially, Herbert was allocated to the 21st Battalion leaving Melbourne onboard *Ulysses* 8 May 1915, after his arrival in Egypt he was promoted to Corporal 25 July 1915. Late in August 1915, the 21st Battalion embarked on the transport ship *Southland* on route to Gallipoli, just a few days out Herbert's transport was torpedoed at 9.43 am on 2 September 1915.[23] Forced to abandon ship Herbert and the rest of the 21st Battalion were later transported to Gallipoli.

Herbert was taken off Gallipoli one month later on 13 October 1915 with Appendicitis. After a stay in hospital at Helouan he was discharged to Zeitoun 16 November 1915, where he joined up with his unit after the withdrawal from Gallipoli. Then in February 1916 Herbert came down with a serious case of Pneumonia. After recovering from that, he was back in hospital with Influenza. Herbert transferred to the 60th Battalion 20 April 1916 with the rank of private then one month later found himself facing two charges, one with appearing on parade unshaven and one of neglect of duty, both cases were dismissed. Herbert was promoted to corporal again on 30 May 1915, he did not enjoy being a corporal and reverted back to private the very next day.

The 60th Battalion left Alexandria for Marseilles 22 June 1916 and made their way to the nursery section near Armentieres where they would take their part in the Battle of Fromelles. When Herbert's battalion arrived in France it had a force of 887 fine Australian soldiers, after the battle there were just one officer and 106 other ranks left that answered the battalion roll call.[24] The battle of Fromelles was a disaster for the battalion, in a single day it was virtually wiped out. As Herbert Evan Jones did not return to his battalion he was listed as missing. His family was notified 5 September 1916 that he was missing and one month later they were told he was still missing. It was not until 25 August 1917 the family of Herbert were told he had been killed in action.

Herbert's older brother, Maurice Theodore Jones who was a priest, decided to join the AIF on 15 April 1918 and was attached to the 8th Field Ambulance.[25] By the time he arrived in France the war was just about over, Maurice made the decision to stay by becoming a Chaplain to continue the search for his brother. Maurice wrote to the Red Cross 6 March 1919 stating that be believed many soldiers from the 60th Battalion who were prisoners of war had returned to England from Germany and again asked after Herbert. The reply on 22 October 1919 to Maurice was that his brother had been killed 19 July 1916.[26] Maurice returned to Australia December 1919 to his church, he died unmarried in 1944, his sister May also unmarried died in 1936.[27]

Another young man never to return to his country was **William Barry [505]** who lost his life on that fateful night. A member of the 31st Battalion, William enlisted 12 July 1915 aged 33 years and 2 months, naming his step father, Mr Shesher/Shearer as next of kin. He stood 5 feet 8 inches tall, his complexion was fresh with blue eyes and brown hair.[28] William's parents, Charles Shearer and Ellen Barry, married 12 June 1877[29] Elizabeth Shearer, their first child, was born 20 January 1879[30] followed by William Shearer 14 May 1881.[31] Why William reverted back to his mother's maiden name when he enlisted and the reason he considered his father as his step father will never be known, his address at the time of enlistment was C/- Mrs Thomas Chayter, King Street, East Brisbane.

Early October 1915 the 31st Battalion travelled by train to Melbourne, Victoria where the battalion embarked on the troopship *Wandilla* 9 November 1915 arriving at Suez 7 December 1915. After travelling to Tel-El-Kebir the battalion settled in for more training. William, on 1 March 1916 was charged with Conduct to the prejudice of good order and Military Discipline – Gambling, for his indiscretion he was awarded 168 hours of Field Punishment No 2.

The 31st Battalion left Alexandria 16 June 1916 arriving in Marseilles 23 June, then travelled to the nursery section where the battalion took part in the Battle of Fromelles. On the night of 19 July, the 31st Battalion suffered 572 casualties, over half its strength,[32] one casualty was William Barry. Base Records wrote to William's step father, Mr Shearer, sadly there was no reply, however, a Mr John Thomas Chayter from Withington Street, East Brisbane wrote to Base Records in regard to William.

Mr Chayter informed the Army that William had been brought up by his mother, Mrs Thomas Chayter, and that he considered himself to be William's next of kin. The Army replied that the next of kin was his step father Mr Shearer. Letters that were sent to William's step father were returned unclaimed which led to the Army, in July 1917, placing advertisements in the papers looking for relations. When there was no reply, Base Records then wrote to Mr John Thomas Chayter asking if he knew of any, Mr Chayter replied stating that William's step father, Mr Shearer had died in 1915, William's sister, Elizabeth had died in January 1918 and his mother, Ellen was an inmate at a Mental Hospital. He also repeated that he had been brought up with William and wish to have a claim on his belongings.

A letter from the Office of The Public Curator dated 18 March 1921 informed Base Records of the death of William's mother, Ellen Shearer on 13 December 1920, as there were no other family members William file was marked Untraceable. In June 1925 Base Records wrote to Mr John Thomas Chayter asking if he would place an inscription for William's headstone, also if he would fill in the Circular for the Roll of Honour. There was no reply. William is buried at the Rue-Petillon Military Cemetery, Fleurabaix, Plot 1, Row K Grave 35.

A young railway employee from Victoria was also killed in action during the night of 19 July, his name was **Philip Athol Fargher [2022]** a member of the 60th Battalion. Philip enlisted in Melbourne 3 July 1915 at the age of 24 years and 11 months, he was 5 feet 8 inches tall, his complexion was fresh with blue eyes and brown hair.[33]

Philip named his mother, Ellen Vannan Stent, 33 James Street, Windsor, Victoria as his next of kin. Philip's record of birth states that he was born 1890, his mother was Ellen Vannan Fargher, father unknown, Ellen married Edwin Stent in 1903.[34] Initially Phillip was allocated to 3rd reinforcements 22nd Battalion leaving Melbourne onboard *Anchises* 26 August 1915, after more training

Philip Athol Fargher AWM DA09925

in Egypt Philip was taken on strength to his battalion at Gallipoli 31 October 1915.

When Phillip arrived, conditions on the peninsula had deteriorated as the wicked winds of winter was making its appearance. Towards the end of November bitterly cold rain began to fall, the rain became sleet and then snow. For two full days and nights the freezing wind swept the peninsula while the men coughed and shivered in their trenches. Although Philip had not been on Gallipoli long, he came down with Diphtheria and was transferred to the Hospital Ship *Oxfordshire* on 12 December 1915. He eventually re-joined his battalion 4 March 1916 transferring to the 60th Battalion on 19 April 1916. As part of the 5th Division the 60th Battalion eventually made their way to France and another young Australian soldier lost his life fighting for King and Country.

Philip's mother Ellen, was notified by cable 28 August 1916 that he was reported as missing, a further cable sent 2 September 1916 stated that Philip has been killed in action 19 July 1916. When Ellen made inquiries after the first cable, a card sent from the Australian Imperial Force Headquarters in London, dated 4 September 1916 stated 'No Report of Casualty'. A letter was sent to London from Base Records in Melbourne explaining that this was not acceptable and they had to think of the families back in Australia and in future the London office should take more care in their reporting.

Philip's mother filled out the Circular for the Roll of Honour stating that he had attended school at Yarra Park. Philip's body was never recovered and he is remembered on the VC Corner Australia Cemetery and Memorial, Fromelles, France on Panel 20.

During the night of 19 July some wounded soldiers were able to make their way back across No-Man's Land to their trenches, some were also helped by their fellow comrades. One soldier who was buried after the battle was **Percy Collier [1057]** he died 20 July 1916. Percy enlisted in Melbourne on 19 July 1915 naming his mother, Sarah Collier, 188 Albert Street, Port Melbourne as his next of kin.[35] At the time of his enlistment Percy was a serving member of the Royal Australian Naval Reserve and had 7 months active service in New Guinea as a Leading Seaman. It appears that there is no list for the first Embarkation Roll of the Naval and Military Expeditionary Force although there is a newspaper article published in the Argus (Melbourne) listing the Victorian Volunteers, Percy's name is on that list.[36]

Percy Collier AWM DA10101

Percy's occupation was Case Maker, he had been apprenticed for 5 years to J Thorpe & Sons in Melbourne. Percy stood 5 feet 5 ¼ inches tall, was aged 21 years and 7 months, complexion was fresh, brown eyes and dark brown hair. Percy also stated he was born in Bendigo, Victoria however, there are no records that confirms his birth.

Percy was eventually allocated to 'A' Company of the 30th Battalion, the battalion was formed at Liverpool, New South Wales on 5th August 1915, about one-fourth of its members consisting of naval ratings of whom the majority came from Victoria.[37] Percy was still wearing his naval uniform at Broadmeadows, Victoria when he had his photo taken which appears on the Australian War Memorial Website. Still in their blue uniforms 'A' Company travelled by train to Sydney to join the other companies of the 30th Battalion. On the 1st September Percy was officially attached to the 30th Battalion changing his blue uniform to khaki.[38]

The 30th Battalion left Sydney 9 November 1915 on HMAT *Beltana* arriving at Suez 11 December 1915. Percy was then transferred to the Machine-Gun Section on 19 March 1916 while stationed at Ferry Post. From 29 May to 3 June 1916 Percy had an attack of Malaria and was transferred to hospital at Moascar. After re-joining his battalion Percy arrived at Marseilles 23 June 1916 heading for the nursery section of the trenches.

The 30th Battalion, of the 8th Brigade, 5th Division went into the Battle of Fromelles 19th July 1916, and Percy's Machine-Gun Section was to be pushed up after the 4th wave to hold the line captured.[39] On 20 July 1916 Percy Collier was killed in action, he was buried the same day at Rue-Petillon Military Cemetery, Fleurbaix, Plot 1, Row K, Grave 68. His medals were sent to his mother, the 1914/15 Star was issued by the Navy.

The battle of Fromelles caused much heartache for many families in Australia, so many of the young men that died left grieving families behind. One such soldier was **Thomas Walker Jones [891]**, the only child of Albert John and Ellen Margaret Jones, he was born in 1893 at Kensington Hill, Victoria. Thomas was the sole support of his mother after his father, Albert John, died in 1907.[40] Thomas enlisted at Melbourne 9 July 1915 naming his mother as next of kin, they were both residing at 102 Railway Place, West Melbourne.[41]

Thomas was aged 21 years and 9 months, occupation Clerk, he stood 5 feet and 5 inches tall, complexion was fair with brown eyes and brown hair. He was allocated to 'D' Company of the 31st Battalion, leaving Melbourne 9 November 1915 onboard the troopship *Wandilla* arriving Suez 7 December 1915. Thomas eventually arrived in the Fromelles area in time for his first engagement of war.

Thomas Walker Jones AWM H06730

Ellen received a letter dated 14 August 1916 reporting that he was wounded then she was notified 25 August 1916 that her son had been missing since 20 July 1916. Ellen had no more word from the Army regarding Thomas and as a result she wrote a letter to the Australian Red Cross on 7 January 1917. Ellen believed that Thomas may be a prisoner of war in Germany and asked if they could give her any information on his where-abouts so that she may communicate with him. A reply was sent back 2 March 1917 informing her that his name does not appear on any prisoner of war list.[42]

Ellen had an agonising wait until 1 August 1917 when Base Records finally informed her that Thomas was killed in action 20 July 1916. His personal effects which consisted of a Note book, Photos, Wrist Watch and Strap were returned to her 10 August 1917. Ellen was granted a pension of £2 per fortnight from 6 January 1917, a small price for her only child. Thomas Walker Jones is remembered on the VC Corner Australian Cemetery and Memorial, Fromelles, Frances, Panel 3.

Another soldier that was killed in action on 20 July 1916 was **Albert Charles Jenkins [883]**. Albert does have a grave with a tombstone marking his final resting place, sadly there is no inscription from his family and the request to fill out the Circular for the Roll of Honour was disregarded. It appears that once he was killed Albert had been largely forgotten by his family.

Albert Charles Jenkins was born in the Bendigo Lying-in Hospital, Victoria to Mary Jenkins, father unknown in 1897, The Lying-in Hospital in Bendigo, was for unmarried mothers.[43] When Albert enlisted at the age of 18 years in the AIF 8 July 1915, he stated that he was born in Fitzroy, Melbourne, Victoria his mother was given as Elizabeth Jenkins and he resided at 217 Napier Street, Fitzroy, Melbourne, Victoria. His age is stated to be 18 years and 0 months which meant he was born in late June or early July 1897; his occupation was Tramway employee.[44]

Elizabeth and her husband William David Jenkins had 10 children, the youngest was Charles Albert Jenkins born in Fitzroy South in 1897.[45] Elizabeth and William also had a daughter, Mary Alice Jenkins born 1883,[46] it is possible that this Mary maybe the mother of Albert Charles Jenkins although she would have been 14 or 15 years of age when Albert was born.

There is a death registration for Albert Charles Jenkins who died at the age of three months in Bendigo, the mother of this Albert Charles was Elizabeth Jenkins. Albert Charles Jenkins was buried at the Kangaroo Flat Public Cemetery Greater Bendigo City in the Roman Catholic section Grave 2461; the date of death given is 18 March 1898.[47] There is no doubt that this child was Charles Albert Jenkins born to Elizabeth as the Albert Charles Jenkins born to Mary would have been at least eight or nine months old. The death certificate for Elizabeth's son does state his name as Albert Charles.[48]

Albert Charles Jenkins enlisted under his correct birth name, there is also written consent from Elizabeth Jenkins stating that Albert Charles Jenkins had her permission to enlist. Albert was assigned to the 31st Battalion leaving Melbourne 9 November 1915 with the rest of his battalion on the troopship *Wandilla*. There is no more information on Albert until 15 May 1916 at Ferry Post when he was Absent from Parade; his award was four days confined to barracks.

Albert's battalion took part in the Battle of Fromelles, the 31st Battalion suffered many casualties especially on the morning of the 20 July when Albert was killed in action. After withdrawing to their own lines, the enemy artillery bombardment was intense and even under shelter of their own trenches the casualties were awful.[49] When Albert was buried, he had no wounds on him but was killed by shell shock.[50]

Albert's 'mother', Elizabeth, applied for a pension which was granted from 29 October 1916, she also received his personal effects and his medals. When it came time to fill out any forms for the Imperial (now Commonwealth) War Graves Commission this was never done, along with the Roll of Honour Circular. His tombstone only has his name and date of death even though Elizabeth was still alive and so were many of her children.

In the aftermath of the battle, No-Man's Land was full of the wounded unable to return to their own trenches and once the sun had risen the shocked soldiers in the front lines looked on in dismay at the suffering of their fellow countrymen. Finally a soldier, Private William Miles, from the 29th Battalion puts on a Red Cross armband and goes into No-Man's Land in search of his Officer, Captain Kenneth Mortimer. While out there he is approached by a German Officer who asks him to return with an officer to see if a truce can be arranged to collect the wounded. Major Alexander Murdoch of the 29th Battalion accompanies Private Miles back to the German lines where Major Murdoch formally asks for a truce.

Major Murdoch returns to the Australian lines full of confidence that they will be able to rescue hundreds of their men, he passes the information on to the Commander of the 5th Division, General McCay, only to hear an immediate answer, NO. Standing orders from General Headquarters that no negotiations of any kind, and on any subject, were to be had with the enemy. Orders were at once sent to put an end to the truce and no soldier was to venture back into No-Man's Land to rescue the wounded. The next day, 21st July, Sergeant Simon Fraser and his mates from the 57th Battalion go out in search of the wounded and are able to bring them in. Night after night the rescues continue saving many of their mates. The whole time ignoring the orders from General McCay. There is no figure on just how many of the wounded were brought back, however the number was in the hundreds, sadly many were left in No-Man's Land to die alone, Fromelles would become the most tragic event in Australian history.

On the day of the Armistice of 11 November 1918, Australia's official war correspondent, Charles Bean, wandered over the battlefield of Fromelles and observed the grisly aftermath of the battle. 'We found the old No-Man's Land simply full of our dead,' he recorded. Soon after the war these remains were gathered to construct VC Corner Cemetery, the only solely Australian War Cemetery in France. It is also the only cemetery without headstones, just a stone wall inscribed with the names of the 1,299 Australians who died in battle nearby and who have no known graves. The unidentified remains of 410 are buried in mass graves under two grass plots in the cemetery.[51]

CHAPTER 3
POZIERES AND MOUQUET FARM 1916

Starting on 23 July and lasting for six weeks the battle of Pozieres and Mouquet Farm took place in northern France. The village of Pozieres is on the Albert-Bapaume Road and lies atop a ridge, nearby the village is the highest point known as 'Hill 160' or 'The Windmill'. An important defensive position for the Germans, the village of Pozieres was an outpost to the second defensive trench system known as the O.G. (Old German) lines.

While the newly arrived Australian 5th Division took over the quiet sector near Armentieres, the 1st, 2nd and 4th Divisions moved south about 64 kilometres from Fromelles to the Somme region. Between 13 and 17 July four attacks were made by British infantry against Pozieres first by patrols, later after heavy bombardment which reduced the village to heaps of rubble. When the British artillery opened up all of their heavy guns, they destroyed every building in the village of Pozieres. After the bombardment was over the British soldiers advanced, but the Germans were still there, coming out of their underground basements, they counter-attacked and drove the British back causing indescribable casualties.

The British Commander Lieutenant General Sir Hubert Gough then met with Major General Harold Walker, Commander of the Australian 1 Division on 18 July 1916 giving him the order 'I want you to go into the line and attack Pozieres tomorrow night….!'[1] Major General Harold Walker objected to the timing and sought a delay until early 23 July to allow his division to prepare. The attack was to be from the south-east on the night of 22/23 July starting at 12.30am. The 3rd Brigade to attack on the right, the 1st Brigade on the left. The 2nd Brigade was to move into position as Divisional Reserve in Sausage Valley. The attacking forces had been in position since the night before in sight of the bodies of British soldiers who tried and failed what they were about to attempt.

While waiting for zero hour the Australian troops endured the German shells that were now falling, killing and wounding many before the attack had started. As the daylight on the 22 July was fading the 1st and 3rd Brigades were issued with two bombs and two empty sandbags each. During the early part of the night the German shelling intensified on the Australian trenches and all across No-Man's Land flares turned the area bright as day. By late evening on 22 July the Allied artillery was firing their guns as fast as they could reload, with the German artillery replying.

The bombardment which started the battle for Pozieres became famous among the many later ones on the Western Front. Just after midnight the first wave of the attacking battalions of the 1st Division crept out of their trenches into No-Man's Land following a line of tape which had previously been laid. Now they had to lay still hoping the Germans did not see them. This stage of an attack was always an anxious one; if the Germans discovered the troops out of their trenches unimpeded machine-gun fire and artillery shells would destroy them.

As the 2nd and 9th Battalions crept closer to the German lines, they were clearly seen and came under attack from machine-gun fire taking what cover they could within shell holes. At 12.30 am on 23 July the whistles blew and the first wave of the brave and courageous Australian soldiers stood up and charged. By 4.00 am the main attack had seized the village south of the Bapaume Road except for two or three ruined houses at the extreme north-east.[2] Many young Australian soldiers died during the Battle of Pozieres and Mouquet Farm which became the greatest sacrifice of this country's men in our military history.

Inscribed on a stone plinth at the site of the Windmill Charles Bean's epitaph simply states: *The ruin of Pozieres Windmill which lies here was the centre of the struggle in this part of the Somme battlefield in July and August 1916. It was captured on August 4 by Australian troops who fell more thickly on this ridge than on any other battlefield of the war.*[3]

A young Australian soldier who lost his life on that fateful night was **William Patrick Buchan [4147]**. William was living in Brisbane, Queensland when he enlisted 28 August 1915, giving his age as 23 years and 3 months. Stating he was born in Melbourne in 1892 he stood 5 feet and 5 ½ inches tall, his complexion was dark with grey eyes and light brown hair, religion was Roman Catholic. Occupation Labourer, and next of kin was his guardian Miss Ellen McCann who lived at Timor West, Via Maryborough, Victoria, William was allocated to the 13th reinforcement 9th Battalion [4]

There is no birth record for a William Patrick Buchan in any Australian birth records although, records show that William was admitted on 20 November 1895 to the St Joseph's Home for Destitute Children at Surry Hills, Victoria. His age at that time was 2 years and six months old, born at Melbourne, his mother's name was Buchan and his religion was Catholic. William was educated and raised at St Joseph's until the age of 10 when he was adopted by Miss Ellen McCann of Timor West via Maryborough on 11 July 1902.[5]

William left Brisbane onboard the troopship *Kyarra* 3 January 1916 arriving Alexandria 19 February. After a short stay in Egypt, he boarded the *Transylvania* for Marseilles disembarking on 4 April 1916, William was taken on strength to the 9th Battalion 25 May 1916. William's battalion spent some time in the trenches at Fromelles before leaving to go south with the rest of the 1st Division to take part in the battle that would end his life. It is not known when William was killed however the 9th Battalion was at the forefront of the attack and for six hours the battalion saw hand to hand fighting. During this time the fortunes of both sides sank and rose until finally the enemy was pushed back to his second strong post.[6]

William's effects were sent to Miss McCann, they consisted of; 1 Devotional Book, Holdall, 1 Hair Brush, 1 Razor, 1 Shaving Brush, Comb, 2 Kit Bag Handles, Housewife, Lead Pencil, Boot Pad, Post Cards and a Book of Views. On 24 March 1917 Mr W J Harding from Gormanston, West Coast, Tasmania wrote to the Army requesting information on William, the Army then informed Mr Harding that William had been killed in action. What connection this person had to William is not known.

Miss McCann filled out William's Roll of Honour Circular stating that she believed William was about 19 years when he was killed, he was 24. William does not have a grave instead he is commemorated at the Villers-Bretonneux Memorial in France. Ellen McCann died in the Timor district aged 86 in 1952.[7]

An Englishman by the name of **Charles Henry James Davis [2660A]** also died during the initial stage of the battle. Charles was born in 1889 at Hampstead Heath, London. He enlisted at Lismore, New South Wales 18 August 1915 where he worked as a Carter, his address was C/- Mrs J Morgan, Orion Street, Lismore. Charles stated his age as 26 years and 5 months, his complexion was fair with grey eyes and light brown hair, he was 5 feet and 5 ¾ inches tall, his next of kin was a friend, Samuel McLean also from Lismore. Charles was initially allocated to 6th reinforcement, 25th Battalion then later transferred to the 9th Battalion after his arrival in Egypt.[8]

Joining his unit 28 February, he left Alexandria on the troopship *Saxonia* arriving at Marseilles 3 April 1916. Charles was posting as missing until a Court of Enquiry held on 2 July 1917 found that he was killed 23 July 1916 by a shell in No-Man's Land. The Army notified Samuel McLean of Charles's demise and when asked if he knew of any blood relatives Mr McLean wrote back to say that Charles was all alone and had no relations at all. There are no definite birth records for Charles or any supportive records to show when he arrived in Australia, however, F Elms who lived at 39 New End, Hampton, London wrote to the Red Cross 15 April 1917 stating that Charles, a cousin, had not been heard from.[9] Later a Miss Violet Staines from 30 Manor Park Road, East Finchley, London wrote to the Army stating that she was engaged to Charles and when he was next in London on leave, they were to be married.

Miss Staines forwarded to the Army letters that she had received from Charles while he was in the trenches to support her claim, also she sent a copy of Charles' will naming her as his sole beneficiary and that she was claiming his medals. The Army then wrote to Miss Staines to ask if she knew of any blood relations. She replied that Charles was a deserted child from the age of one month and was adopted by her great uncle and aunt and that she was a second cousin to Charles. She went on to say that Charles had left England for Australia in 1909, however this is difficult to prove as many men by the name of Charles Davis arrived in Australia prior to the outbreak of war. The Army then made the decision to allow Miss Violet Staines to receive his medals. Charles has no known grave; he has been commemorated at the Villers-Bretonneux Memorial in France.

The 9th Battalion was one of the first troops ashore at Gallipoli in the early hours of 25 April 1915, and even though the battalion was divided with the re-organisation of the AIF early in 1916 many of the original Gallipoli troops remained with the battalion. One such Gallipoli veteran was **Cecil Raymond Heaton [493]** who enlisted at Toowoomba, Queensland 29 August 1914.

Cecil claimed he was born in 1877 in the Parish of St Marys, Nottingham, England, his occupation was Fitter, he had spent 4 years and 10 months with John Jardine at Nottingham. It is possible his apprenticeship was at the Jardine's lace making machines in Nottingham. He named his next of kin as his father, Cecil Heaton, at the Langham Hotel, Radford Road, Nottingham. He also stated that he had served 12 years with the 16th Queens Lancers, however research has failed to locate his service under that name. Cecil stood 5 feet 7 inches tall, his complexion was fair with grey eyes and brown hair, he also had a scar on the back of his right wrist, Cecil was allocated to the 9th Battalion.[10]

In spite of extensive searching, no records at all can locate any birth record for Cecil or any record of his arrival in Australia, there is an entry for a Cecil Heaton, occupation Engineer who was admitted to a workhouse, St George's Union at Westminster.[11] His admission date was 2 March 1910 and discharge 24 March 1910, his year of birth was noted as 1872 it is possible this could be the same man who enlisted in Toowoomba, Queensland in 1914. He may have had some military training as he enlisted as a private, became a lance corporal 4 September then a sergeant two days later on 6 September. This did not last as he was reduced to the ranks 26 September and given 16 days detention while enroute to Egypt onboard the troopship *Omrah* which left Brisbane 24 September 1914.

During the initial landing on Gallipoli, Cecil received the Distinguished Conduct Medal for bravery near Gaba Tepe on 25 April 1915 when he rescued and brought in, under heavy shell and machine-gun fire, a wounded man. Cecil was again promoted to corporal three days later on 28 April. Cecil was Mentioned in Despatches by General Sir Ian L M Hamilton on 12 June 1915 'For gallant and distinguished services in the Field'.[12] Cecil stayed with his battalion on Gallipoli until 19 June 1915 when, at 5.30am Corporal Heaton was hit by shrapnel on the arm.[13] His wound was critical enough to send him to the 1st Australian General Hospital in Cairo before being discharged back to Australia 14 August 1915 onboard *Themistocles.*

While he was back in Australia Cecil met up with a journalist who reported a meeting with Sergeant 'Skinny' Heaton, this story was printed in the Adelaide paper, The Register 11 October 1915. The journalist remarked that on his uniform he wore ribbons that showed he had been in the North-West Afghanistan with Sir George White; in the Tirah Campaign, under Sir Power Palmer; the Egyptian campaign; in the Sudan with Sir Francis Wingate and in the Boer War, where he was made a Queen's Sergeant.[14]

Cecil recuperated in Brisbane from his injury which included a fractured forearm and badly damaged hand and fingers. In his

Service Record it is noted that Cecil, while recovering from his wound, gave his occupation as an Electrical Engineer. Once he had fully recovered, he embarked with the 13th reinforcements of his battalion at Brisbane 3 January 1916. When he re-joined his unit in France 22 April 1916, Cecil had the rank of sergeant. Before Cecil left Brisbane, he made a will dated 2 January 1916 leaving all of his property to two different ladies. First, he left to Miss Lucy Elizabeth Dunn the Langham Hotel in Nottingham plus the 8 shops next to the hotel which he claimed to own. To Miss Esme Theila Jean Newman he left his Insurance Policy Number 1050 amounting to £700, there is no name for the policy.

Shortly after arriving in France Cecil found himself in trouble again, this time on 6 May 1916 at Steenwerck when he was charged with being drunk and could not maintain order in his billet. Cecil was severely reprimanded by the Commanding Office of the 9th Battalion however; he kept his rank of sergeant. While taking part in the attack on Pozieres Cecil Raymond Heaton was killed in action 23 July, he is buried at the Pozieres British Cemetery, Plot 3, Row L, Grave 14.

The usual cablegram was sent to Cecil's father at the Langham Hotel in England but was returned stating that Mr Cecil Heaton was unknown at the hotel, this was very strange as Sergeant Heaton claimed to be the owner of hotel. When Base Records received Cecil's will, correspondence was sent to Miss Dunn asking if she knew of any relatives, she replied stating that he had no relations as both parents were deceased, she would be claiming his property including his medals.

Solicitors, W H Wilson & Hemming from Brisbane, then wrote to Base Records stating that they were representing Miss Dunn and had engaged solicitors in England in relation to the property left to her by Cecil. Base Records in Melbourne advertised in Australian and English papers trying to locate anyone who knew Cecil however this was unsuccessful. When Cecil's Distinguished Conduct Medal was available this was forwarded to Miss Dunn.

Grave of Cecil Raymond Heaton Nation Archives of Australia

The fact that Cecil did not own what he claimed became apparent to his beneficiaries, they eventually did not answer any letters from the Army forcing Base Records to mark his campaign medals as Untraceable. The Roll of Honour Circular for Cecil was never filled out, a letter sent to Miss Dunn 22 January 1924 giving her the opportunity to place a personal inscription on his permanent headstone was never answered.

Cecil Raymond Heaton did appear to exaggerate his past, clearly he did not own the property he claimed and were his previous campaign ribbons his or did he embellish his military experience to impress? Much research was done on the various campaign ribbons that Cecil wore however no proof has been located to confirm his involvement. It is thought, although difficult to verify, that Cecil Raymond Heaton was not his real name. Obviously, Cecil was a brave and courageous soldier and there is no denying he did receive a Distinguished Conduct Medal and was Mentioned in Despatches.

Another Gallipoli veteran to fall on 23 July 1916 was **John Edward Kenyon [741]**, an Englishman from Southampton, Hampshire, who answered the call of his motherland and enlisted into the AIF 27 August 1914. His gave his age as 34 years old, occupation Bush Worker who lived in Kyogle, New South Wales. Travelling to Brisbane to enlist he gave the name of a friend, M E Halstead, who resided in Brisbane, as next of kin. John was 5 feet 7 ¼ inches tall with dark complexion, brown eyes and black hair, he was allocated to the 9th Battalion, and promoted to Lance Corporal 10 September 1914.[15]

One of the first ashore at Gallipoli, John soon showed his courage by earning a Distinguished Conduct Medal on the day of the landing. His citation states: *On 25 April, in the face of heavy shrapnel and rifle fire, Kenyon returned from the firing line to collect reinforcements and assist in leading a successful bayonet charge to the brow of hill, which was eventually held against great odds.*[16] John was promoted to Sergeant on 28 April 1915. John again proved he was a capable soldier as on 24 August 1915 he was Mentioned in

Despatches, for Gallant and Distinguished services in the Field.[17] Towards the end of the Gallipoli campaign John was in and out of hospital due to the deteriorating conditions on the peninsular that affected many troops. After the withdrawal from Gallipoli the 9th Battalion eventually moved onto the Western Front in April 1916 spending time in the quieter trenches known as the nursery.

On 11 May 1916 while in the Sailly area John was charged with leaving a parade without permission. At a hearing held 15 May John was severely reprimanded but kept his rank of Sergeant. On the night of 1 and 2 July 1916 volunteers from the 9th Battalion took part in a raid on the enemy trenches in the Fleurbaix (Fromelles) region of France. For his action that night Sergeant John Edward Kenyon received a Military Medal. His citation reads; *During the successful raid carried out by 9th Battalion on the night 1/2 July 1916 in company with his officer was first into enemy trenches where they tackled 21 Germans in a large dug-out. In spite of the fact that rifle and revolver fire was directed at them from the dug-out these two went in returning the enemy fire eventually killing seven and disarming and capturing the remainder. Throughout the raid this NCO proved absolutely fearless and set a splendid example of gallantry. He has already been awarded the DCM for gallantry on Gallipoli.*[18]

Sadly, Sergeant John Edward Kenyon died during the initial battle of Pozieres 23 July 1916, John has no grave and is remembered on the Villers-Bretonneux Memorial. The Army wrote to his next of kin, a friend named M E Halstead, this person seemingly did not know John. His will which was made 24 April 1915 named a Maud Cobb as his beneficiary. Maud was engaged to be married to John and made a claim for his medals, Base Records made the decision on 28 July 1920 to pass all of John's medals to her, by now she had married and was Mrs M Haupt.

One year after John's death the Cobb family placed a notice in a Brisbane paper in memory of John. The notice read; *In memory of our dear friend Jack who was killed in action in July 1916. He like a soldier fell. Inserted by his friends, Mrs Cobb, Mrs Haupt and Mrs Devine.*[19]

Mrs M Haupt did fill in the Roll of Honour Circular for John stating that he had been born in Berks, England, had arrived in Australia during 1904, and aged 42 when he died. The birth records for John Edward Kenyon have been problematic due to the various ages stated and location of his birth, the same for his arrival in Australia. Mrs Maud Haupt did state that he did not have any relatives alive back in England.

Another Englishman to join the AIF when war was declared was **Frederick Howard Arnold Horsfall [177]** who enlisted 19 August 1914. Frederick was born 1890 at Gravesend, Kent, England, he stood 5 feet 5 inches tall with fair complexion, brown eyes and dark hair, he gave his occupation as a Sailor.[20] Frederick was the only child of Frederick Peel and Louise Mary Horsfall. From an early age Frederick travelled with his father onboard his ship to all parts of the world until the age of seven years old. His schooling was at Pitman's College London.[21]

The family based themselves in Nova Scotia and Victoria, British Columbia, Canada where Frederick became an expert sailor. On the death of his father, Frederick and his mother moved back to England where he joined the Queen's Own (Royal West Kent) Regiment in March 1913.[22] After one year of service Frederick resigned from the Regiment in 1914 with the idea of moving to Australia to start a new life for himself and his mother.

Frederick arrived in Sydney 18 June 1914 onboard the *Osterley* leaving his mother behind until he was settled,[23] however Frederick enlisted within days of war being declared. He was allocated to the 2nd Battalion, one of the first infantry units raised in New South Wales, the 2nd along with the 1st, 3rd and 4th Battalions formed the 1st Brigade. Frederick and the rest of the 2nd Battalion left Australia just two months later arriving in Egypt 2 December, 1914. Frederick took part in the Anzac landing as part of the second and third waves on 25 April, enduring all the severity of Gallipoli until the 2nd was withdrawn back to Egypt.

During February 1916 Frederick was promoted to Lance Corporal before leaving for the Western Front, France. Just

Frederick Howard Horsfall AWM H0666

before the battle for Pozieres was to start, he was again promoted this time to Corporal, on 17 July 1916. Frederick's war ended 23 July 1916 when he was killed in action by a small piece of shell splinter which struck the back of his head just below his helmet.[24] Frederick's body was never recovered, he has no grave but is remembered on the Villers-Bretonneux Memorial. When his mother filled out his Roll of Honour, she also sent a photo of Frederick, her only child, requesting that it was to be forwarded to the War Memorial.

A member of the 1st Battalion who was severely wounded during the initial attack, was **Richard 'Dick' McDonald [5182]** born in the region of the Burdekin River, North Queensland 25 April 1883. There are no birth records for Richard, what is known about Richard is that he was aboriginal and when he enlisted 3 December 1915 at Liverpool, New South Wales, he stated that he had no next of kin.[25] His address was C/- Post Office Kiama, New South Wales, he stood 5 feet 9 ½ inches tall, complexion was dark with brown eyes and black hair. He stated that he was still serving with the 37th Infantry Band. The photo of Richard McDonald is reproduced from the Queensland State Library.

At a recruiting meeting held in the Oddfellows Hall in Kiama on Thursday, 25 November 1915, Richard volunteered to become a Waratah and proved to be one of the most popular recruits on the march.[26] At the Kiama send off, he accepted a safety razor and match box from the Military and Recruiting Association, a presentation from the band, and a kit bag from the Red Cross. He was the guest of honour at a farewell organized by the local cricket club, his friends waiting patiently for him to arrive home on leave, aboard the 8pm train.[27]

Richard left Australia with the Waratahs 1 April 1916, aboard *Makariai* disembarking at Suez 2 May. He then left Alexandria 9 May arriving at Marseilles 17 May, finally joining the 1st Battalion 11 July 1916, Richard's war was about to begin. After a route march on 20 July the 1st Battalion arrived at Contalmaison where it took over the front line in readiness for the attack on Pozieres.

Richard McDonald Queensland State Library

The night of 22/23 July was a very costly one for the courageous Australian soldiers, one victim was Richard who suffered a gunshot wound to the abdomen. Richard was taken to South Midlands Field Ambulance where he succumbed to his wound dying 24 July 1916. He was buried in the Warloy-Baillon Military Cemetery, 5 miles west of Albert.

Richard left a will leaving his estate to Miss A M Morrow from Dapto, New South Wales, his effects consisted of Photos, Pipe, Wallet, Wrist Watch and Strap plus 2 Devotional Books. As Richard had previously stated he had no next of kin, Major Lean from Base Records, Melbourne contacted Miss Morrow in an attempt to find some blood relatives. Her reply was that he was 'absolutely without a living relative' and as a result Richard's medals were classified as Untraceable.

Richard may not have had any living relations however; he had many friends that thought a great deal of him as shown in a local newspaper: *ROLL OF HONOUR. PRIVATE DICK McDONALD. There seems little doubt that Private R McDonald, no relatives, referred to Dick McDonald, who left Kiama as a Waratah, since the Sydney papers announced such to be case; and a man, unwept and unmourned, for he had a warm place in Kiama's heart, and many honoured the white soul of him who so earnestly wanted to do his bit. His dark skin it was said, stopped his acceptance when he tried first to enlist and when he finally was accepted, no happier man set out on the great adventure, than did he. A recollection that will long remain with those that saw it, was his childlike delight in the presents that were showered upon him at the public send-off to the Waratahs. After the meeting he spread them out, taking a joy in each one. "It was just like at Xmas time" he said, with the bright smile that was his own. In the national kinship that binds us close in these days of stress and struggle for our Empire, Dick McDonald, who fine physique and manly qualities, gentleness of nature and kindly soul, gained him many friends and well-wishers, as his patriotism gained our admirations, passes away sincerely mourned. He died of wounds in France, and far from the old district he rests, but his name will live in honoured remembrance with those who went forth from our midst, and were called upon to give their greatest gift, for their country.*[28]

On 25 April 1917, the anniversary of Richard's birth a Moreton Bay fig tree was planted in his memory on a Kiama reserve where the old Council Chambers had once been located. An initiative of Mr W G Walker of Manning Street, Kiama, the

4pm ceremony was attended by 50 cadets along with quarrymen and cricketers. Sadly, today the tree which was planted in memory of one of Kiama's fallen heroes has since disappeared.[29]

Major Lean from Base Records sent Miss Morrow a Roll of Honour Circular which she filled out and sent back, even though she did not know where he was born, she did state that: 'He was a very keen cricketer and sportsman, very popular among men.' In 1926 Miss Morrow wrote asking if she could have photos of his grave and asked if she could place a personal inscription on his tombstone. Richard's tombstone in France has the wording *My Friend*. Miss Annie May Morrow died at Wollongong in 1949, she never married.[30]

Richard's Bible was located in a box of second-hand books at Surry Hills, Sydney in 2006, the Bible was received on behalf of Kiama Library by the Mayor, Sandra McCarthy, at a small ceremony at Kiama Library 7 July 2011.[31]

On 25 July the 5th Battalion was brought into the attack taking their objectives during the day which were O.G.1 and then onto O.G.2. But owing to a solid counter attack by the enemy accompanied by a strong bomb attack made it advisable to withdraw back to O.G.1 making sure of holding and consolidating it. Casualties were heavy being 6 officers and 39 other ranks killed, 6 officers and 242 other ranks wounded and 1 officer and 158 other ranks missing.[32]

One of those missing was **Albert Roberts [1641]**, it was later found that Albert had been killed in action 25 July. Albert was born in 1887 at North Melbourne to Albert and Totten Roberts,[33] he was their only child. When he enlisted, 2 December 1914 Albert named a friend as his next of kin, J A Burrell, as his parents had died when he was a young child. Albert stood 5 feet and 5 ¼ inches tall, his complexion was fresh with blue eyes and brown hair, he was allocated to the 3rd reinforcements of the 5th Battalion.[34]

Albert was taken on strength to the 5th Battalion at Anzac Cove 5 May 1915 in time to join the 2nd Brigade that left that night for Cape Helles. Arriving back to Anzac Cove 17 May 1915

Albert stayed on the Gallipoli Peninsula until the 5th Battalion was withdrawn during December 1915. After confirmation of Albert's death, the Army informed his next of kin which revealed that Julie Annie Burrell was the sister of Albert Roberts senior and that she had raised young Albert after the death of his parents and that he was an only child. After consideration from the Army his aunt was granted his medals.

By the 26 July the 5th Brigade which included the 20th Battalion was holding the front when at 7am, the German bombardment again descended on Pozieres. The enemy fire this day was as severe as that of the previous and far heavier than that of the 24 July.[35] During this heavy shelling a very young Australian soldier was killed at the tender age of 16 years. He was **Edward Sydney Cawe [2342]** who was born 21 November 1899 in Surry Hills, New South Wales, although his birth was not registered until early in 1900.[36] He was the only child to Edward Sydney Cawe and Jessie Maria Weekes who had married in Sydney during 1899. Young Edward's father found himself on the wrong side of the law even before he married Jessie spending numerous times in Gaol for various offences including embezzlement, stealing, shop breaking and neglect to comply with order of Courts. His offences started in 1898 and went through to 1905. He also had many aliases which included Edward Cove, Edward Corr and George Brown.[37]

In 1905 while Jessie and young Edward were living at 252 Devonshire Street, Surry Hills Jessie filed for divorce from her husband citing wife desertion, at that time Edward senior was in Gaol for neglect to comply with order of Courts.[38] Jessie also stated that she was forced into service to make a living which could explain why she allowed her sister, May Eveline Lowry and her husband, to adopt young Edward. Mr & Mrs Lowry lived in the Unanderra region of New South Wales where Edward had his schooling. Mr Lowry worked for the Railway and on 22 October 1914 young Edward commenced his employment with the Railway as a Junior Porter.[39]

Edward carried out his duties with the Railway, until the 11 July 1915 enlisting into the AIF at Liverpool. Even though he was fifteen years of age, the Attesting Officer did not question him when Edward stated his age as 18 years and 1 month. Edward put his address down as Brunswick Street, Brisbane, Queensland, the same address as his mother who he named as his next of kin. Edward was obviously unaware that his mother had remarried 4 October 1913 to Vincent Walter Berry in Queensland.[40]

Edward was a tall lad for his age standing 5 feet 7 inches and weighing in at 130lbs so he had no problem enlisting, his complexion was dark with blue eyes and black hair.[41] The day after he enlisted Edward got himself baptized in Sydney 12 July 1915, the record showed that he lived in Dapto.[42] Edward was then granted leave from the Railway to join the Army 24 July 1915.

Edward embarked on the troopship *Ballarat* on 5 September 1915 and after arriving in Egypt he appeared to be very excited about the sights of Cairo. He wrote to his aunt stating *that he was one of 2,000 doing picket duty in the streets of Cairo during Xmas and New Year weeks in consequence of some pranks played by some soldiers in the streets of Cairo. Previous to that on New Year's Eve he had supper at 12 0'clock at Kasr-el-Nil barrack on the banks of the river Nile.*[43]

Edward was taken on strength to the 20th Battalion 19 January 1916 at Tel-El-Kebir, eventually arriving in Marseilles 25 March 1916. Edward's war was now beginning. During the heavy shelling on 26 July 1916 young Edward was first listed as missing, believed killed. After an enquiry which was held 6 March 1917, it was found that he had been killed in action. Edward's aunt Mrs Lowry received a letter from Sapper F Midgley who stated that *Edward who was in the machine gun section was heavily shelled by the enemy.* Sapper Midgley concluded by saying that *Private Cawe was liked by all who knew him.*[44]

Edward's medals were sent to his mother in Brisbane along with the Roll of Honour Memorial Circular, however, this was filled out by his aunt and uncle confirming that he was 16 years of age when he died. Edward's name is on the Villers-Bretonneux Memorial in France.

During the early morning of the 26 July 1916 **Charles Miller [1044]** was killed as the 20th Battalion made their charge. Charles was born sometime between 1894 and 1897, there is no record of his birth due to the fact he was adopted and was given his name by his adopted parents. He enlisted 7 May 1915 claiming he was 19 years and 6 months old; his occupation was Farm Labourer and was living with his adopted mother, Esther, at Nicholson Street, Burwood, New South Wales. Charles stood 5 feet and 7 ¾ inches tall, complexion dark with hazel eyes and dark hair.[45]

The 20th Battalion left Sydney 25 June 1915 onboard the troopship *Berrima* arriving in Egypt then left Alexandria for Anzac Cove where Charles went ashore with his battalion 22 August. On the 22 September he received 14 days Field Punishment No. 2 for falling asleep on duty at Gallipoli, after his indiscretion Charles behaved himself for the remainder of his time on the Peninsular arriving back at Alexandria 9 January 1916. On 21 January, while at Tel-El-Kebir, Charles was absent for 2 hours resulting in 3 days Field Punishment No. 2.

Charles travelled to France with the rest of the 20th Battalion arriving in Marseilles 25 March 1916 before moving to Steenbecque, a quieter part of the front line. At the end of June, the 20th moved again and at 10.10pm on the 24 July into the British old front line at Sausage Valley. 26 July saw the 20th take part in an attack which was launched at 3.21am in three columns. Many companies were badly cut up by rifle and machine-gun fire and held up by uncut enemy wire. The estimated casualties were 2 Officers wounded and 200 ordinary ranks killed, wounded and missing.[46]

Charles Miller was killed during the early morning attack, listed as missing until 24 March 1917 when Private F J Murphy [1049] stated that he saw Charles fall in the charge about 4.00am. He saw him again in another charge 28 July lying in No-Man's-Land and was sure he was dead.

The Army wrote to Esther Miller asking if his father was alive, this was when Esther explained that her husband had died in 1902 and that Charles had been adopted from the Central Methodist

Charles Miller AWM H06782

Missions Children's Home "Dalmar" in Croydon on 20 March 1901, he was her only family. Charles was aged four at that time and before she allowed her son to enlist Esther contacted the Children's Home to make sure no one had been asking after him. The Army agreed to give Esther Charles' medals. Esther filled in the Roll of Honour Circular stating that Charles was aged 19 and 6 months when he was killed, and he attended the Grammar School at Tamworth.

Another member of the 20th Battalion that was killed 27 July 1916 was **Henry Edwards [538],** a Gallipoli veteran. Henry had enlisted at Liverpool, New South Wales on 15 March 1915. Born in London, England in 1883 he gave his mother, Jane Ware who lived at 76 Denmark Road, Kilburn, London as his next of kin. Henry was 5 feet 5 ¼ inches tall with a fair complexion, blue eyes and fair hair, occupation was Labourer.[47]

Leaving Sydney on the troopship *Berrima* Henry sailed to Egypt before heading to Gallipoli arriving at Anzac Cove with the 20th Battalion 22 August 1915. While at Russell's Top 5 September Henry received a shell wound to his face and ear which was serious enough to send him back to Egypt. He eventually rejoined his battalion in January 1916, arriving in Marseilles 25 March 1916. One month later 28 April he was charged with being out of bounds for which he received 4 days Field Punishment No 2. Henry seemed to get in trouble again as in early July he was charged with breaking out of billets and AWL from 1 July to 3 July, this time he received 14 days of Field Punishment No 2.

Henry was reported as missing but was found to be killed in action after a Court of Enquiry was held 29 July 1917. Correspondence sent to his mother in England was returned with the note, gone away. As notices placed in the English newspapers in 1917 and 1918 brought no response for anyone who knew Henry, his medals were marked as Untraceable. Searches of English records for Henry's birth has proved futile, there is no record of his mother Jane Ware that can be located, it is also unknown when Henry arrived in Australia. Major Lean from Base Records in Melbourne searched through Henry's effects that were returned to Australia. Nothing was found to help find any clue to his relations back in England. Henry's name appears on the Villers-Bretonneux Memorial in France.

Another Gallipoli veteran was **Ernest Hogan [2036B],** Ernest enlisted at Liverpool, New South Wales 17 March 1915. Ernest, born about 1882 in Sydney, New South Wales stated his occupation as Cook, he stood 5 feet 8 ½ inches tall, his complexion was fair with grey eyes and brown hair. Initially he stated that he had no next of kin then the name of Miss May Brennan, 8 Evans Place, Surry Hills was given, this was later changed to Miss Tess Young, 1 Taggart Street, Surry Hills. First, Ernest was allocated to the 3rd Reinforcement 20th Battalion, however after arriving at Anzac Cove 29 September 1915 he was taken on strength to the 18th Battalion.[48]

Surviving Gallipoli, Ernest was back in Egypt when he went AWL 22 January 1916, his award for that indiscretion was 168 hours of Field Punishment No.2. After arriving in France Ernest was charged 4 April 1916, with being Drunk and Insolence to a Superior Officer. The award was 28 days Field Punishment No. 2 and 28 days' pay. Ernest decided to go AWL again, this time from 28 June to 30 June, he was awarded 168 hours Field Punishment No. 2. Ernest died 28 July 1916, the War Diary for the 18th Battalion stated there were casualties due to shelling on their position from their own artillery.[49]

Ernest had made a will naming Tess Young as his beneficiary, as a result Tess did receive his personal effects. Base Records wrote to Tess asking if Ernest had any blood relation in order to pass on his medals. Tess replied stating that the parents of Ernest had died when he was very young and he had been brought up by strangers, she then asked if she could have his medals, Base Records replied saying this was not possible. The Army did try to contact Miss May Brennan, the letter was returned marked as Unknown, as a result his paperwork was marked as Untraceable. Ernest has no grave; his name is on the Villers-Bretonneux Memorial in France.

By the early hours of 5 August 1916, the 5th Brigade which included the 20th Battalion had captured a majority of the OG (Old German) lines. The German response was quick, launching a brutal artillery barrage. Sometime during the 5 August 1916 **Frederick Fawkner [864]** from the 20th Battalion was killed when hit by a shell. Frederick enlisted at Liverpool, New South Wales 29 March 1915 stating his occupation was Station Hand. He named a sister, Mrs Margaret Floyce/Floyd who lived at Curzon Street,

North Melbourne as his next of kin. Frederick was aged 28 years and 10 months old, his place of birth was St Kilda, Victoria, he stood 5 feet 6 ¾ inches tall with fair complexion, grey eyes and brown hair.[50] A search of birth records in Australia has failed to locate his birth along with Margaret, his sister, there is also no record of his sister's marriage.

Frederick arrived at Gallipoli with the rest of the 20th Battalion surviving until the evacuation back to Egypt. On 14 January 1916 Frederick was awarded 14 day's detention for AWL from 8 to 12 January. He seemed a model soldier from there and was promoted to Lance Corporal on 23 May 1916 after arriving in France. After Frederick's death the Army wrote to his sister, Margaret, however all mail was returned stating that the person was not known.

A letter dated 26 April 1917 was sent to Base Records from Mr W G Balfour, Killara Estate, Culcairn, New South Wales, the employer of Frederick. Mr Balfour claims he had a letter passed onto him from J Dale, who also worked on the Estate, and that Frederick was a good friend of Mr Dale. Fredrick's letter to his friend was written 1 November 1915 from Gallipoli stating, *I gave your name and address as my next of kin stating that you were no relation. My previous papers leave a married sister's address Curzon Street, N Melbourne but I don't know where you would find them now. At my rate if I get bowled over have a try for it yourself, there will be a few quid left to come for me.*

Mr Balfour went on to say that Mr Dale wanted to know where he now stood? Frederick's paperwork was never changed to Mr Dale and as a result the Army replied to Mr Balfour that the next of kin was Fredrick's sister. Base Records did try to locate his sister by advertising in all newspapers however, this proved unsuccessful. Searches for any evidence of Fredrick or his sister, Margaret, prior to Frederick's enlistment has proved to be useless. Frederick's medals were classified as Untraceable, his name appears on the Villers-Bretonneux Memorial.

On the night of the 5/6 August a heavy bombardment took a substantial toll on the 2nd Division and were relieved by the 4th

Division. On 7 August orders were issued for the 4th Brigade to launch on the night of 8 August, the first of a series of advances along the summit of the ridge towards Mouquet Farm. During this advance a young native of Switzerland, **Peter Pedretti [5405]** was killed in action.

Pietro (Peter) Pedretti was born 2 February 1890 in the small village of Brusio, located in the valley of Val Poschiavo. An Italian speaking area of Switzerland, Brusio is situated on the Bernina Pass which connects Italy and Switzerland. At the age of 18 years, he decided on a new life in Western Australia embarking on the ship *Bremen* from the Italian city of Genoa arriving in Fremantle 5 March 1909.[51] From Fremantle Peter travelled to Collie in the south west region of Western Australia, about 60 kilometres from Bunbury. There was already a family living in the town of Collie with the surname of Pedretti and it is possible they were related to the Pedretti family from Brusio. Peter was residing in the small town called Bila, near Collie, when he applied to become a naturalised Australian 2 December 1914. It is likely that Peter worked as a teamster transporting sleepers from Bila to Collie. To support his application Peter supplied a reference from the local Police Constable from Collie stating that he had lived in the area for five years and was of good character. He was naturalised by the local Magistrate 17 December 1914.

Peter enlisted 6 January 1916 giving his occupation as a Teamster, his next of kin was his father, Michele (Mick) Pedretti, Brusio, Switzerland. Peter stood 5 feet 8 inches tall with sallow complexion, grey blue eyes and dark brown hair.[52] He was assigned to the 17th reinforcement of the 16th Battalion 'D' Company; 4th Brigade of the 4th Division. After training at Blackboy Hill Camp, he left Fremantle aboard the troopship *Aeneas* 17 April 1916 bound for Alexandria.

On the same troopship was Lieutenant Charles Dan Brown, Peter was later assigned to the Lieutenant as his batman. Peter stayed at Alexandria until 14 June 1916 when he left for Marseilles and finally taken on strength to his unit 19 July. Peter's 'D'

Company went on the attack at midnight on the 9 August 1916 and sometime during the initial battle Peter was wounded.

He was told by Lieutenant Brown to make his way back to their line in No-Man's Land, which he did, to have his wound attended to however, Peter was never seen again. The Red Cross Files at the Australian War Memorial states that he was seen being hit by a shell and was killed outright. Peter's body was never recovered and was listed as missing until a Court of Enquiry, held 4 April 1917, found that he had been killed 10 August 1916. His effects and medals were sent to his father, Michele (Mick) Pedretti back in Switzerland, his father later sent back to Australia the Roll of Honour Memorial Circular for his son. Peter's name is on the Villers-Bretonneux Memorial in France.

Between 8 August and 3 September, the Australian launched nine separate attacks in a bid to capture Mouquet Farm. They were forced back each time due to fierce German counter-attacks. A young soldier by the name of **Frank McKinnon [3088]** was killed in action during one attack 14 August.1916. Frank was the only child of Catherine McKinnon, he was born at Maclean, New South Wales in 1895. Frank enlisted at Lismore, New South Wales 12 August 1915, he stood 5 feet 10 inches tall with fair complexion, blue eyes and brown hair. His occupation was Watchmaker and nominated his mother, Catherine McKinnon as his next of kin.[53] Catherine was living in River Street, Maclean with her sister, Elizabeth McKinnon who apparently was Frank's foster mother and aunt. When Frank enlisted, he awarded 3 shillings a day to his aunt, this probably was due to his mother Catherine, already working as a nurse. Frank also made a will naming his aunt as sole beneficiary.

Frank was initially allocated to the 9th Battalion but after his arrival in Egypt he was transferred to the 49th Battalion on 25 February 1916. The newly created battalion was part of the 13th Brigade and the 4th Division. Frank was killed outright by shellfire, his body was never found, his name is on the Villers-Bretonneux Memorial. Base Records sent his effects and medals to his mother,

Frank McKinnon Australia's Fighting Sons of the Empire

sadly she never filled out the Roll of Honour Memorial Circular. Frank died one year and two days after his enlistment, his mother wrote to Base Records saying that Frank was all she had.

By 16 August 1916 the battalions of the 1st Division had been rotated back into the front lines, the next day the 3rd Battalion came under substantial bombardment from Allied artillery. Communication was very poor resulting in a two-hour delay for a runner to pass the message back to headquarters for a ceasefire.[54] This caused many casualties, amongst the dead was **George Henry Walker [1645]**.

George Henry enlisted at Liverpool, New South Wales 12 December 1914 stating that he was 22 years and 1 month old. Born at Cootamundra he gave his mother, Mrs N Walker, Cootamundra, New South Wales as his next of kin, the same address was given on his Embarkment Roll. George Henry stood

5 feet 9 inches tall, his complexion was fair, with brown eyes and light brown hair, occupation was Labourer.[55] George Henry left Sydney onboard *Seang Choon* 12 February 1915 for Egypt then eventually landed with the 3rd Battalion at Anzac Cove 25 April 1915. He came down with Pleurisy 23 June 1915 and was admitted to hospital in Malta. When fully recovered, George Henry was sent to Egypt 4 March 1916 re-joining his unit at Serapeum 21 March 1916.

After George Henry's death Base Records sent notification to Mrs N Walker, Cootamundra, New South Wales, the mail was returned saying that she was unknown. George Henry had made a will naming as his beneficiary a Miss Violet Taylor, Eungai Creek Post Office, New South Wales. After efforts to locate Mrs Walker proved futile the Army contact Miss Taylor in an attempt to find any blood relations. Miss Taylor replied stating that George Henry had told her that he had no father, mother, brother or sister, he was entirely alone. She also stated that he had moved to the Eungai region two years before he enlisted.

There are no birth records for a George Henry Walker, however there is a George Richard Walker born in Sydney 13 September 1892. This George Richard appeared before a magistrate, in Cootamundra, 9 March 1901 charged with 'habitually wandering or loitering about the streets in no ostensible lawful occupation'. His mother, Ellen Sullivan, stated that she was often away from home working and George would not attend school, she wished him to be sent to an Industrial School. She claimed his father was Thomas Walker, a Blacksmith, his whereabouts were unknown. George Richard was sent to the Training Ship *Sobraon* at the age of nine years where he would have stayed until 18 years of age.[56] There are no more records that relate to this George Richard Walker and it is thought that George Richard and George Henry could be the same. George Henry's body was never recovered, he is remembered on the Villers-Bretonneux Memorial in France. His paperwork and medals were marked as Untraceable.

While the battle for the capture of Mouquet Farm was taking place the 9th Battalion of the 3rd Brigade was issued orders for an attack on the enemy's trenches south west of Mouquet Farm.[57] **William Patrick Bradshaw [5051]** was wounded during the attack with a gunshot wound to his shoulder. Enlisting at Townsville, Queensland William stated he was 33 years old, born at Nhill, Victoria, occupation was Seaman, his address was Innisfail, Queensland. Standing 5 feet 8 ¼ inches tall his complexion was fair with blue eyes and light brown hair, he gave a friend's name as next of kin, Miss Sarah Strathie.[58]

William was initially allotted to the 33rd Battalion, leaving Sydney 31 March 1916 onboard *Star of Victoria* arriving in Egypt 5 May 1916. After travelling to France William was transferred to the 9th Battalion 13 August 1916 just one week before he was wounded. Taken to the 26th General Hospital at Etaples on 24 August William finally died from his wound on 2 September 1916. He is buried in the Etaples Military Cemetery (Plot 11, Row B, Grave No. 2A). Miss Strathie told Base Records that she had no knowledge at all of his relations, as a result his file was marked Untraceable.

By 3rd September the 4th Division was rotated back into the front lines which include the 49th Battalion who was ordered to attack the enemy trenches, although they had some success the causalities were substantial. One killed that day was **John Lynch [3401]** a 32-year-old Farm Labourer from Bangalow in the northern region of New South Wales. Enlisting at Brisbane, Queensland 9 August 1915 John stood 5 feet 5 inches tall, his complexion was fresh, with blue eyes and brown hair. His next of kin was noted as friend, Mr Nies, Inspector of Police, Walgett, New South Wales. John also stated that his previous military experience was with the New South Wales Mounted Rifles serving in South Africa, this has been difficult to locate as there were more than one John Lynch that served.[59]

John was initially allocated to the 11th reinforcements of the 9th Battalion leaving Brisbane 5 October 1916 on the troopship

Warilda. Shortly after arriving in Egypt John was in hospital at Cairo suffering from the Mumps. When discharged he was allotted to the 49th Battalion and was taken on strength to his unit 29 February 1916. John arrived in Marseilles 12 June 1916 and while in the field he was promoted to Lance Corporal 25 August 1916. During the attack John Lynch was killed in action 3 September 1915.

His personal effects, a Razor, Chain and a Silver Locket, were returned to his next of kin, Peter Joseph Nies who later informed the Army that John Lynch was his adopted son. There are no birth records for John however, research reveals that he was born in 1884, his father was Bernard Lynch. In 1885 Bernard died which resulted in John being placed into the care of the Sydney Benevolent Asylum. John was then discharged 11 November 1886 to the care of the State Children Relief Board 12 November 1886, his age then was 2 years and 6 months. He was placed, by the Board, to the No 3 Home at Mittagong 16 July 1887 stating that his father was deceased and his mother was living a dissipated and dissolute life, her whereabouts unknown.[60]

Peter Joseph Nies and his wife Anna then adopted John when he was aged about 4 years old, educating and raising him as their own. When it came time for John's medals to be forwarded, Mrs Nies wrote to say that her husband was now deceased and she requested that the medals be sent to her. Mr Nies had accidentally drowned while swimming in the Bong Bong River at Moss Vale chasing ducks in February 1922.[61] The Army sent John's medals to his foster mother, Anna. There is no grave for John, he is remembered on the Villers-Bretonneux Memorial.

The attack to capture the trenches in front of Mouquet Farm by the 49th Battalion, was a costly one even though their attack was successful the Germans launched counter-attacks. On 4 September **Patrick Walsh [5222]** from 'A' Company was first reported missing then killed in action. Patrick was born in Manchester, England about 1881 stating that he was 33 years and 7 months old. Enlisting on 23 October 1915 at Townsville,

Queensland he gave his address as South Johnstone Mill, Innisfail, Queensland, standing 5 feet 2 inches tall his complexion was dark with brown eyes and dark hair, when asked about his next of kin he stated he had none.[62]

On his Attestation papers Patrick stated that he served with the Kimberley Light Horse and the Scottish Horse during the Boer War. Research has shown that Patrick joined the 1st Imperial Light Horse as a Trooper with a service number of 1639 on 28 November 1900 before transferring to the 1st Battalion Scottish Horse on 2 January 1902, his service number then was 36972 during the Boer War.[63] After he had served his time in South Africa nothing more is known about Patrick until he enlisted at Townsville.

Initially he was allocated to the 33rd Battalion before transferring to 16th reinforcements of the 9th Battalion, leaving Sydney on the troopship *Star of Victoria* 31 March 1916. While in Egypt Patrick transferred again this time to the newly formed 49th Battalion on 24 May 1916. Arriving in France 12 June 1916, the 49th moved into the trenches of the Western Front for the first time 21 June. The battalion fought is first major battle at Mouquet Farm, suffering heavy casualties during the assault on 3 and 4 September.

Patrick was listed as missing until a Court of Enquiry held 31 July 1917, found that he had been killed in action. Sergeant Alf Cooper from the 49th Battalion stated that he saw Walsh go into action at Mouquet Farm on 4 September. He did not see or hear of him again. He went on to say that it was the roughest stunt he had been in. As Patrick did not have anyone noted as next of kin, Base Records was forced to mark his Service Record as Untraceable. As Patrick had no grave his name is recorded on the Villers-Bretonneux Memorial in France.

A young soldier from the 49th Battalion, by the name of **Alexander Charles Traise [2253]** was also killed in action on 4 September 1916. Aged just 18 years and 10 months it appears that Alexander did not ask for his parents' consent to enlist. He was the youngest son of Charles Edward and Agnes Ellen Traise, born in Brisbane, Queensland 27 November 1896. His older brother, **Jack Herbert Traise [354]** enlisted 25 September 1914, Jack was born 30 January 1895 and produced a consent from his father to enlist.[64]

Jack, who was attached to the 15th Battalion was killed 29 May 1915 at Gallipoli, the heartbroken parents were given the news of their eldest son's death 19 June 1915. Shortly after their other child Alexander enlisted, just what his parents thought of this will never be known. His Service Record does not contain much information on Alexander other than his age, his next of kin, his occupation was Department Assistant and his religion Presbyterian. There is no Certificate from the Attesting Officer in his Service Record and no signature by Alexander for his Oath, it is thought that Alexander may have enlisted shortly after the news of his brother. Initially Alexander was allocated to the 4th reinforcements of the 25th Battalion which left Brisbane 18 September 1915 onboard the troopship *Armadale*. The ship left two days after his Attestation paperwork was filled out, this is not feasible, and searches have been made on the 4th reinforcements to see if Alexander enlisted under another name, nothing has been found.

After Alexander's arrival in Egypt, he was transferred to the 9th Battalion 4 March 1916 then the 49th Battalion 2 April 1916. Arriving in Marseilles 21 June 1916 Alexander's war had begun, sadly he was killed 4 September 1916. His family were notified 8 October 1916 that he was wounded then 24 February 1917 he was listed as wounded and missing. His mother Agnes wrote seeking more information, she had already lost one son and now her remaining son could not be found. After an enquiry held 31 July 1917 the parents of Alexander Charles Traise were eventually informed their son was killed in action 4 September 1916.

Alexander's body was never recovered, his name is on the Villers-Bretonneux Memorial in France. His brother Jack is buried in the Shrapnel Valley Cemetery in Gallipoli. No words can describe the pain and sorrow felt by Charles and Agnes in the loss of their only children sacrificing both young men to the war. Agnes died in August 1928; Charles died July 1943.

On the 5 September the 49th Battalion launched another attack north of Mouquet Farm, commencing at 6.00am this attack was successful but the battalion had a hard time. The Germans bombarded so heavily; any wounded left out would have been killed. One soldier that died that day was **James Clarke [3728]**, James enlisted 13 November 1915 at Toowoomba, Queensland. His Service Records states that he was aged 42 years and 10 months old, born in Sydney about 1872, his birth record cannot be located. Occupation was Cook but sadly he did not give any next of kin stating that he had none. James stood 5 feet 6 inches tall, had a ruddy complexion with hazel eyes and brown hair.[65]

Initially he was allocated to the 9th Battalion leaving Brisbane 30 December 1915 onboard the troopship *Itonus*. As with many from the 9th Battalion, James was transferred to the 49th Battalion 29 February 1916. Base Records in Melbourne could not locate anyone that may have known James and as a result his paperwork was marked as Untraceable. James Clarke is buried in the Courcelette British Cemetery.

The intense fight to capture Pozieres and Mouquet Farm took a terrible toll on the three Divisions during the seven weeks they were in battle. The Australians paid a dreadful cost that amounted to 23,000 casualties including 6,900 killed in action or died of their wounds. The Australians now left for Ypres and a rest leaving behind many of their mates while back in Australia mothers, wives, and girlfriends mourned for the young men never to return.

FALLEN NOW FORGOTTEN

Grave of James Clarke National Archives of Australia

CHAPTER 4
FLERS 1916

The fighting from which the Australians had emerged was in some respects, the heaviest they had ever experienced. The Australian force in France had, in less than seven weeks, suffered more than 28,000 casualties. The 1st Division 7,700, the 2nd 8,100, 4th 7,100 and the 5th had lost 5,500 at Fromelles.[1]

At the end of August and beginning of September the Australian forces were withdrawn from the Somme to take over from the Canadians at the southern half of the Ypres Salient. In the past the Salient had been a dangerous sector of the British front. The decision to send them to Ypres for a rest did not sit well with some of the troops believing they had been sent there for another offensive. As a matter of fact, the Germans were also sending their tired divisions to the Ypres sector, resulting in a peaceful time unknown to the soldiers. The main task for the troops was the improvement of the defences of the Salient which appeared to be in a dangerous and weak state. With winter approaching the soldiers were put to work making their position more tenable before the winter rain.

Meanwhile back at the Somme, Field Marshall Douglas Haig Commander in Chief of the British Forces in France, decided to make a tremendous push above the Somme. His plan of attack was to be towards the villages of Courcelette, Flers, Gueudecourt and then on to Bapaume. By late September the rain had started, eight days of it. The battlefield was a complete bog made even worse by the shelling. Douglas Haig wanted all attacks to go ahead in spite of the weather and the churned-up battlefield, after all he was living in a dry crater-free landscape at his General Headquarters which was situated at Chateau de Beaurepaire, Montreuil, Pas-de-Calais.

Throughout September each attack failed and worse was to come for the British troops. They were living on cold food; the men were standing up to their knees in mud, and were exhausted. General Haig believed he could continue through the winter but the weather was rapidly deteriorating and the battlefield turned into a quagmire. A period of fighting in terrible weather in which the heavy, clinging, chalky Somme mud and the freezing, flooding battlefield became as formidable an enemy as the Germans.

For the Australian troops it came as a nasty shock when they received news to prepare to return to the Somme. The 5th Division was the first, reaching Ailly-le-Haut-Clocher on the 18 October followed by 1st, 2nd and 4th Divisions.[2] On 25 October the 5th Division received orders to attack, however, with rain falling constantly it was postponed.

Major British offensives were occurring at Le Transloy from 1 to 18 October and it is believed that during this period an Australian serving with the British Army was severely wounded. He was **Captain William Malcom Stewart** of the 23rd Machine Gun Corps, William was born 10 April 1881 at Port Pirie, South Australia. His parents were Robert Walter Stewart and Gertrude Theodora Fidell Lindsay. William had an older sister Eleanor Charlette, born 1879 and a younger sister Clarice Geraldine born 1883, both were born at Port Pirie, South Australia.[3]

William's father was a respected surgeon in the Port Pirie district but had moved to Brougham Place, North Adelaide when his son had died from his injuries. Dr Stewart had been born in Plymouth, England, migrating to South Australia in 1875 he married Gertrude in 1878 at Victor Harbor. William attended St Peter's College in Adelaide for his education where in his final year 1899, participated and exceled in swimming, athletics, football and cricket. William represented the school in cricket and at times took part in out of state matches excelling as a wicket keeper.[4] During 1900, at the young age of 19 years William travelled to South Africa to join the Imperial Light Horse.[5]

The Nominal Roll for the Imperial Light Horse reveals that William enlisted as a Sergeant 21 January 1901 with the Service Number of 1959.[6] Towards the close of 1900 a second regiment of the Imperial Light Horse was raised, and at once took the field in the Eastern Transvaal. Major D M'Kenzie was given command of the 2nd Regiment and it is believed that William may have been allocated to the new regiment.

Since taking the field the 2nd Imperial Light Horse had been almost wholly employed in the Eastern Transvaal under Major-General Smith-Dorrien with many skirmishes. On 6 February 1901 the 2nd was fiercely attacked by General Botha at Bothwell, Lake Chrissie with two killed and four wounded, the attack was driven off, the enemy leaving twenty-five dead. During February and March Major-General Smith-Dorrien's column took part in a push driving the enemy to the borders of Zululand, taking many prisoners and capturing all their artillery. Throughout February the Imperial Light Horse were involved with constant skirmishing and many stiffly contested rear-guard actions, at times engaging with General Christiaan de Wet's forces.[7]

Back in South Australia the 5th South Australian Imperial Contingent was formed arriving at Port Elizabeth 23 March 1901. On arrival the 5th Contingent was taken to the Kroonstad district where they joined Colonel De Lisle, later joining with the 6th Contingent. Even though the Imperial Light Horse became the most distinguished irregular regiment of the Boer War, William decided to be discharged, at Johannesburg, 29 July 1901 to enlist with the 5th South Australian Imperial Contingent.

For the rest of the Boer War the 5th and 6th Contingents fought many battles with the Boers, taking part in the driving operations in the north-east of the Orange River Colony throughout January, February and March 1902. During these operations the outpost work was so arduous that the general ordered the officers to take their turn on sentry. The casualties of the regiment were 14 killed and 28 wounded, they were never three consecutive days in one place.[8]

The Regiment sailed for home leaving South Africa early April 1902 on two ships, *Manchester Merchant* and *Columbian*. The Port Pirie Recorder and North Western Mail, on 14 May 1902, told of the Enthusiastic Reception for the members of the Fifth and Sixth Contingents at the International Hall.[9]

After the close of the Boer War William travelled back to South Africa where he obtained a commission in the Rhodesian Military Police, how long he stayed there is unknown.[10] When talk of war began in 1914 William immediately travelled to England enlisting 20 August 1914 as a Second Lieutenant with the 3rd Devonshire Regiment. William fought many battles in France; however, he did manage to return to England to marry Kathleen Mary Dicker in September 1915, before returning to France.[11]

During the early part of 1916, William Malcolm Stewart was promoted to Captain transferring to the 23rd Battalion Machine Gun Corps. William died 27 October 1916 from wounds received while fighting, mostly likely, at the Battle of Le Transloy. William is buried at the Grove Town Cemetery Meaulte, France. He is remembered in Australia on the Commemorative Roll at the Australian War Memorial and also, on the Memorial Honour Roll at St Peter's College in Adelaide to recognise his service in the Boer War. William's father, Robert Walter Stewart died 1921, his mother, Gertrude, while on a visit to England, wrote to the British Army 24 February 1924 requesting an Emblem, her address then was given as Mrs R W Stewart, Queens Court Hotel 25 Earls Court Square. Gertrude and her two daughters, Eleanor Charlotte and Geraldine travelled from Adelaide to Marseille in 1925 perhaps to visit William's Grave.[12]

William's wife Kathleen Mary applied for probate of William's will 6 December 1916 which amounted to £129.4s 5p.[13] It is believed that Kathleen Mary re-married in 1921 to Harold Walter Cornwell, William and Kathleen's union did not produce any children. William's mother, Gertrude died 1946, his youngest sister Geraldine died 1957, his older sister, Eleanor Charlotte died 1966, neither sister had married.

After spending time in the front line trenches the soldiers of the 55th and 56th Battalions were relieved for a rest as the constant rain forced the Generals to keep delaying the attack. Then on 30 October the 55th and 56th Battalions were sent back to the front-line for the attack on 1 November even though the rain persisted. General Elliott of the 15th Brigade did report to the Commander of the 5th Division, Major-General McCay that to attack over such mud-soaked ground was sheer madness.

With the rain increasing, the attack for the 1 November, was again postponed until the 5 November. The War Diary for the 56th Battalion states that *the Battalion was relieved by the 53rd Battalion, during the relief the enemy shelling increased and a fair number of casualties occurred. The shelling was due, no doubt to the fact that all the Companies moved over open ground in preference to relieving through the trenches. The trenches were in an awful condition, being in most places up to, and over, the men's knees in mud and slush.*[14] During that day 10 ordinary ranks were killed, one of those killed was Private **William James Day [5361].**

William Day was born at Waterloo, Sydney stating his age as 21 years and six months when he enlisted at Liverpool, New South Wales on 25 January 1916. For his next of kin, William claimed that his mother was Margaret Day, her address 72 Gerrard Street, Alexandria, New South Wales the same address where William was living.[15] There is no record of William's birth, it is not known who his mother was. Margaret, named as his mother and next of kin, was his grandmother, Margaret Day (nee Lamb). His grandfather was James Day who died in 1915. William's father was James Day born 1876 at West Maitland, New South Wales, the son of James Snr and Margaret Day, there is no record of birth for James, the father of William.

William was 5 feet and 10 ½ inches tall, his complexion was dark with brown hair and brown eyes. After some initial training

William was assigned to the 17th reinforcement 4th Battalion leaving Sydney 14 April 1916 onboard *Ceramic* arriving Suez 17 May. While stationed at Tel-El-Kebir William was transferred to the 56th Battalion 25 May 1916, he arrived at Marseilles in France 29 June. On 8 September William was sent to the Trench Mortar Battery re-joining his battalion the next day, then 13 October William was sent to the Divisional Bomb School but returned to his battalion the same day.

William's family placed a notice advising of William's death on 1 November 1916 at the age of 20 years and 4 months.[16] The article was inserted by his father, grandmother, uncles, aunts and cousins. As his body was never recovered William is commemorated on the Villers-Bretonneux Memorial, which could be the reason why his father, James Day enlisted at Redfern on 17 January 1917.

James Day Junior, the father of William James, stated he was 40 years and 6 months old when he enlisted naming his mother, Margaret as next of kin.[17] James stood 5 feet 7 ½ inches tall, his complexion was fair with blue eyes and brown hair, he also noted that he was a widower although no marriage can be found for him. James left Sydney 7 February 1917 onboard *Wilshire* and while in France he spent a large amount of time AWL, perhaps searching for information on William. On his Service Record James was discharged because his age was 45 years and 5 months old on 12 December 1917. He was returned to Australia and discharged 3 April 1918; James died in 5 June 1925 at Prince of Wales Hospital, Randwick, his mother, Margaret had died in 1918.[18]

Base Records, on 25 May 1933 wrote to the Repatriation Commission asking if records disclose the present whereabouts of next of kin or other relatives of young William James. The Deputy Commissioner replied that James Day (a widower) was the father of William. At the time of James' death his next of kin was recorded as, brother Mr Albert Day, 51 Raglan Street, Redfern. Base Records wrote to Albert 7 June 1933, the letter was returned. Albert Day had died three years earlier in May 1930.[19] Base Records was then forced to mark William James Day's medals as Untraceable.

The rain kept coming down, turning the trenches and No-Man's Land into a muddy mess, even though the attack was not to start until the 5 November men were still dying while trying to withdraw. Retrieving the wounded fell to the stretcher bearers of the Field Ambulance, their task was both strenuous and dangerous, at times they were in thigh deep mud. Stretcher bearers were non-combatants, unarmed and protected only by their 'S B' armband, they often worked under direct fire, carrying the wounded.

One stretcher bearer who received a gunshot to his chest 2 November 1916, was **Alfred John Hopkins [6869].** Alfred born at Unley, South Australia in 1895 was the son of Alfred Stanley Hopkins and Clara Bails, he had a sister, Edna, who was two years older. Alfred enlisted 8 June 1915 at Keswick, South Australia at the age of 20 years and four months naming his mother, Clara as next of kin. Alfred stood 5 feet 5 ¼ inches tall with fair complexion, blue eyes and fair hair, his occupation was Draughtsman, his parents gave consent to his enlistment on the grounds he served with the Australian Army Medical Corp.[20]

Alfred was educated first at Sturt Street Public School, then at the Adelaide High School and completed a successful career at the Adelaide School of Mines and Industries in mechanical and electrical engineering. Prior to enlisting he was employed at Messrs. Bagshaw & Sons, of Mile-End, as Junior Draftsman.[21]

After his initial training Alfred was allocated 1 August 1915, to the 8th Field Ambulance as a driver, he left Melbourne onboard the troopship *Ascanius* 10 November 1915 for Egypt. In February the next year Alfred was transferred to the 15th Field Ambulance leaving Egypt 19 June 1916 for Marseilles. The 15th Field Ambulance was attached to the 15th Brigade of the 5th Division, which had been brought up to strength after the battle of Fromelles. During October the 15th Brigade moved to the Somme in readiness for an attack which included the 15th Field Ambulance. On 22 October a Bearer Subdivision from the 15th Field Ambulance was sent to the 8th Field Ambulance to assist in recovery of wounded.[22]

Within a week the bearers were becoming exhausted with the exceedingly difficult conditions under which the wounded were excavated. The bearers were forced to travel in thigh high mud to get the wounded back to an aid station, conditions were deplorable. Alfred's war was to end 2 November 1916 when he received a shrapnel wound to the chest while on duty with the 8th Field Ambulance. He was immediately taken to the 38th Casualty Clearing Station but died on the same day, Alfred is buried in the Heilly Station Cemetery, Mericourt-L'Abbe.

Alfred's parents placed an obituary for their son which stated: *Private A J Hopkins, only son of Mrs and Mrs A S Hopkins of Mildura, Victoria, late of Wayville, S A died in France on November 2, 1916, at the age of twenty-one. He left South Australia in November, 1915, thus putting in one year-the first part training in Egypt and the last months in the thick of the fighting in France. It may be helpful to others to know that Jack was not only true to King George and a brave soldier, but was true to the King of kings. In a letter lately received from a chum of his, it stated that Jack not only helped the wounded soldiers bear their pain, but also helped them spiritually. This is a noble testimony to so young a man, and should lead us on to aim at the higher life and so worthy when heaven's portals opens to meet such a pure soul. May his saintly life be the means of winning many souls for Christ's kingdom. He was a member of the Unley Methodist Church and young men's class, and in his last letter testified "to the good influence that he had received there. His letters were always cheerful, with a vein of mirth running through them that made one feel that if there was a joke about Jack would be sure to see it. He was loved by all, and died true to his country and his God."*[23]

Alfred's parents wrote many letters to Base Records requesting the return of his personal effects, none were forthcoming. His sister, Edna never married, she died aged 83 and was buried beside her parents at Centennial Park Cemetery, Pasadena, Mitcham City South Australia.[24]

Many soldiers that fought during World War 1 did not necessarily die in the heat of battle; some were in reserve trenches waiting for their turn to move back into the front lines. One such soldier was **Harold Edgar Burton [379]** who was killed 2 November 1916. When Harold enlisted at Melbourne 9 July 1915, he stated his age as 21 and named his mother, Martha Howson as next of kin. He stood 5 feet 5 ¾ inches tall with a pale complexion, grey eyes and brown hair, his occupation, Pastrycook. Harold was allocated to the 29th Battalion, 'A' Company.[25]

The 29th Battalion, attached to the 8th Brigade of the 5th Division was formed in Victoria 10 August 1915, and when Harold enlisted, he would have known of the large number of casualties at Gallipoli. The 29th Battalion carried out their training at Broadmeadows eventually embarking on the troopship *Ascanius* which left Melbourne 10 November 1915. The battalion served briefly in Egypt on garrison duty before being sent to the Western Front arriving at Marseilles 23 June 1916.

The 8th Brigade arrived in the Fromelles region on the night of 10/11 July 1916 in preparation for an attack that was to start on 19 July. Harold survived the attack which claimed the lives of many young Australian men, devastating the whole of the 5th Division of the AIF. August and September, the 29th Battalion spent time in the quieter area waiting for reinforcements to boost the numbers of the 5th Division. In October the battalion had moved to Bussus where it experienced heavy rain.

On 18 October a very pretty French wedding was celebrated in the local church which was well attended by all ranks. Rice in abundance was thrown at the happy couple. The latter incident will be remembered owing to a subsequent Orderly Room case in connection with the disappearance of rice from the Quarter Master Stores.[26] By 22 October 'A' and 'B' Companies went forward into the front lines at Flers to relieve the English.

The trenches were despicable, with the constant heavy rain they were full of mud, there was no sanitary arrangements and from the trenches the Australians could see the dead English and Germans soldiers still laying in the battlefield. On 24 October the two companies of the 29th Battalion were relieved in very heavy rain to the Reserve Trench in front of Flers.

Harold was killed 2 November 1916; his death was witnessed by a fellow soldier. Private H H Kroger told an Enquiry Bureau that on that day the battalion was in the reserve trench in front of Flers, they were having tea, when a shell exploded killing Burton and four others (McKean, Lennox, Lewis and Swanton). They were all killed instantly. The pioneers collected the pay books and discs, and buried the bodies in a shell hole behind the trench. No Padre officiated, and it was impossible to hold a burial service. A wooden cross was erected over the grave bearing soldiers' names, numbers and battalions. Private Kroger knew Burton well and came from Australia with him on SS *Anchises*.[27]

When it came time to forward Harold's medals to his family it was revealed that Harold's mother, Mrs Martha Howson, was his foster mother stating that she adopted Harold when he was eight months old. A search of the Victoria Births, Deaths and Marriages Indexes does not show a birth for Harold in the year of his supposed birth of 1894, however there is a birth for a Harold Burton born Carlton, Victoria in 1891, mother Ellen Burton, father unknown.[28] Martha did have a son named William Thomas Henry Burton who was born approximately 1877, although this birth was never registered. This William died in 1921 aged 44, the index shows the mother was Martha, father was Archibald Burton.[29] Harold Edgar Burton is buried at the Bulls Road Military Cemetery, 8 miles east north east of Albert. His foster mother, Martha, did not fill out the Circular for the Roll of Honour nor did she put any inscription on his tombstone.

The 2nd Division newly arrived from Ypres was to relieve the infantry of the 5th Division as the planned attack had been postponed to 5 November but at nightfall on 4 November the rain came down again. There was talk of postponing for 24 hours however, this was rejected and the planned attack was to go ahead. At 12.30am 5 November, General Paton of the 7th Brigade reported that No-Man's Land was fairly good, but the trenches were knee-deep in mud and some of the assembly trenches could not be found.[30] The 27th Battalion of the 7th Brigade found that getting to the assembly point was exhausting, as the conditions were unimaginable and they were worn out even before the attack had started.

The 27th Battalion was to attack the enemy position in Bayonet Trench which they held for 1 ½ hours when a withdrawal was necessary as no reinforcements were available. The casualties for the 27th Battalion 5 November were 5 Officers, and 72 other ranks killed.[31]

One young Australian who died that day was **Arthur Henry Hooper [833],** the only child of Alfred and Eliza Hooper.

Arthur was born in Adelaide 2 August 1891,[32] and was 23 years and 6 months old when he enlisted 19 February 1915 at Keswick, South Australia with his friend, John Thomas Madigan [863]. Arthur stood 5 feet 6 ¼ inches tall, his complexion was fair, with brown eyes and brown hair. His occupation was Labourer and he lived with his parents at Ashbrook Avenue, North Norwood, South Australia naming his mother, Eliza, as next of kin. Initially Arthur was allocated to Base Depot Infantry then transferred, with his friend, John Thomas Madigan to 'D' Company 27th Battalion. After some training Arthur left Adelaide 31 May 1915 onboard the troopship *Geelong* bound for Egypt where the battalion undertook more training for another 2 months.

The 27th Battalion landed during the night at Anzac Cove 10 September 1915 where the battalion took over Cheshire Ridge until 10 November 1915. The conditions on Gallipoli were, by now, becoming unsustainable with sickness causing many of the troops to be taken off the peninsular. Arthur was one who left 5 December 1915 and was sent back to Egypt 14 December to convalesce. At the end of February 1916 Arthur was assigned to the School of Instruction at Zeitoun. By June 1916 he attended the 7th Training Battalion for a short time before re-joining his unit in Belgium 17 October 1916.

On 5 November Arthur and his friend, John Thomas Madigan, took part in the attack at Flers by the 27th Battalion which resulted in Arthur's death. Private John Thomas Madigan, when interviewed by the Red Cross on 28 June 1917, stated that Arthur was sniped through the head halfway across No Man's Land on the morning of November 5, 1916 and died almost instantly. Private Madigan had known Private Hooper for a number of years and having been closely connected with him all his life and had been through the campaigns together both in Gallipoli and France.[33] Arthur's body was never recovered, there is no grave for him, instead he is remembered on the Villers-Bretonneux Memorial in France.

Arthur's parents placed a notice in the paper advising of his death stating that he had been educated at Port Germein and the Adelaide School of Mines. They went on to say that he was a fine footballer and fond of sport generally and was of a cheerful disposition. He served on Gallipoli and also in the School of Instruction. From Salisbury Plains he went to France, where he was killed on November 5, soon after landing. He spent his 24th birthday on Gallipoli and his 25th at Salisbury Plains.[34]

Among the soldiers from the 27th Battalion that died 5 November was Swedish born **Private Charlie Alvin Akerlind [1661A]**, Charlie was born near Stockholm, Sweden 15 September 1882, he arrived in Australia July 1909 and was naturalised 7 August 1915.[35] While residing at Lameroo, South Australia, Charlie enlisted 27 October 1915 at Adelaide, he stood 5 feet 5 ¾ inches tall, complexion was fair with blue eyes and fair hair. He named his mother Mrs Erica Anderson as next of kin, her address was near Stockholm, Sweden, research cannot find any record of his birth.

After some initial training Charlie was posted to the 43rd Battalion leaving Adelaide 9 June 1916 onboard the troopship *Afric* arriving in England 24 July 1916. He was transferred to the 27th Battalion 9 September 1916 leaving for France two days later joining his battalion 28 September at Steenvoorde.[36] After a short stay at Ypres, Belgium the 27th returned to the Somme in October and the muddy trenches in preparation for the attack on 5 November. Charlie's mother, Erica Anderson was notified of her son's death signing a receipt for his effects which was sent to the Royal Swedish Consulate General in London. Erica Anderson applied for and was granted a pension however nothing more was heard from Charlie's mother; the Roll of Honour Circular was compiled by the Official Historian Staff. There is no grave for Private Charlie Alvin Akerlind, his name is listed on the Villers-Bretonneux Memorial in France.

Five days later a young Australian was to die tragically while helping the wounded from the battle. His name was **William Charles Bannister [131]** from Broken Hill, New South Wales. William was the only child of Otto Wagenknecht and Mary McKenna, born 13 April 1894 at White Cliffs, New South Wales,[37] the parental grandparents of William were both born in Germany. Two years after William's birth a younger brother was born, Otto, he died at the age of nine weeks, one year later his mother, Mary died when William was just three years old, the family was living in Broken Hill, New South Wales.[38] William became an orphan at the age of ten when his father, Otto died in 1904,[39] his mother's sister, Helen Bannister took care of William, sadly she also died 1 January 1907,[40] another aunt, Susannah Frew then raised William.

William Charles Bannister enlisted 20 August 1914 at Adelaide, it is possible he took on the name of Bannister due to his German ancestry, naming his aunt Mrs Leslie Frew as his next of kin. William's occupation was Stenographer, he stood 5 feet 7 inches tall with fair complexion, brown eyes and fair hair, he also stated that he was a member of the Militia 'C' Section of the 19th Australian Medical Corp.[41] Initially William was a private, however due to his previous experience he was promoted to Sergeant 1 September 1914, assigned to 'B' Section, 3rd Australian Field

Ambulance, attached to the 3rd Brigade which included the 9th, 10th 11th and 12th Battalions. William left Adelaide onboard the troopship *Medic* 20 October 1914 bound for Egypt.

The 3rd Field Ambulance were one of the first onshore with the battalions of the 3rd Brigade serving throughout the Gallipoli Campaign until December when the unit was advised to prepare to withdraw from the Peninsula. William left a little earlier than his unit as he was placed on a hospital ship 17 December 1915 suffering from Bronchitis. He recovered while in Egypt and rejoined his unit 4 January 1916 receiving a promotion 16 January 1916 as Staff Sergeant of Nursing Duties.

The 3rd Field Ambulance arrived in France 27 March 1916 and prepared themselves for the coming attacks. On 9 September 1916 William was recommended for an award. *131 Staff Sergeant William Charles Bannister. The work of this N.C.O. has always been of the highest standard of efficiency whether in charge of Nursing Duties or of the Orderly Room of this Unit. He has shown himself thoroughly reliable in the discharge of his duties thereby rendering the greatest assistance to his officers.*[42]

After Pozieres William was back in the Somme Region for the attack on Flers, where he died on 11 November while tending to his patients. At 00.40 on the morning of the 11 November an enemy aeroplane flying low dropped six bombs on the 1st Anzac Corps Rest Station. Five patients were killed outright, thirty-three wounded more or less seriously, and three slightly. Of the personal at this station, one was killed, four seriously wounded and one slightly wounded. All of these belonged to No 3 Australian Field Ambulance. One bomb was dropped on the Orderly room, destroying a number of the records of the station and of the unit. Damage was done to four marquee tents and eight bell tents. The distinguishing lamps were burning brightly at the time the attack was made.[43]

William was buried at the Heilly Station Cemetery, Mericourt-L'Abbe, Picardie, France. His aunt, Susannah Frew received his effects and medals. On 24 November an obituary was printed

William Bannister's Grave http://discoveringanzacs.naa.gov.au

in the local paper. *Mr and Mrs Leslie A Frew, of Leyton, Zebina Street, Broken Hill, have received a message sent by Major Hardie, D.A.H.G., 4th Military District, informing them that their nephew, Staff Sergeant W C W Bannister of the 3rd Field Ambulance, had died from the effects of gunshot wounds in the legs, on November 11, at the 38th Casualty Clearing Station, France. Staff Sergeant Bannister was one of the first in Broken Hill to enlist. He was a member of the A M C branch of the Citizen forces, and he enlisted in August 1914, into the A M C for active service abroad. Being already well trained, he did not stay long in camp, but left in the first contingent in November 1914. He saw service in Egypt, was through the Gallipoli campaign, in Egypt again and finally in France.*

Before enlisting, deceased had been correspondence clerk in the Central Mine Offices, where he had been employed for between, four and five years. He was a lacrosse player, and was an exceedingly popular young man in many circles.[44]

Another Australian soldier to die on 11 November during the bombing raid on the 1st Anzac Corps Rest Station was **William Millar [759]** from the 12th Battalion. There are no birth records for William, his mother, Elizabeth Armstrong was married to

Alexander McDonald. William enlisted at Morphettville, South Australia 5 September 1914, aged 35 years, his occupation was Carpenter, he stood 5 feet 5 inches tall and named his mother, Mrs A McDonald as next of kin.

William was allocated to the 12th Battalion, the 12th was one of the first infantry units for the AIF, with the 9th, 10th and 11th Battalions it formed the 3rd Brigade. William left Melbourne 17 September 1914 aboard the troopship *Geelong* for Egypt where he undertook more training. William took part in the landing at Gallipoli in the early hours of 25 April 1915, the battalion was involved in establishing and defending the front line of the Anzac position.

During the hot summer months, the conditions at Gallipoli were becoming unbearable with troops falling ill every day. William was one who reported sick when he was taken back to Egypt 2 August 1915 with diarrhoea, as his condition deteriorated, he was transferred to England 28 August. After he had recovered, William was sent to the Australian Intermediate Depot at Abby Wood 19 November 1915, while there he spent some time AWL for which he received punishment. William re-joined his unit 9 August 1916 but was again sent to hospital 7 November 1916 with Scabies. On 11 November 1916 William was killed during the bombing raid on the 1st Anzac Corps Rest Station, he was buried at the Dernancourt Communal Cemetery.

William's mother Elizabeth McDonald, now a widow, received his personal effects and was granted a pension. When it came time to fill out the Circular for the Roll of Honour and place an epitaph on William's tombstone this was not done as Elizabeth McDonald had died aged 70 in 1923,[45] the paperwork was returned to Base Records.

As November wore on the conditions became appalling with the rain and mud creating the most trying period ever experienced by the troops. The journey into the trenches through the deep thick mud left the men totally exhausted as they had to carry their greatcoats, waterproof sheet, one blanket, 220 rounds of ammunition, two bombs, two sandbags and two days reserve rations.

By 18 November the battle on the Somme was drawing to a close, when it wasn't raining a cold and bitter wind was blowing making life in the trenches unbearable. On that day another young Australian died. He was **William Adam Kinross [3857]** from South Australia. William enlisted 6 October 1915 at Adelaide at the age of 32 he stated that he was born at Parkside, South Australia and named his mother Mrs Annie McKinley, as next of kin. William stood 5 feet 9 ¼ inches tall with fair complexion, hazel eyes and dark hair, his occupation was Horse Driver.[46]

William was born 12 August 1882, his birth record shows that his father was William Kinross and his mother was Annie Lott.[47] When his widowed mother, Annie applied for a pension she admitted to the authorities that William was an ex-nuptial child. After some training William was allocated to the 27th Battalion leaving Adelaide 7 February 1916 onboard *Miltiades* for Egypt. While in Egypt he was transferred to the newly created 50th Battalion 2 April 1916 arriving in Marseille, France 12 June 1916.

One month later, 20 July, 1916 he decided to go AWL and was also charged with drunkenness which result in a fine and punishment. The 50th Battalion saw action at Mouquet Farm from 13 to 15 August where it suffered many casualties. 2 September William was placed in hospital suffering from dyspepsia, a gastric condition but was back with his unit at Flers 31 October 1916. On 18 November while in the front-line, enemy shelling wounded William, he died later that day. William was buried at Flers however, his grave was never located after the war instead his name has been placed on the Villers-Bretonneux Memorial, France. A Miss H Du Rieu wrote to Base Records asking after William, on behalf of his mother, saying that she was his intended wife and that he was Annie McKinley's only child.

Throughout the November attacks many of the soldiers were wounded and some were sent back to England for further treatment. There was no penicillin or any sort of antibiotics to treat the wounds of the soldiers and many died weeks later from infections. One of these was **Sydney Campbell [1111]** who died 28 November 1916 at the 1ˢᵗ South General Hospital, Birmingham, England.

Sydney was born in Perth, Western Australia on 8 March 1893.[48] He was placed in Clontarf Orphanage, Victoria Park, when he was about 3 or 4 years old. He enlisted 7 October 1914 at Blackboy Hill, Western Australia naming a friend William Bailey of Loco Shed, Mount Magnet, Western Australia as his next of kin, William was also raised in the orphanage. Sydney stood 5 feet 7 inches tall, his complexion was fair, with brown eyes and fair hair, his occupation, Farm Hand,[49] He was allocated to the 1ˢᵗ reinforcements of the 11ᵗʰ Battalion. Sydney embarked from Melbourne, Victoria onboard *Themistocies* 22 December 1914 bound for Egypt.

After further training the 11ᵗʰ Battalion set sail for Gallipoli, the 11ᵗʰ along with the 9ᵗʰ, 10ᵗʰ and 12ᵗʰ Battalions formed the 3ʳᵈ Brigade, the first to go ashore on the Peninsula. Sydney's battalion landed on the beach at 4.30 am one mile south of Fisherman's Hut, Gallipoli under heavy musketry and machine gun fire. They stormed the cliffs about 300 feet high pushing back the Turks and occupied the position.[50]

The 11ᵗʰ Battalion was heavily involved in defending the front line of the Anzac beachhead and throughout the time on Gallipoli took part in many attacks. After the withdrawal from Gallipoli the 11ᵗʰ Battalion was back in Egypt where 23 January 1916, Sydney decided to go AWL from 6 am till 9 pm, for punishment he forfeited 1 days' pay. The 11ᵗʰ Battalion sailed for France arriving at Marseilles 5ᵗʰ April, Sydney was appointed Lance Corporal on 20 May. Pozieres, in the Somme Valley was the first action the battalion had in France during July 1916.

While at Pozieres Sydney suffered a gunshot wound to the left arm, and was admitted to Royal West Sussex Hospital, Chichester, England 28 July, he eventually re-joined his unit 17 September. November 9 the 11ᵗʰ Battalion was heavily shelled by the enemy which resulted in Sydney receiving another wound this time it was his right arm. He was admitted to 1ˢᵗ Southern General Hospital, Birmingham, England, his condition was reported as serious.

Lance Corporal Sydney Campbell died from Septicaemia 28 November 1916 and buried 2 December in Lodge Hill Cemetery, Birmingham, Grave No 405, Section B 10. Today he has no tombstone instead his name is on the Commonwealth War Graves Commission Screen Wall B10 as his burial site could not be located. Base Records wrote to William Bailey to enquire if Sydney had any relatives, William replied that Sydney did not know of any and that he had grown up with Sydney in the same orphanage. Sydney's will left half of his estate to William Bailey and half to the Clontarf Orphanage, as a result it was decided that Mr Bailey should receive Sydney's medals.

The close of the Somme battle left the Australian divisions to face what would be the most terrible winter of the war. Unaccustomed to the cold and snow that had started falling the men suffered terribly, the bitter cold causing trench foot and frostbite.

CHAPTER 5
BAPAUME TO BULLECOURT 1917

In the first months of 1917 the Australian troops were to face their heaviest fighting in France. They suffered disease outbreaks in the extreme weather conditions of January and February. In mid-January the winter freeze set in, the constant rain gave way to snow that turned the muddy ground to ice. Meanwhile General Haig, back at his chateau, decided to keep pressure on the Germans with an attack on Stormy Trench. The 15th Battalion attacked on 1 February taking the trench but the Germans counter-attacked re-taking the trench, the 15th suffered 144 casualties.[1]

The 15th Battalion was relieved in the front line by the 13th Battalion 2 February with orders to attack Stormy Trench again. This time the attack by the 13th was to be launched on the night of 4/5 February starting at 10pm. Lieutenant-Colonel Durrant the Commander of the 13th, loaded the men with bombs, the infantrymen stuffed their greatcoat pockets with them, 'A' Company carried more than 2,000 grenades.[2] This time the attack was successful even though the Germans counter-attacked throughout the night the men of the 13th Battalion fought back. Although the 13th only had 26 hours' notice of the attack, the men had never been so well prepared for one, and knew more of the details of what they had to do than ever they had done before. The reconnaissance of the ground by all Officers and C. Os proved invaluable. Three men from the battalion were recommended for the Victoria Cross.[3]

It is during the night of 4 February that **Martin Hamann** **[1401]** a member of the 13th Battalion died, Martin had enlisted in Sydney 19 November 1914. He stated on his Attestation papers that he was 22 years of age and his birth place was Riga, Russia. Martin stood 5 feet 6 inches tall, his complexion was fair with hazel eyes and fair hair, his occupation was Seaman, he gave the name of his sister, Annie who lived in Riga, Russia as next of kin.[4]

Riga, a port city was the capital of Lativa, Martin could not travel back to his hometown as Germany in August declared war on Russia, he was accepted into the AIF. Martin was initially allocated to 'A' Company of the 13th Battalion. After some training at Broadmeadows, Victoria he left Melbourne 22 December 1914 on board the troopship Ulysses. With the 14th, 15th and 16th Battalions they formed the 4th Brigade the commander of the 4th Brigade was Colonel John Monash.

The 13th Battalion landed at Anzac Cove in the early hours of 26 April, Martin spent about one month on Gallipoli then somehow fractured his shoulder 29 May 1915 which resulted in a stay on a hospital ship. He re-joined the 13th on 25 July 1915 but on 10 August at Walkers Ridge Martin received a gun-shot wound to his left arm. He was sent back to England four days later to recover; and was back with his unit 15 January 1916.

While at Tel-El-Kebir on 3 March 1916 Martin was charged with drunkenness and creating a disturbance, he was given 3 day's Field Punishment No. 2. Just two days later he transferred to the 4th Division Artillery and was taken on strength to 37th Battery of the 10th Field Artillery Brigade 16 March 1916 arriving in Marseilles 17 May 1916. While at the 4th Division Base Depot 16 August 1916 Martin went AWL for three days and was also charged with being in possession of some rum. This time he was given 28 days Field Punishment No 1 and forfeited 32 day's pay.

Martin transferred back to the 13th Battalion 16 November 1916 in time to spend some distressing months in the muddy and cold trenches. After Martin was killed 4 February 1917, Base Records in Melbourne wrote to the Russian Consul General in

Melbourne in March 1917 to inform the Russian authorities of Martin's death. His medals were sent to London to be passed onto his sister, sadly all were returned due to the ongoing war in Russia. His medals were marked as Untraceable. Martin Hamann's body was never recovered, he is remembered on the Villers-Bretonneux Memorial, France.

Another Russian born soldier who joined the AIF was **Abdul Genivahoff [1703],** Abdul was born in 1886 at Kazan, the capital of the Tatarstan Republic, Russia, he enlisted at the Melbourne Town Hall 18 February 1916 stating that his occupation was Seaman. He named a friend, Mr Henry Donald Nicholson as his next of kin, Abdul gave his address as Surf Side, 7 Esplanade, St Kilda, the same address as Mr Nicholson. Abdul stood 5 feet 6 inches tall, his complexion was fresh, with brown eyes and dark brown hair. Initially allocated to the 37th Battalion he transferred to the 2nd reinforcements of the 2nd Pioneers.[5]

Abdul left Melbourne 8 April 1916 onboard the troopship *Aeneas* for Egypt. While at Tel-El-Kebir he had a bout of measles 16 May 1916 which required a transfer back to England 11 June 1916. After his recovery he returned to the 2nd Pioneer Battalion in France 14 July 1916, then 27 July 1916 Abdul and his unit relieved the 1st Pioneers in the line at Pozieres. On the night of 4/5 August four detachments of the 2nd Pioneers took part in an attack by digging communication trenches which was quite successful.[6] During this attack Abdul was wounded although he decided to remain on duty.

Abdul stayed with the 2nd Pioneer Battalion throughout the rest of 1916, then 11 January 1917 he was transferred to the 19th Battalion. On 26 February 1917 the 19th Battalion relieved the 20th at Flers. The next day the 19th took part in a bombing attack on Malt Trench, that day 27 February 1917 Abdul was one of three men killed during the attack.[7] When it came time to locate relatives of Abdul, Base Records in Melbourne realised that he had none. The friend, Henry Donald Nicholson, was actually the Non-Commissioned Officer who filled out his Attestation papers.

When Abdul told him his only family were his parents who were deceased and he did not know anyone in Australia Mr Nicholson offered to place his name down as Abdul's next of kin.

Private Abdul Ganivahoff's body was never recovered, he has no tombstone, instead Abdul is now just another name on the Villers-Bretonneux Memorial, Picardie, France and on the Australian War Memorial Roll of Honour. Abdul's file was marked Untraceable, after dying at the age of 31 years Abdul has been forgotten by time with no one to remember his sacrifice.

Towards the end of February, the Australians discovered some of the German trenches were empty, they had withdrawn back to what became known as the Hindenburg Line. For a short time, the soldiers would experience life out of the trenches. As the Australians advanced with caution, they still came across some German machine gun posts and after firing the Germans would scamper off.[8] By March the weather started improving and on 17 March the Australians were in Bapaume, however the Germans had destroyed everything in the town along with other surrounding villages.

On 7 April the 10th Battalion moved to the front-line north of Louverval to relieve two companies of the 12th Battalion, the 10th sent in 'B' and 'C' Companies. At 0300 the line advanced 1,000 yards, strong opposition was met by 'B' Company resulting in two Officers and 40 Other Ranks killed.[9]

Albert Butler [1907], from 'B' Company was killed during the advance. Albert was born 21 August 1895 at the Lying-in Hospital for Destitute Women in South Australia. His mother was Jane Butler nee Woods, Jane named as the father, James Bradley who was a knockabout hand at Eagle Tavern, Hindley St, Adelaide. The authorities wrote to James Bradley on 11 September 1895 but there was no reply. Jane's husband was William Henry Butler; however, he had divorced Jane in October 1893 and as she had nowhere to go Jane and young Albert stayed in the hospital for the next six months. Jane and Albert were sent to Mrs Barber, Vaughan's Mansion, Roman Catholic Refuge

25 February 1896, on 22 May 1896 a visit by the Authorities to check on young Albert found the child was alive and well but address of mother was unknown, he was to become a Ward of the State until the age of 18 years.[10]

Albert Butler Photo courtesy of Macclesfield RSL

Albert enlisted 29 December 1914 at Oatlands, naming Mr O'Malley as his next of kin, he had been raised by the O'Malley family from a young age. He was a tall lad standing 6 feet with fair complexion, blue eyes and fair hair.[11] Allocated to the 10th Battalion, Albert embarked at Adelaide on the *Hororata* 20 April 1915 and was taken on strength to the 10th Battalion at Gallipoli 8 August 1915. Staying on the Peninsula the 10th Battalion returned to Egypt 29 December 1915 then onto France disembarking at Marseilles 3 April 1916.

Albert, while in France came down with Influenza 12 May 1916 which turned out to be Malaria, he was sent back to England and was admitted to hospital 17 May. After his discharge from hospital 25 July Albert was allocated to the Provost Staff in England. He re-joined the 10th in France 16 January 1917 and was promoted to Lance Corporal after four days. Just a week later Albert came down with the Mumps so back to Hospital 27 January re-joining his battalion 6 March 1917. Albert made a will 13 March 1917 leaving all he had to his childhood friend, Mr O'Malley.

Albert was killed during the attack at Lagnicourt by machine gun fire, his mates tried to bury him but they had to retire due to counter-attacks by the Germans, he was eventually buried 10 April 1917.[12] When it came time to dispose of Albert's medals, Base Records wrote to Mr O'Malley requesting information on his relatives, Mr O'Malley replied that Albert had no one and was raised by his mother, the late Mrs J O'Malley.

Base Records sent Albert's effects to Mr O'Malley, they consisted of a Prayer Book, Handkerchief, Record Book and Religious Book. Base Records also decided to send Albert's medals to Mr O'Malley. The Roll of Honour Circular was never filled out by Mr O'Malley and his burial site was never discovered after the war. Albert's name is on the Villers-Bretonneux Memorial in France.

By 9 April the Australians were in front of the Hindenburg Line with its barbed-wire entanglements, the soldiers were now facing the Germans and their machine-gun posts. A plan was hatched to attack around the ruined village of Bullecourt but first the barbed wire had to be destroyed. General Hubert Gough approved the use of tanks to crush the wire with the infantry to follow. The Australians were told to be ready to assemble at 3 am on the 9 April however, this was cancelled when the tanks did not arrive.

Late on the night of the 10 April the wind howled and it started to snow, the artillery would lay down a barrage until 4.30am, then the tanks were to line up in front of the infantry and go forward to the Hindenburg Line. On reaching their objective they would signal for the infantry to cross the open ground. At 4.15 am the tanks still had not arrived, the troops were lying out waiting for their arrival, at 5 am still no tanks. With daylight the Germans would see the Australians lying out in the snow, the tanks had been held up by the snowstorm, again the attack was called off. The attack was to go ahead around dawn on 11 April the next day with a minor change, the infantry would go forward fifteen minutes after the tanks.

Once more the troops got into position for the attack, that night the weather was cold and windy. The Australian infantrymen waited in the snow for the tanks, at 4.30 am three were in position in front of the 4th Brigade and one near the 46th Battalion another one appeared but it soon broke down. The infantry left the tanks behind and advanced with a few of the troops finding their way through the barbed wire and into the German trenches, the whole time the Germans were cutting the men down. Eleven tanks set out and by 10 am all were destroyed or disabled. Many died on 11 April in a courageous battle that became known as the First Bullecourt, the Germans counter-attacked causing many casualties.

On 11 April **Captain Henry Stanley Davis** was killed in the early stage of the attack. Henry was born 25 May 1889 at Drysdale, Victoria to John and Caroline Davis, he had an older brother Frederick Gordon born 16 June 1887. Frederick died 1889 and in 1890 Henry's mother, Caroline, died, his father later remarried Esther Eva Carter in 1908.[13] Henry applied for a Commission in the AIF on 22 July 1915. After he qualified for his appointment as 2nd Lieutenant, he was allocated to the 10th reinforcements of the 14th Battalion. He gave his occupation as Student Municipal Engineer. His schooling was State School, Technical School and Private Tuition, father John, was named as next of kin. Henry stood 5 feet 10 inches tall and had 2 ¼ years commission service Senior Cadets and was a Lieutenant in the 69th Infantry.[14]

Henry left Melbourne onboard *Port Lincoln* 16 October 1916 for Egypt however soon after his arrival he was admitted to hospital at Abbassia 4 December 1915 suffering from Mumps, he returned to the 14th Battalion 7 January 1916. Henry was then transferred to the 46th Battalion 12 March 1916 in readiness for the move to France. The 46th Battalion was involved in the battle for Pozieres during August 1916 and in letters written by Henry to his father described the bombardment which occurred during the battle.

In one letter dated 19 August 1916 he wrote: *It's like a combination of sounds of, say a very heavy swell on a rocky shore, several express trains, heavy thunder, and ten thousand immense kettles boiling furiously. That may give a faint idea of what our bombardment sounds like on the enemy's line. When we are getting it, we're too busy hugging the parapet of the trench and expecting every moment to be blown to 'kingdom come' or be buried, to notice what it sounds like.*[15]

While still in the Somme region Lieutenant Davis was recommended for an award by Brigadier General J C Robertson, the recommendation reads: *For conspicuous gallantry and devotion to duty at Gueudecourt on 12 November 1916 during relief under heavy enemy shell fire, a shell burst killing his Company Commander and wounding several others and stunned Lieutenant Davis. Immediately he recovered took command and set a magnificent example of courage to his men.* Lieutenant Davis received the Croix de Guerre on 19 January 1917.[16]

Henry's Company Commander was Captain Purnell, and with his death Henry was promoted to Captain 14 November 1916 to 'C' Company 46th Battalion. On 28 December 1916 he was detached to 4th Divisional School as Adjutant and Quartermaster eventually re-joining his unit 2 April 1917. The War Diary for the 11 April gives an insight to the problem facing Captain Davis and the tanks that the British Commanders placed all of their trust in for the advance onto the Hindenburg Line. *Infantry will not advance until 15 minutes after the tanks pass the jumping off trench. At 5.10 am Captain Davis who commanded the centre sector of the attack spoke to me on the telephone to the following effect only one tank has passed our jumping off trench we can't see any of the others – are we to advance? I at once ordered the advance and communicated my action at once to 12th Brigade Headquarters.*[17]

It is believed that Captain Henry Stanley Davis was killed in No-Man's Land, his batman, Private Frederick John Bascombe 2283, was beside him when he was shot through the head. Private Bascombe tended to his wound then went to find a stretcher bearer but on returning could not find his body. Henry is remembered at the Villers-Bretonneux Memorial in France.

Henry's father had kept all of his son's letters and the diaries in which Henry described his experiences up till his death. In 1932-33 John Davis donated the diaries to the Australian War Memorial, he also allowed the Memorial to transcribe Henry's letters. These are available for viewing on the Memorial's website. Included is a letter from Brigadier General J C Robertson, 12th Brigade dated 22 April 1917 to John Davis in part it says: *Your son had been with the Brigade for some considerable time and his sterling qualities as a soldier were well known to all. He was a particularly capable and trustworthy officer, courageous in the extreme. His Battalion went into action early on the morning of 11th inst., attacking the formidable Hindenburg Line. It was a magnificent effort – unfortunately the effort will be his last. I am indeed sorry Mr Davis, but I hope the glorious nature of his last act and his great sacrifice will help to soften the grief that must surely be with you.*[19]

Henry's body was buried by the Germans, probably in an unmarked grave however his disc was forwarded to the London Branch of the Red Cross by the Berlin Branch.

Artillery played a large part in the First Battle of Bullecourt especially the Howitzer Batteries, one such battery however was totally destroyed by German artillery. It was a gun from the 110th Howitzer Battery attached to the 4th Division Artillery receiving a direct hit destroying the gun and killing the crew. **Henry Leslie Beeson [18636]** died on 11 April 1917 while manning his gun.

Henry was the eldest son of Charles and Alice Beeson born 1883 in Melbourne, Charles and Alice had two more children, Alice Maud born 1886 and Charles born in 1889.[20] The family lived in Melbourne, Victoria however after Charles Senior died in 1910 Alice moved to the Sydney Region. Henry enlisted in Warren, New South Wales 12 January 1916 naming his mother Alice as next of kin. Henry's occupation was Boilermaker, he stood 5 feet 9 inches tall, his complexion was florid with brown eyes and brown hair, his address was 20 Salisbury Street, Waverley.[21] Henry's younger brother Charles had already enlisted 11 August 1915, he was allocated to the 53rd Battalion then transferred to 114th Howitzer Battery attached to the 5th Division Artillery.[22]

Henry left Sydney 11 May 1916 onboard *Argyllshire* arriving in England 15 September. Initially Henry was allocated as a Gunner to 23rd Howitzer Battery, 3rd Division Artillery before finally he was taken on strength, in France, to the 110th Howitzer Battery 9 March 1917. Sergeant J G Pike of the 110th Howitzer Battery was able to relate to the Red Cross on how Henry was killed: *Informant states that they both belonged to 110th Howitzer Battery. On 11 April 1917 the battalion was in action at Bullecourt. About 10 am while Beeson was at his gun a shell fell near by blowing the gun up and hitting Beeson so badly that according to what Informant was told, he died soon afterwards. A good few were hit by the same shell. Informant was on another gun 20 or 30 yards away and saw the whole occurrence, but on account of the confusion after the shell fell, did not see Beeson. He had, however, seen him at the gun shortly before the shell fell. According to the Informant Beeson was a well thought of chap.*[23]

Henry is buried at the Ecoust Military Cemetery, Ecoust-st. Mein, France along with four of the gun crew who were killed by the same shell. After Henry's death Charles Beeson applied to the Army for six months leave back in Australia as now, he was the only support for his widowed mother and invalid sister. Charles was granted leave then the Army discharged him 4 December 1917 after he arrived back in Australia.

Alice received Henry's personal effects which were, Belt Clasp, Knife, Pipe, Metal Mirror, Comb, Testament, Tobacco Pouch, Electric Torch, 3 Notebooks, Metal Wrist Watch, Fountain Pen, Photos, 2 French Books, 2 Badges, Regimental Colours. Alice returned the metal wrist watch as it belonged to another soldier and asked about his razor which was in a silver case. She never received the razor.

Alice's daughter, Alice Maud died 6 June 1919[24] her youngest son, Charles, her only remaining child died 31st January 1920 from injuries he received when he fell from a tram in Sydney.[25] Alice had lost all three of her children, she died 10 January 1930 aged 78.[26]

Hurtle William Emery [2611A] was a soldier reported as missing on 11 April 1917, he was attached to the 4th Australian Light Trench Mortar. Hurtle was born to James and Mary Emery 12 April 1891 at Rosewater South Australia, he had seven brothers and sisters, sadly six died as infants.[27] Hurtle enlisted 26 May 1915 at Keswick, South Australia naming his mother, Mary, as next of kin, his address was 10 Gliddon Street, Rosewater, South Australia. He stood 5 feet 8 ½ inches tall with fair complexion, blue eyes and brown hair.[28]

Hurtle was first allocated to the 8th reinforcements of the 16th Battalion leaving Adelaide 26 August 1915 onboard *Morea*,

Hurtle William Emery South Australia State Library

he was taken on strength to his unit on the Island of Mudros 23 October 1915. Hurtle arrived in France with the 16th Battalion 9 June 1916 however, by the 30 June he had been transferred to the 4th Australian Light Trench Mortar. He was promoted to Lance Corporal 25 August 1916 then 15 January 1917 was promoted to Corporal. Nothing more is known of Hurtle until his Service Record states he had been missing since 11 April 1917, an enquiry held 1 December 1917 found he had been killed in action. His name is on the Villers-Bretonneux Memorial, France. Hurtle's surviving brother, Ernest John, died in 1962, he never married.

Later, during the morning of 11 April 1917 **William John Ireland [1937]** was killed although it was not until a Court of Enquiry held 29 December 1917 found that William indeed was killed in action 11 April. William enlisted 10 February 1916 at Adelaide, naming his mother, Florence Ireland as next of kin, Florence also gave him permission to join as he was 18 year and 9 months old. He stated his occupation as Farm Hand, William stood 5 feet 8 ¾ inches tall with dark complexion, brown eyes and dark hair.[29] William was the youngest child of John and Florence Ireland born 5 May 1898 at Norwood, South Australia, his older brother, Thomas James Ireland, was born 3 May 1896, they were the only children of John and Florence.[30]

Thomas James Ireland [1885] was the first to enlist 2 February 1916 at Adelaide, he was allocated to the 5th Pioneers, William was eventually assigned to the 3rd reinforcement 48th Battalion. When William enlisted, he was first allocated to the 10th Battalion, then 1 March 1916 he transferred to the 3rd Light Horse. Finally, 20 April 1916 he was transferred to the 48th Battalion. William left Adelaide 13 July 1916 onboard *Seang Bee* arriving at Plymouth 9 September 1916. He arrived in France 4 December 1916 and was taken on strength to his unit 22 December 1916.

By the 8 April 1917 the 48th Battalion was at Noreuil near Bullecourt two days later the 46th and 48th Battalions were ordered to attack the enemy trench on a frontage of about 600 yards. The attack was called off when the tanks failed to appear. In a Report on Operations of Tanks, on 11 April, Captain Raymond Leane, Commanding Office of the 48th Battalion was very scathing.

The men would have gone forward and successfully occupied the objective under an artillery barrage without suffering such heavy casualties which undoubtably resulted by the failure of the tanks to start in time and they're not advancing beyond the first 'Jumping Off' trench. Why the tanks stopped and opened fire from the 'Jumping Off' trench perhaps is best known to the O.C. tanks. It was certainly bad tactics because it promptly brought a barrage right on to the men waiting to advance. I am of the opinion that the tanks absolutely failed to carry out their part in the attack. I consider had they shown more dash and initiative things would have been better and perhaps we might have been still holding the line captured today.[31]

William was declared missing which caused a lot of anxiety for his brother and his parents back in South Australia. Thomas wrote to the Red Cross requesting information on his brother. Sadly, Thomas was killed in action 4 November 1917 in Belgium, before William was declared killed in action at a Court of Enquiry held on 29 December 1917. Vera Deakin from the Red Cross wrote to Thomas after Private Yates had told them that: *He was in the same gun team and that Yates bandaged him up. Had to leave him as they had to withdraw, they were unable to retain their ground.*[32]

During 1918 it appears that John and Florence Ireland had separated as John had one address when he wrote to Base Records and Florence had another. Florence did place a notice in a newspaper telling of her grief at losing her only sons:

W J Ireland (1937) previously reported missing April 11, 1917 now reported killed in action at Bullecourt; also, T J Ireland (1885) killed in action November 4, 1917, in Belgium.
No loving mother's gentle hand to wipe the death drew from their brows.

No token of love in that far-off land to mark the spot where they sleep now.
No loved one stood around them to bid a fond farewell.
No word of comfort could I give to the son's I loved so well.[33]

The medals of William and Thomas were sent to John Ireland their father.

During the First Battle of Bullecourt 1,170 soldiers were taken prisoner, the largest capture of Australian prisoners in a single action on the Western Front, **William Guest [2756]** was one of the prisoners. William was born 1890 in Maryborough Victoria, his parents were George and Maria Guest, one of four children born to the couple. William had a younger brother, Edward who was born 1892 in Bendigo, Victoria. The boys had two sisters, sadly both girls did not live past infancy, their father, George died in 1899 leaving Maria to raise her young sons by herself.

William enlisted 2 July 1915 at Melbourne naming his mother as next of kin, his occupation was Butcher, aged 23 years, he stood 5 feet 4 ½ inches tall with dark complexion, brown eyes and black hair.[34] William was allocated to the 8th reinforcement of the 14th Battalion leaving Melbourne 15 September 1915 on *Makarini*, and was taken on strength to the 14th at Gallipoli 13 November, 1915. When William joined his unit at Durrant's Post, Gallipoli he would have found conditions very arduous, the weather had turned cold and snow was starting to fall. A month later, 12 December 1915, the 14th Battalion received orders to have the ranks ready to move out. By midnight on 18 December William embarked on *Hazel*, sailed to Mudros then onto Alexandria 31 December 1916.

France was William's next country sailing into Marseilles 8 June 1916 with the 14th, he survived Pozieres, however, at the beginning of September his unit was down to 29 Officers and 634 ordinary ranks. The 14th Battalion had reached Noreuil 9 April 1917 in readiness for the attack on the 11 April. 2nd Lieutenant

S J J Carton from the Lewis Gun School gave a report to the Red Cross concerning William: *I was in charge of 'A' Company and saw Guest on right of Bullecourt about 11.00am badly wounded in the thigh in the German trench. I put him in a dugout and his wound was dressed by H A Black 3031. The Germans drove us out and came over the ground. Never heard more of him. I do not consider he was fatally wounded.*[36]

William was captured by the Germans on 13 April and placed in a hospital dying 15 April from his wound which was from grenade shrapnel to his thigh. The Germans buried him 17 April in the Military Cemetery, Bugnicourt, France, his mother was notified of the death and place of burial 6 December 1917. By then her youngest son, **Edward Guest [2670]** had also been killed in action 10 August 1917 during the Third Battle of Ypres. Edward probably knew of his brother's demise as he had transferred to the 14th Battalion 18 February 1917 probably to fight beside his older brother.

A report on the attack 11 April, 1917 from the Commanding Officer of the 14th Battalion was scornful: *The Tank Co-operation in the attack made on the Hindenburg Line on the night of 10/11 April was useless, or worse than useless. The whole outfit showed rank inefficiency and, in some cases, tank crews seemed to lack 'British tenacity and pluck, and that determination to go forward at all costs', which is naturally looked for in Britishers.*[37] William's effects were sent to his mother, they consisted of 2 French Notes, 4 Coins, 1 Razer, 1 Watch (damaged) 1 Money Belt, 1 Pair Gloves, Letters and 1 Pencil. His disc was recovered and passed onto Maria when he was re-interned in the Cabaret Rouge British Cemetery. The body of Edward, William's younger brother, was never recovered.

Despite the failure of the First Battle for Bullecourt, another attack by the Allies was planned for 3 May. The 5th and 6th Brigades of the 2nd Division were chosen for the attack on the Hindenburg Line. Zero hour for the 19th Battalion was 3.45am, the battalion was to be the right flank battalion for the whole attack. The enemy brought heavy machine gun fire on the right flank as the men left the trenches leaving 12 Officers and 347 other ranks killed, wounded or missing from the 19th Battalion.[38]

Amongst the missing was **Norman Frank Callaway [5794]**, a young man with a brilliant cricketing career in front of him. Norman was born in 1896 at Hay, New South Wales, his parents were Thomas and Emily Callaway. A sister Jessie was born in 1898 however after her birth there are no records available for Jessie Callaway, perhaps she may have died shortly after her birth. In 1912 another son was born his name was Ernest, sadly Ernest died in 1912.[39] After the death of Ernest the Callaway family moved to Sydney residing at 22 Ebley Street, Waverley.

Before the family moved to Sydney Norman played a lot of cricket in the area around Hay, once in Sydney his cricket career drew the attention of newspapers and the sporting community. It wasn't long before Norman was chosen to play, in January 1914, with the New South Wales Colts against the Victorian Colts at the Melbourne Cricket Ground, he was aged 17. He made his first-class debut aged 18 for New South Wales in a match against Queensland at the Sydney Cricket Ground. He became the first batsman to score a double century on a first-class debut scoring 207.[40]

When he enlisted at Sydney 27 June 1916, he claimed to be 21 years, adding a year to his age so that he did not require his parent's permission. Norman stood 5 feet 7 inches tall, his complexion was fresh with blue eyes and brown hair, his occupation was Clerk, he was allocated to the 19th Battalion.[41] Norman left Sydney 7 October 1916 onboard Ceramic arriving in Plymouth 21 November 1916. He was eventually taken on strength to his unit in France 5 February 1917 while the battalion was in the Le Sars, Eaucourt region. Norman was to experience the worst winter of 1916/17 which the Australian soldiers had to tolerate, however, after February the weather warmed a little.

On the morning of 3 May Norman received a fatal wound while waiting for the advance on the Hindenburg Line. Private

Matthews was later interviewed who gave the following account. Private Matthews stated that he was in the same shell hole when a shell hit Norman's head. He fell across Matthews; he was so shocked at the time that he never thought of taking his disc or paybook or any proof of identity.[42] It wasn't until 27 October 1917 that Norman's parents received the news that he was killed in action. Emily Callaway, believing that her only son will have a grave choose the wording for his tombstone; *A soldier and a man he died, honored by all! His country's pride*. There is no grave for Norman, he is remembered on the Villers-Bretonneux Memorial in France.

At the Waverly Oval pavilion a large photo of Norman was hung with the lines of the poet, Robert W Service, attached:

And though there's never a grave to tell, nor a cross to mark his fall,
Thank God! We know that he "batted well". In the last great Game of all.[43]

The 17th Battalion was also involved in the attack that was to commence 3 May, one soldier from the battalion was wounded during the advance, he was **William Allen Newman [2762A]** receiving a gun-shot wound to the left thigh and face. William had been born 29 December 1891 at Northamptonshire, England and was baptised 7 August 1892 the only child of Henry and Harriett Newman. It is thought that William's mother Harriett may have died as on 2 February 1909 William and his father, Henry, left England onboard *Wilcannia* a ship from the Lund's Blue Anchor Line bound for Sydney.

William enlisted 9 June 1916 at Kiama, New South Wales naming his father, Henry as his next of kin. William stood 5 feet 6 ½ inches tall, his complexion was fresh with blue eyes and brown hair. Henry's address given as 22 Johnson Street, Annandale, New South Wales while William's address was 'Burland' St. George's Crescent, Drummoyne, Sydney. Before William left Australia he filed three documents with the Army, the first; *I hereby give Mr Horace Gilbert of Henley, Sydney full permission to take over my affairs whilst I am on Active Service and away from Sydney. This gives him full access to my trunks and belongings and also unquestionable right to handle my money matters (whatever they may be) without fear of any legal proceedings caused by any person or persons whatsoever.* The document was signed by William.

The second document, a will naming Mr Horace Gilbert as sole beneficiary to all of his property. The third document stated; *I William Allen Newman hereby give Mrs Dutton of 'Burland' St. George Crescent, Drummoyne, Sydney the authority to refuse to allow any person or persons (except Mr Horace Gilbert of Henley, Sydney) to handle or in any way interfere with my trunk, cases, belongings and etc, unless a written order is produced, written and signed by me. Note: In case of my death the above articles to be moved to Mr Horace Gilbert, Glenare, William St Henley, Gladesville, Sydney.* One can only assume, from the wording in the documents that William and his father had a strained relationship.

William was initially allocated to the 53rd Battalion leaving Sydney onboard the troopship *Ceramic* 7 October 1916 bound for Plymouth, England before heading to France 28 February 1917. He spent a short time with the 53rd Battalion before transferring to the 17th Battalion on 23 March 1917, his service number had an A added to 2762. William Allen Newman died from his wounds 5 May 1917 at the 3rd Casualty Clearing Station. He is buried at Grevillers British Cemetery, in the Pas de Calais region of France. His father, Henry placed the following inscription on his tombstone; *In memory of the dearly loved son of Mr H Newman of Sydney.*

William's effects were sent back to his father, they consisted of: Wallet, Battalion Colours, Cards, Photos and Receipt. When William's documents, regarding his wishes, came to light the Army wrote to Mr Newman requesting the personal effects to be returned, this did not happen, his father did receive all of his son's medals. He also filled out the circular for the Roll of Honour.

During the Second Battle for Bullecourt the Australians managed to seize part of the German lines, however the Germans counter-attacked causing many casualties with the troops experiencing intense trench warfare. On 7 May 1917 another young man lost his life, he was **2nd Lieutenant John Pauling Sives** born 1893 in Manchester, Lancaster, England. John, the only child of Elizabeth Sives, left England 18 August 1911 onboard *Ormuz* for Sydney.[46] His mother Elizabeth arrived later, her sister Annabel and brother-in-law Hugh Kellie also came to Australia, the family were all living at Chisholm Street, Greenwich, Sydney.

John enlisted at Liverpool, Sydney 24 April 1915 naming his mother as next of kin, he stood 5 feet 5 ½ inches tall, his complexion was fair with hazel eyes and brown hair, his occupation was Clerk. He was initially allocated to the 9th reinforcements of the 4th Battalion and given the Service Number of 2228. He left Australia 16 June 1915 aboard the troopship *Karoola*, joining his battalion 4 August 1915 on Gallipoli. Just two days later he was in the thick of it when the 4th attacked Lone Pine. During the attack John suffered shock from the shelling and was sent back to England to recuperate, spending the rest of 1915 at Wandsworth Hospital in London.

John re-joined his battalion 5 January 1916 at Tel-El-Kebir, just a month later 6 February he was sent to the School of Instruction at Zeitoun. Transferring from the 4th Battalion to the Machine Gun Company of the 1st Infantry Brigade on the 12 March 1916 may not have been to his liking as four days later he was back with the 4th. John arrived in France 30 March 1916 taking part in training for the upcoming battles on the Western Front. He received his first promotion to Lance Corporal 8 May 1916.

John's next action was at Pozieres, France where his bravery earned him a Military Medal, his citation reads: *At Pozieres, France on 25 July 1916 Lance Corporal Sives in an attack on a German Trench did splendid service. He was extremely cool and courageous under fire and by his judicious and dashing handling of the Lewis guns helped the bombers to gain and retain their positions.*[48] Shortly after John was promoted to

Temporary Sergeant 31 July 1916, another promotion was to come his way 30 September 1916, when he received his appointed as 2nd Lieutenant. John and the 4th Battalion went on to spent a cold and miserable winter in what has been described as Europe's worst.

John's courage was to shine through again 15 April 1917 when he was Mentioned in Despatches for devotion to duty during the enemy attack on Demicourt and Boursises. Less than a month later 7 May John was killed in action during an attack on Bullecourt between Diagonal Road and Ostrich Avenue. His mother, Elizabeth was devastated when news of her son's death was conveyed to her, she placed a notice in the Sydney Morning Herald 6 June 1917 saying *He lived honourably, fought bravely, and died nobly.*[50]

Elizabeth never recovered from his death dying herself shortly after 2 August 1917. Her brother-in-law, Hugh Kellie took over her affairs informing the Army of her death, he was the Executor of her will naming her sister, Annabel, her sole beneficiary. The Army sent John's medals and effects to Annabel Kellie. John does not have a grave; he is remembered at the Villers-Bretonneux Memorial in France. His Military Medal and Lotus Leaf (Mentioned in Despatches) were sold recently in England.[51]

On 5 May 1917 the 11th Battalion moved to Noreuil to hold the line in front of the village of Bullecourt and was still there 8 May when **Peter McKinlay [2648]** was killed in action. Peter was born 1890 Collingwood, Victoria, the youngest of three children to Peter and Bethia McKinlay, the eldest was Janet Pender born 1886, next was Elizabeth born 1888, sadly she died one year later, all were born at Collingwood, Victoria. Peter's father, Peter McKinlay, died 1891 leaving Bethia to raise her young family. She later marred Daniel Landy in 1895.[52]

Peter enlisted 19 June 1915 at Blackboy Hill in Perth, Western Australia naming his sister, Janet McKinlay as his next of kin. Peter's address at enlistment was 141 Bulwer Street, Perth, Western Australia while Janet lived at 165 Vere Street, Abbotsford, Victoria. Peter stood 5 feet 7 ½ inches tall, his complexion was

Peter McKinlay AWM H06470

bronzed with blue eyes and light brown hair, his occupation was Orchardist. As part of the 8th reinforcement of 11th Battalion Peter left Fremantle onboard the troopship *Anchises* 2 September 1915.[53]

Peter joined his battalion 12 December 1915 at the Sarpi Rest Camp on Lemnos Island, on the day he arrived Diphtheria was infecting the soldiers resulting in isolation for the battalion, Meningitis was also causing a problem for the 11th. While back in Egypt Peter found himself in and out of hospital for various ailments finally re-joining his unit in France 23 June 1916. One month later the 11th Battalion took part in an attack on the night of 22/23 July 1916, one of the 11 wounded was Peter suffering a gunshot wound to the right leg and face. The wound was considered slight however, he was returned to England and admitted to the 1st Auxiliary Norfolk War Hospital.

After some more training in England Peter finally travelled back to France to re-join his unit 15 March 1917 in preparation for the 2nd Battle of Bullecourt. The 11th Battalion took over the front line on 5 May 1917, Peter was killed three days later just before the battalion was due to be relieved. The Army informed Peter's sister Janet of his death and as he left a will naming her as his sole beneficiary Janet received all of his personal effects. They consisted of 2 Wallets, Photos, Letters, Cards, Unit Colours, 7 Stamps, Gold Strip, Key, 2 Coins, Notebook, Armlet Purse, Burn's Poems, Leather Cup, Leather Writing Case, Scissors, 2 Handkerchiefs, 2 Pencils, Coin on Ribbon and a Fountain Pen. Janet wrote back asking if they could tell her how Peter died, a Private A McKenzie informed the Red Cross that he was with him holding the line in front of Bullecourt village when part of a shell hit about the face killing him instantly. He body was still there when the battalion was relieved that night.[54]

Janet later wrote to Base Records informing them that she was leaving Australia for Canada 25 March 1919 giving them her new address. The Army replied asking the whereabouts of Peter's parents or brothers. Janet replied that Peter had no one except her and she was his only next of kin. Janet neglected to say her mother was still alive and living in Melbourne, why, this will never be known. Janet later moved to America, she never married, even though Janet received the Circular for the Roll of Honour, this was not filled out. Peter's body was never recovered, instead he is remembered on the Villers-Bretonneux Memorial in France. Peter's mother, Bethia Landy died October 1947 in Melbourne, her death notice named her children, Peter as deceased and Janet living in USA.[55]

By 10 May the 58th Battalion of the 5th Division was at the Hindenburg Line east of Bullecourt, the battalion was brought into the attack 12th May which resulted in some heavy fighting. During the attack **Frederick Arthur Caddy [158]** was killed. A Gallipoli veteran, Frederick had enlisted at Melbourne 18 August 1914 stating his age as 21 years and 7 months, born at Ballarat. He named his mother Mary Jane Williams as next of kin, he stood 5 feet 8 inches tall with fair complexion, blue eyes and brown hair, his occupation was Clerk, the family was living at 87 Yarra Street Abbotsford, Victoria.[56]

Allocated to the 6th Battalion he left Melbourne for Egypt onboard the troopship *Hororata*, for training before the landing on Anzac Cove. The 6th Battalion as part of the second wave landed 25 April 1915. In early May the 2nd Brigade which included the 6th Battalion was transferred to Cape Helles. The attack 8 May on the village of Krithia was costly as the 6th and 7th Battalions were ordered to attack across open country against a growing storm of rifle-fire, the 6th losing a third of their men. Frederick survived and returned to Anzac Cove 16 May where he received a gun-shot wound to his right forearm 4 June 1915. Frederick was taken off the Peninsula and sent to the Cottonera Military Hospital at Malta for treatment until the 15 June 1915.

Unable to return to his unit on Gallipoli, Frederick returned to Egypt where he took on a clerical role until his arm was fully healed. He soon found himself back in hospital at Alexandria 10 December where he was treated for Venereal Disease, he was discharged 12 January 1916. Shortly after Frederick was transferred to the 58th Battalion 17 February 1916 as part of the re-organisation of the AIF, the 58th would become part of the 5th Division. During 1916 Frederick was promoted to Corporal, despite requesting that he would prefer to stay a private, he was made a Corporal again and again, finally he became a Sergeant 4 March 1917.

When Frederick was killed Base Records notified Mr James Frances Williams as Mrs Mary Jane Williams had already died. The Army was aware of Mrs Williams death and as Frederick had written a will leaving his estate jointly between Mr Williams and Frederick's brother, William Caddy, the Army wished to pass Frederick's medals to his brother.

Mr Williams wrote back stating that before his wife died, she told her husband that neither Frederick or William were her sons and William Caddy was no relation to Frederick. Frederick was the illegitimate son of Mary Jane's sister, Annie Teresa Voges, his real name was Ernest Frederick Voges, his mother did not want to raise him so Mary Jane took him and raised him from a baby. At the time Mary Jane was living with a man with the surname of Caddy so Mary Jane gave that name to Frederick, at the same time she also took in a William Nicholas giving him the surname of Caddy. After Mr Caddy's death Mary Jane posed as the widow Caddy with two children, when Mr Williams married Mary Jane, he always believed they were her sons, the boys always believed she was their mother.

Frederick's real mother now known as Annie Bartlett knew of Frederick death, as she registered his birth, 14 June 1917, with the Victorian Birth, Death & Marriages stating that he was born 16 January 1896. Five days later Annie filled out a Statutory Declaration informing the Army that she was his mother; she also requested a Death Certificate for her son. After Mr William's explained the situation and that he had raised Frederick since 1904, the Army decided that he did have the right to Frederick's medals even though Frederick's grandfather Mr Voges also wanted to claim his estate.

The Circular for the Roll of Honour was forwarded to Mr Williams but was never filled out. His body was not recovered instead he is remembered on the Villers-Bretonneux Memorial.

The Second Battle for Bullecourt continued while more young men lost their lives in an ill-conceived and deplorably executed charge that ended in a stalemate. On the 15 May 1917 another young man was mortally wounded; his name was **Herbert Creagh [4758].** Herbert enlisted 28 August 1915 at Warwick Farm, Liverpool, New South Wales stating he was 18 and 7 months old. He stood 5 feet 9 ½ inches tall with fresh complexion, brown eyes and black hair, giving his father John as next of kin. He was initially allocated to 'C' Company 15 reinforcements 2nd Battalion leaving Sydney onboard *Star of England* 8 March 1916.[57]

Not long after his arrival in Egypt Herbert was transferred to the 54th Battalion 20 April 1916 while stationed at Ferry Post. The 54th Battalion arrived at Marseilles 29 June 1916 then fought its first major battle at Fromelles, the battle was a disaster for the 5th Division, however Herbert survived. The 54th spent an extreme winter in the trenches which took its toll on Herbert, he suffered from Trench Feet and was in hospital from 1 January until 30 January 1917.

The 54th on 11 May 1917, made preparations for moving to the front line to relieve the 53rd Battalion. During the early morning of 15th May the battalion's front line and support trenches were subject to a heavy bombardment from enemy artillery. A message was received at Battalion Headquarters at 6.45am which read: *Enemy is attacking all along the line. Situation at present is doubtful as our right company was wiped out previous to the attack. No reports to hand from dawn. Will inform you later re situation.*[58] During that morning Herbert received a gunshot wound to his head. Taken to the 29th Casualty Clearing Station he died from a cerebral herniation 18 May 1917.

Herbert was the eldest of three sons born to John and Alice Creagh, Alice had died in 1912,[59] John (Jack) was born 1899 and Arthur Frederick was born 1902.[60] Jack, even though he was underage, decided he too would enlist on 7 August 1916 stating his age was 18 years and 6 months, he was given the Service Number 6723. He named his father as next of kin, Jack served overseas until he was discharged 17 April 1918 because he was underage. Jack returned to his father and younger brother in Auburn, after their father's death the two brothers lived together until they died. Jack and Arthur Creagh never married. Herbert is buried at the Grevillers British Cemetery.

Even though the Second Battle of Bullecourt was considered over by 17 May 1917 men still died, **James Kerr [2512]** was killed in action 18th May. James enlisted 2 August 1915 at Liverpool, Sydney claiming he was 23 years and 2 months old, born at Newcastle on Tyne, England. He stood 5 feet 2 inches tall with dark complexion, brown eyes and dark hair, his occupation was Mono Operator. James named his father, Franklin G Kerr living at 152 Victoria Street Darlinghurst, as his next of kin.[61] Initially James was allocated to the 15th reinforcements of the 18th Battalion leaving Sydney on board the troopship *Themistocles* 5 October 1915. James claimed, at enlistment, he was born in 1892, however, he was born early in 1898.[62]

On the day James left he was transferred to the 55th Battalion, over time he was promoted a number of times however, each time he would revert back to private. Finally, he accepted the promotion of Sergeant 2 May 1916, shortly after James arrived in France 29 June 1916 with the 55th Battalion. Back in Australia, James's father, Franklin Gilroy Kerr enlisted 23 July 1916, leaving behind his wife, Sara and his youngest son, Franklin Gilroy Kerr Junior. Franklin Gilroy claimed he was 40 years and 4 months old, however, he did put his age down by 2 years.[63]

James was transferred to 4th Army School 17 October 1916, another promotion 11 February 1917 to 2nd Lieutenant required him to attend Corps Intelligence School from 26 February 1917, re-joining his unit 11 March 1917.

Early April James and the 55th were involved in the attack at Doignies then 15 May the Germans made a final attempt to dislodge the Australians from Bullecourt, they failed. The 18 May the 55th was ordered forward to relieve the 56th Battalion, 2nd Lieutenant Kerr was killed by an enemy shell whilst proceeding from Noreuil to the front lines.[64] James is buried at the Noreuil Australian Cemetery, his mother Sara was informed of his death. She penned the words for his tombstone: *Greater love hath no man than this that he laid down his life for his country.*

Franklin Gilroy Kerr served abroad for two years and 296 days with the 8th Battalion, he was discharged and returned to Sydney 16 October 1919 returning to his wife and son. Sadly, Franklin Gilroy Snr died 1921, a newspaper report explaining his death. *Sydney Harbour Accidentally Drowned. One of two bodies found in the harbour this morning was identified this afternoon as that of Franklyn Gilroy Kerr, formerly of New South Head Road, Double Bay. On the body, which was picked up off Kirribilli, were papers and war bonds bearing the deceased name.*[65] Franklin Gilroy Kerr Jnr became a Bank Clerk, he died 10 July 1945 at his residence Stratford, 15a Lower Wycombe Road, Neutral Bay, beloved son of Mrs Sara Kerr aged 43 years.[66] Sara Kerr, last of the Kerr Family, died in Sydney at the age of 82 in Crows Nest, Sydney, New South Wales in 1959.[67]

CHAPTER 6
MESSINES 1917

Major General John Monash, the commander of the 3rd Division, was pleased his men would be entering a battle for the first time. The division was anxious to prove itself worthy of the reputation of the other veteran Australian divisions; the village of Messines in Belgium was to be the target of the attack. The village was located on the Messines Ridge, a ten-mile-long piece of high ground south of Ypres. The battle was an attempt by the Allies to capture land and gain control of the higher ground in the Ypres salient, 7 June 1917 was the date the battle would commence. For a week before the attack the tried and tested artillery assault started with over 2,400 artillery guns pounding the German lines to inflict serious damage.

The day before the attack began the 42nd Howitzer Battery moved further towards the front lines for the preparation of the creeping barrage needed to protect the attacking troops. One of the 42nd Battery, **Gunner Frank Robert Warlward Osborne [1900]** was mortally wounded. Frank, the only child of James Robert and Nellie Osborne was born in Rochester, Victoria in 1896. The family were living at Hagita, a coconut plantation, at Milne Bay, Via Samarai, Papua. Frank's father, James Robert Osborne, a former Wesleyan missionary and managing director of a Milne Bay Rubber Company took over the lease of the plantation in 1910.[1] Frank had his early schooling in Melbourne at Wesley College moving with his family to the plantation when he was about 14 years old. Frank travelled by boat down to Cairns enlisting in Townsville 13 September 1915. He stood 5 feet 9 ½ inches tall with dark complexion, blue eyes and dark brown hair, his occupation was given as Planter, his father was next of kin.[2]

Frank's father, James Robert Osborne wrote a letter to the Army giving his permission for his son to join, stating that his son was 19 years old on 10 April 1915. Frank was first allocated to the 2nd Light Horse Regiment leaving Sydney 22 January 1916 onboard the troopship *Boonah,* after arriving at Heliopolis he was taken on strength to the 1st Light Horse 6 March 1916. Another transfer 21 April 1916 saw him become a Gunner with the 11th Field Artillery Brigade, which was part of the 4th Division, eventually arriving in France 10 June 1916.

Frank in January 1917 was at Flers before moving the next month to Delville Wood spending February and March in the area. By early June Frank and the 42nd Howitzer Battery were in

Frank Robert Osborne. The Queenslander 28 July 1917 Page 22

position ready to assist the infantry in their attack. At some time during the Battery moving forward, Frank received a gun-shot wound to the head and chest. Taken to the 77th Field Ambulance, Frank never recovered from his wounds and died 6 June1917. He is buried at the Westhop Farm Cemetery in Belgium, his parents wrote the inscription on his grave, *Lo I am with you always Jesus*.

Not long after their only child was killed James and Nellie returned to Victoria where Nellie received his effects, they consisted of: Letters, Franc Note, Knife and Note-Book. On 25 April 1927 Nellie misplaced her Mother's Badge, she immediately wrote to the authorities telling them of her loss, she was heartbroken to think she had lost another part of her son, her badge found on St Kilda Road was returned to her. James Robert died in 1941 and Nellie in 1949.[3]

At 3.10 am, Zero Hour, on the 7 June 1917 a number of big guns began to fire and then the trench-walls rocked. To the left, near Wytschaete a huge bubble was swelling mushroom-shaped from the earth and then burst to cast a molten, rosy glow on the under-surface of some dense cloud low above it. The nineteen great mines had been exploded.[4] Since 1916 the Allies had been digging tunnels under Messines Ridge, in all 19 mines were exploded. It became the biggest man-made explosion in history until the Atom Bomb in World War 11.

Two brothers who took part in the battle had joined up together, they were **Eric Burton Chapman [28]** and **Edward Laurie Chapman [Lieutenant],** both enlisted 23 August 1915 at Warwick Farm, New South Wales. They were the only sons of Edgar Chenhalls Scott and Emily Chapman, there was an older brother, Lydill Edgar Elliott Chapman, born 1883 at Dubbo, New South Wales. Lydill was attending Berkeley University in America when he was tragically drowned 8 May 1906 while trying to save a female friend, both died in the accident.

Eric, was born 2 January 1890[5] he stood 5 feet 5 ¾ inches tall, his complexion was fair, with blue eyes and fair hair, occupation was Surveyor.[6] Eric was allocated to the 33rd Battalion which formed part of the 3rd Division. The battalion trained at Casula, New South Wales before moving to England. Eric was appointed Acting Sergeant 29 December 1915 then became a Sergeant 4 May 1916.

The 33rd Battalion left Sydney onboard the troopship *Marathon* 4 May 1916, the day he was promoted to Sergeant. Arriving in England 9 July 1916 the 33rd Battalion undertook more training

Eric Burton Chapman AWM P12157.022

with Eric proving he was a capable soldier as on 6 September he was sent to a training school at Tidworth. The 3rd Division under the command of Major General John Monash moved to France late November 1916 in time for one of the coldest winters in history. Eric was promoted to 2nd Lieutenant 8 February 1917 transferring to the 35th Battalion 18 February 1917, leaving behind his brother Edward who was still with the 33rd Battalion.

In the early months of 1917 the 3rd Division carried out raids, the biggest on 27 February, used 854 men.[7] At 12.15am 7 June, eight attack battalions of the 3rd Division began their approach through Ploegsteert Wood in the battle for Messines Ridge. At zero hour after the mines were blown up the 3rd went over the top into the dust, smoke and flame. Before 4.00am the 3rd had control of its target however Eric was not among the conquerors. A report within his Service Record states; *he was last seen a few minutes before zero hour (3.10am) on the morning of 7 June.* Eric's body was recovered and buried by the battalion chaplain, Rev. J E Osborne, the site of his burial was lost due to further battles in the region. Eric is remembered on the Ypres (Menin Gate) Memorial in Belgium.

Edward, Eric's younger brother was born 12 June 1891.[8] He stood 5 feet 6 inches tall with fresh complexion, brown eyes and brown hair, his occupation was Stock and Station Agent, he was also allocated to the 33rd Battalion.[9] Edward applied and was granted a commission as a 2nd Lieutenant 6 January 1916 while still in the Casula camp. After his arrival in England, he was promoted to Lieutenant 1 August 1916 before attending the Hayling Island School 27 August then onto the Lewis Gun School at Grantham.

Two days after the start of the battle, 9 June 1917, Edward was wounded in action however he stayed on duty, by then he would have known of the death of Eric. On 12 July 1917 while still in Messines, Edward was sitting in his dugout when a shell exploded at the entrance killing him. Edgar and Emily now have lost both their sons, Emily did find it difficult to accept the fact

(Edward Laurie Chapman AWM P12157.003

that Edward had also been killed. On 26 July 1917 a letter was sent to Base Records from the Blayney War Service Committee making an enquiry on behalf of Mrs Chapman. She believed that the telegram notifying them of Edward's death was a mistake and that the Army was again reporting Eric's death. She could not lose both sons so close together. Edward is buried at the Kandahar Farm Cemetery Belgium, the epitaph for Edward's tomb; *His Son Went Down In The Morn*. Edgar and Emily had three sons; none have a grave in Australia.

The 52nd Battalion of the 4th Division was also brought into the attack on the 7 June, a soldier from the battalion also killed was **Harry Wentworth [2755]**. Harry enlisted at Brisbane 6 June 1916 stating he was born 1895 in London, England, he named a sister, Mrs Alice Wentworth of Essex, England as next of kin. The Mrs was latter crossed out on his paperwork. Harry stood 5 feet 10 inches tall with dark complexion, brown eyes and light brown hair, he had many tattoos on his arms and chest, occupation was Cook.[10] Harry left Sydney onboard *Ceramic* 7 October 1916 arriving in England 21 November 1916. On 2 December charged with resisting arrest by Military Police at Codford, he received 24 hours detention. Arriving in France 28 December 1916 he was taken on strength to his battalion 2 January 1917. Harry took part in the battle at Noreuil on 2 April 1917 before moving into the line ready for the attack at Messines. It was in the afternoon that Harry took a direct hit from a shell killing him instantly. The authorities tried to locate his sister however, the address given was insufficient.

A Private Henry Hansen gave a statement on 11 September 1917 revealing why the Army could not locate any relations of Harry. Private Hansen knew Wentworth in Mackay, Queensland as Harry James. He was a labourer, single, his people lived in London. He would not take leave to visit them as he was using an assumed name. This was because he was in debt in Australia.[11] Base Records forwarded everything to England hoping that his family may be located, that did not happen and his Memorial Plaque was returned to Australia 12 July 1946. Harry Wentworth is buried at Messines Ridge British Cemetery and a family in England never knew what happened to Harry James.

Messines Ridge was taken on the first day of the battle, however the Germans counter-attacked, they did not want the ridge to fall into the hands of the Allies. The battle continued for another week, over that time more Australian men died. One was **James Emanuel Callard [1641]** who died 8 June 1917, he had enlisted at Broken Hill, New South Wales 24 February 1916. His age at enlistment was 21 years and 7 months, he stood 5 feet 9 inches tall with dark complexion, grey eyes and dark brown hair. James was a station hand at the Morden Station near Tibooburra, New South Wales.[12]

James' mother Mildred Callard was named as his next of kin, he was the only child of the widow Mildred. Mildred and her husband, James Emanuel Callard had four sons and one daughter while living at Broken Hill, New South Wales. Richard, was born and died in 1892, James born 1894, Thomas G born and died 1896, Helen born and died 1898 and Thomas B born and died 1899.[13] Tragedy stuck the family again in 1907 when Mildred's husband, James, died from natural causes at the Wounamonta Tank, near Milparinka.[14] It appears that James Emanuel Callard Senior was born in England as his mother placed an advertisement in an Adelaide paper in 1909 stating that her son was missing. She said that her son was Emanuel Hutt but now goes by the name of James Emanuel Callard, who had come to Sydney in March 1883, his last letter to her in England, from Broken Hill was in 1897.[15]

James was joined by three brothers, Messrs. R Monaghan, J Monaghan and M Monaghan, from Morden Station for a farewell at the Milparinka Hall on the 4 April 1916 which was the most successful and enthusiastic gathering that had taken place in Milparinka.[16] James was assigned to the 2nd reinforcements of the 48th Battalion leaving Adelaide onboard *Aeneas* 11 April 1916. While in Egypt, on 17 May 1916, he took ill with Bronchitis and Influenza, when he recovered, he attended the 12th Training Battalion finally arriving in France 29 December 1916. He was taken on strength to the 48th Battalion 6 February 1917.

James and the 48th Battalion took part in the First Battle of Bullecourt, the 48th suffering many losses, the battalion later moved to Belgium ready for the attack on Messines. The war for

James ended 8 June 1917, Mildred was living in Adelaide when she received the news of her only child, she was sent James' effects which consisted of a Notebook, Photos, Cards and Letters, sadly she did not fill out the Roll Honour Circular for her son.

Leslie Edward Lee [224] a member of the 10th Machine Gun Company also died 8 June 1917. Leslie enlisted 11 March 1916 at Melbourne, Victoria stating that he had been born in Brunswick, Victoria, his age was given as 21 years and 3 months. He stood 5 feet 11 ¼ inches tall with fair complexion, brown eyes and auburn hair, occupation was Labourer, giving his next of kin as father George Lee. His address at time of embarkment was c/- Mrs Simcock 30 Murphy Street, North Richmond.[17]

Leslie was allocated to the 10th Australian Machine Gun Company, attached to the 3rd Division leaving Melbourne 27 May 1916 onboard *Ascanius* bound for England. While in England Leslie was a star player in an AFL match between 3rd Australian Division and the Australian Training Units at Queen's Club, West Kensington on Saturday 28 October 1916, the 3rd Division won. Back in Australia Leslie had been a promising player for Richmond AFL Club. The 10th trained at Lark Hill, England before heading for France 22 November 1916. Leslie spent a cold winter at Armentieres, France where he first saw action finally moving to Belgium beginning of June 1917. The War Diary for the 10th Machine Gun Company states that Private L Lee was wounded 8 June 1917.[18] There was no other news on Leslie that the Army could give other than he was declared wounded and missing. Finally, in February 1918, after enquiries from other members of Leslie's company, he was officially noted as killed in action. When the family was informed of his death, more information on Leslie came to light.

George Lee, who was named as his father, had died in 1917.[19] The wife of George, Eliza, wrote to the Army updating her address stating she was the mother of Leslie and all mail should be directed to her. Shortly after correspondence from an Isabella Turner Roberts to the Army claimed that she was the mother of Leslie and Eliza Lee was her sister. Leslie was born as Edward Leslie Barnes

Leslie Edward Lee AWM H05990

Cooper 21 November 1894 at Parkside, South Australia, mother Isabella Turner Barnes and his father was Edward Cooper.[20] Isabella and Edward were never married and when Edward deserted Isabella and young Edward in 1897 Isabella sent Edward to live with her sister, Eliza and George Lee. Edward stayed with the Lee family for four years, the whole time Isabella financially supported Edward, she even allowed her son to use the name Leslie Edward Lee.

Isabella married in 1910 to Arthur James Roberts[21] which enabled her to have Edward with her, he apparently did not get along with his step father and decided he would live with another aunt, Mrs Annie Simcock. Isabella continued supporting her son until he could fend for himself, he was still with his aunt, Mrs Simcock, when he enlisted. Major Lean, from Base Records required Isabella to sign a Statutory Declaration which she did, Isabella was able to receive all of her son's medals. There is no grave for Isabella's son, he is remembered on the Ypres (Menin Gate) Memorial in Belgium, she also received a pension for Leslie.

The 43rd Battalion, formed from South Australian recruits, attached to the 11th Brigade, of the 3rd Division arrived in France 25 November 1916. A member of the 43rd was **John Edward Harold Norman St Claire [2261]** who was killed in action 12 June 1917. John's battalion was in the process of being relieved by the 16th Battalion under shell fire when he was killed.[22] John enlisted at Adelaide 15 May 1916 aged 38 years and 5 months claiming he was born in Skibbereen Ireland, he stood 5 feet 6 ¼ tall, complexion was fresh, with blue eyes and dark brown hair.[23] Two months later John married Jean Young 11 July 1916, the index shows John's father as Michael St Claire and Jean's father as George Young.[24]

John's previous military experience revealed he spent 3 years with the USA Cavalry, 2 years Light Artillery and 1 year Infantry, he also served in the China Boxer Rebellion then was discharged. None of this can be proven, there was a Gunner C St Clair from the Royal Garrison Artillery that served in the Boxer Rebellion however, this person was later located in England in 1917.[25] There is no birth record for John anywhere in the County of Cork or in Ireland, he does not appear to exist until he enlisted and then married. John was initially allocated to 4th reinforcement of the 50th Battalion before transferring to the 43rd embarking 12 August 1916 from Adelaide onboard the troopship *Ballarat* arriving at Devonport 30 September. He was taken on strength to the 43rd in England 25 October leaving for France 25 November 1916.

John's wife, Jean placed a notice in the local paper advising of his death stating his name as Private J E H N (Pat) St Claire and that he was well known on the west coast of Australia.[26] The body of Private St Claire was never located, he is remembered on the Ypres (Menin Gate) Memorial, West-Vlaanderen, Belgium. Jean was awarded a pension of £2 fortnightly from 28 August 1917, she received his effects which consisted of Letters, Comb, Purse, Rosary Beads, Badge, Padlock, Razor Blades, 4 Booklets, Knife and Photo. His medals were sent to her along with other paperwork, however in May 1922 the King's Message and the Memorial Scroll were returned. Jean had changed addresses many times after her husband enlisted and letters from Base Records sent in June and September 1922 were returned.

Jean St Claire left South Australia and moved to Queensland where she was located in 1925 living at the Club Hotel, Nambour.[27] Also, at the same address was a John Edward St Claire who apparently took over Private St Claire's identity, during that year the couple had moved to Galah Street, Longreach. Jean, as she was a widow, married James William Williams in Longreach 16 January 1926.[28] John Edward St Claire continued living in Longreach until his death 31 March 1959, the index does not contain any names of his parents.[29]

Even though the Battle of Messines was over, troops were still being killed while manning the front-line trenches, one such soldier was **Ralph Oswald Kirby [29321]**. Ralph was born 29 November 1891 in Rockhampton, Queensland,[30] his parents were Henry and Mary May Kirby. By the time he had enlisted the Kirby family were living in Sydney, New South Wales where he attended the enlistment venue at Queen's Park, Waverley. Ralph enlisted 25 May 1915, he stood 5 feet 9 inches tall, his complexion was dark, with hazel eyes and dark hair. His occupation was Clerk and named his father, Henry as his next of kin. Ralph immediately embarked onboard the troopship *Ajana* on 31 May 1915 along with the 5th Field Ambulance, he joined the MEF at Gallipoli 16 August 1915.

Ralph had one sister Geraldine, born 31 December 1889 and three brothers, Walter Humphrey born 8 March 1894, Owen Bruce born 13 May 1897 and Lawrence Charles born 29 July 1899.[31] Owen also enlisted 27 March 1916 with the Service Number 2093, initially he was attached to A Company of the 3rd Battalion before he was transferred to the 36th Battalion 11 November 1916, the same battalion as his older brother Ralph. Owen was only 19 when he enlisted, both parents gave their consent.

After Gallipoli, Ralph transferred to the 15th Field Ambulance 21 March 1916 while at Tel-El-Kebir, leaving for France 26 June 1916. He was able to take leave while in France from 8 October to 24 October 1916. Ralph found the winter of 1916/17 difficult as it was one of the toughest winters the troops had to endure. He became very ill and required hospitalisation from 21 December 1916 until 8 January 1917. On his release Ralph was transferred to his brother's unit the 36th Battalion 27 January 1917. The 36th Battalion spent the next few months in and out of the front lines until the night of 6/7 June when the Battalion commenced their approach march for the battle of Messines.

During the battle Ralph was awarded the Military Medal, within his Service Record it states: *The Bde Commander has much pleasure in placing on record the name of this soldier who was conspicuous for his bravery and gallantry in the recent offensive.* He was awarded the medal 23 June1917. Just days later Ralph was killed 3 July 1917, he is buried at Messines Ridge British Cemetery in Belgium. His brother **Lieutenant Owen Bruce Kirby [2093]** was killed in action 17 April 1918, he is remembered at the Villers-Bretonneux Memorial. The sister and two brothers never married.

Ralph and Owen Kirby AWM 2017.6.245

CHAPTER 7
THIRD BATTLE OF YPRES 1917

After the battle of Messines, the Australians then fought in one of the most costly and horrific campaigns of World War 1, the Third Battle of Ypres. The Australian Artillery had been brought in to support the British attacks which began 31 July 1917. On 20 September 1917 the 1st and 2nd Australian Divisions were to take part in the battle of Menin Road. During the night of 19 September steady rain started to fall, turning the area from dust to mud. The battle was to start at 5.40am the next morning.

Even though the battle was a complete success, the Australian casualties were high. One who was killed on 20 September was **Leslie Charles Edwin Beard [1717]** from the 8th Battalion. Leslie was born about 1896, St Kilda, Victoria, his unmarried mother Elizabeth Lillian Beard did not register his birth. He enlisted 31 December 1914 at Melbourne, aged 18 years and 3 months. His mother Elizabeth Sincock now married, gave her consent for Leslie to join. Leslie stood 5 feet 8 ¾ inches tall, his complexion was fresh with blue eyes and fair hair. Leslie's occupation was Fruiter and he resided with his mother and step father at 15 Rowan Street Elsternwick, Victoria.[1]

Leslie was allocated to 4th reinforcements of the 8th Battalion leaving Australia 14 April 1915 onboard the troopship *Wiltshire*, eventually joining his unit on Gallipoli 26 May 1915. While Leslie's battalion was at Lone Pine, he was wounded in action 10 August but rejoined his battalion four days later. One week later Leslie refused to obey an order by a NCO, he was awarded 28 days Field Punishment No.2. Leslie, along with many on Gallipoli suffered from Diarrhoea, he was transferred to Base at Imbros 8 September then onto Alexandria 11 September to recover. Leslie rejoined his unit 19 December 1915 in Egypt before becoming an Orderly at Cario 26 June 1916. He transferred back to 8th Battalion 10 September 1916 in Belgium.

Throughout late 1916 and early 1917 Leslie found himself in trouble time and time again by going AWL which finally earnt him 44 days Field Punishment No. 2. He survived the harsh winter of 1916/17 and was in and out of the front line over the next few months. By 20 September the 8th Battalion found the move to the Assembly Point greatly hampered by the slushy state of the ground.[2] During the afternoon of 20 September Leslie and eight others, while taking cover in a shell hole from their own artillery, took a direct hit killing all. Sgt. T P Masters buried all but while still under shell fire there was no ceremony and no crosses put up. Later a cross was erected for Leslie.[3] Leslie's burial location is now Tyne Cot Cemetery in Belgium, His mother received his personal effects which consisted of 1 Identity Disc, 1 Diary, 2 Note Books, Rosary, Cards, Photo and Letters.

With the success of the first stage, plans were under way to capture Polygon Wood, the second stage was to take place 26 September using four AIF brigades. One was the 15th Brigade commanded by Brigadier-General 'Pompey' Elliott which contained the 58th Battalion, the advance began at 5.50am. One young soldier from the 58th Battalion who lost his life that day, **Arthur Noel Russell Blayney [2745]** at the age of 19 years old.[4]

Arthur was 18 years and 1 month old when he enlisted 22 June 1916 at Brunswick, Victoria, with the consent of his parents. His occupation, Bank Clerk, next of kin was his father Oliver Blayney. Arthur was a lofty lad for his age, standing 6 feet 4 inches tall, complexion florid, eyes blue with fair hair. Allocated to the 6th reinforcements of the 58th Battalion, Arthur left Melbourne onboard *Nestor* 2 October 1916 with the rank of Lance Sergeant; he reverted back to private on arrival at Plymouth 16 November

1916. After further training in England, Arthur sailed to France and was taken on strength to his unit 28 May 1917 at Havre. Over the next few months while in France, Arthur and the 58th Battalion carried out more training in preparation for the second phase of the Third Battle of Ypres.

The 58th Battalion moved into their position at Polygon Wood by 10pm on the night of the 23 September ready for the attack the next day.[5] At 12 noon on the 26 September 1917 Arthur Noel Russell Blayney was mortally wounded. Initially Arthur's father Oliver Blayney was notified that his son was missing in action, nothing more was forwarded to Arthur's family.

On 30 January 1918, Mr H W Osborne, Manager, Western District Factories Co-op, 4957 King Street, Melbourne wrote to Base Records stating that his son, Private J B Osborne [2755] 58th Battalion had written to him 19 November 1917 stating that Arthur Blayney had been killed. Base Records asked for a copy of Private Osborne's letter. As a result, a Court of Enquiry was held in the Field 17 February 1918 by order of the CO of the 58th Battalion to determine Arthur's fate. A statement by Private Cockroft [3093] 58th Battalion stated: *I was in a shell hole at Polygon Wood about 12 o'clock (noon) on that date, when a shell killed Private Blayney and Private Saunders and wounding myself*[6] The family was then officially notified of the death of their only child. Their other child, Nancy Mary Blayney born 1903 had died aged 8 in 1911.[7] Arthur has no grave, he is remembered on the Ypres (Menin Gate) Memorial in Belgium.

A soldier from the 29th Battalion also lost his life during the battle of Polygon Wood, **Thomas Carlin [4013]** died between 26 and 27 September. Thomas was aged 28 years and 8 months when he enlisted 14 August 1916 at Melbourne, he lived at 308 Spencer Street, Melbourne. Thomas claimed he was born in Montreal, Canada, he stood 5 feet 9 ½ inches tall, complexion fresh, brown eyes and hair, he did not name any next of kin.[8] Thomas was allocated to the 10th reinforcements of the 29th Battalion leaving Melbourne 21 October 1916 onboard *Port*

THIRD BATTLE OF YPRES 1917

Arthur Noel Russell Blayney AWM P05413.010

Melbourne for England where he was assigned to the 8th Training Battalion at Hurdcott. Thomas found the Army life not to his liking, going AWL many times resulting in various awards such as Field Punishment No. 2 and forfeiting many days' pay. Thomas arrived in France 19 June 1917, joining the 29th Battalion 13 July 1917, where he undertook more training before finally moving to Belgium in September.

There is no defined date for the death for Thomas, his file states that he died between 26 and 27 September. As the 29th Battalion was waiting to advance it was heavily shelled by gas, the next day the Germans counter-attacked.[9] By the end of the month the 29th had lost 40 killed in action with 19 missing. Thomas Carlin was declared killed in action by a Court of Enquiry 3 October 1917, his body was never found. Thomas is remembered on the Ypres (Menin Gate) Memorial.

A Miss B Spriggins wrote to Base Records 10 November 1919 asking for all records on Thomas as she had some urgent matters to attend to regarding his estate. Base Records replied asking if she knew of any blood relation for Thomas. Miss Spriggins responded stating that Thomas was an American and his parents and one sister had died. There was one married sister, she believed, still living in America however Thomas had lost touch with her many years before. Miss Spriggins also made application for his medals, this was refused and Thomas' file was marked Untraceable.

Another soldier that died on 26 September 1917 was **Marten Peater Hansen [2917]**. Marten enlisted at Emerald 29 September 1916 stating that he had been born at Ipswich, Queensland. Aged 38 years and 5 months old he was a tall man standing at 6 feet 3 inches. His complexion was fresh with blue eyes and brown hair, his next of kin was a brother, Peater, who lived at Little Ipswich.[10] It is thought that Marten enlisted under an assumed name as there are no official records that relate at all to him or his brother.

Marten left Brisbane onboard *Marathon* 27 October 1916 arriving Plymouth 2 January 1917 where he proceeded to the 13th Training Battalion at Codford. He arrived in France 5 July 1917 and was taken on strength to the 49th Battalion where he was allotted the letter 'A' to his service number. Also, on that day he was admitted to hospital with Scabies, rejoining his unit 10 September 1917, while in hospital Marten made out a will leaving his entire estate to Ipswich Hospital.

Marten moved with his battalion to the Ypres area 21 September, the next few days were spent resting before the planned attack. The 49th moved from their billets in Ypres on the 25th September at 5.30pm, the next day the battalion captured and held the German Line. The War Diary for the 49th records 25 ordinary ranks killed, one of those was Marten.[11]

When the Army tried to notify Peater Hansen of Marten's death all mail was returned unclaimed, as a result Marten's file was marked Untraceable. His effects were sent to Ipswich Hospital which consisted of one Notebook only. Marten has no grave; he is remembered on the Ypres (Menin Gate) Memorial in Belgium.

The 46th Battalion was moved into the front-line 27 September 1917 to relieve the other battalions that had fought at Polygon Wood. One member of the 46th was **Albert James Handley [2215],** the only surviving child of Thomas and Mary Ann Handley who died from wounds 1 October 1917. Albert enlisted at Sale Victoria 18 March 1916 stating his age as 20 years and 7 months. Both his parents gave their consent for Albert to enlist.[12]

Albert stood 5 feet 3 ¼ inches tall, complexion was medium with grey eyes and brown hair, next of kin was his father, Thomas Handley, Albert's occupation, Plumber. After some initial training Albert left Melbourne 16 August 1916 with the 4th reinforcements of the 46th Battalion onboard the troopship *Oronts* arriving Plymouth 2 October 1916. Spending the next couple of months at

Albert James Handley AWM H05966

the 12th Training Battalion at Codford, Albert arrived in France 6 December 1916 joining his battalion 29 December 1916.

Days later Albert was in hospital 6 January 1917 suffering from a sore heel, he was sent back to England 24 January 1917 with Influenza and did not return to France and the 46th until 10 July 1917. Albert received a shell wound to his left arm and abdomen 1 October; his condition was described as critical, he died of his wounds at the No. 17 Casualty Clearing Station at 5.50pm the same day.[13] Albert is buried at the Lijssenthoek Military Cemetery in Belgium. Thomas Handley wrote many letters to Base Records in regard to Albert's personal effects, especially a wristlet watch that his parents have given him when he left. Thomas and Mary Ann, even after many requests, never received anything that belonged to their only child.

The battle of Broodseinde Ridge was the third part of the Ypres offensive, taking place before dawn 4 October, 1917 involving the 1st, 2nd and 3rd Divisions of the AIF. It would become one of the deadliest days for the Australians with 1,279 killed and 5,153 wounded.[14] The infantry followed a creeping barrage however the Germans had the same idea killing many even before the attack began. **John Bradshaw [3025]** died that day.

John enlisted at Holsworthy, New South Wales 24 August 1915 stating he was aged 18 years and 6 months. There are no birth records for John in 1897 however there is a birth registration for a John Bradshaw son of John and Ellen Bradshaw born in 1899.[15] John stated on enlisting at Holsworthy, New South Wales that he believed he was born at Millers Point, Sydney and did not know of any next of kin, giving the name of his best friend Mrs Martha Surman of 32 Botany Street, Waterloo as next of kin. John stood 5 feet 6 inches tall, complexion fair with grey eyes and fair hair, occupation Wool Washer.[16] John left Sydney 20 December 1915 onboard the troopship *Suevic* with the 7th reinforcements of the 19th Battalion. While at Tel-El-Kebir he was transferred 14 February 1916 to the 4th Battalion arriving in France 30 March 1916.

After arriving in France, John and his battalion spent their time training with John seeing action in May. While at Mouquet Farm 19 August 1916, he received a gunshot wound to the head and face which resulted in a short stay in hospital rejoining his battalion 29 September 1916. Early in December 1916 John was back in hospital, this time he was sent back to England suffering from a bad case of Trench Feet. Discharged from hospital John joined the Command Depot at Perham Downs 7 April 1917, before being transferred to the newly created 62nd Battalion.

After the 62nd Battalion was disbanded John went back to the 4th Battalion arriving in France 21 September 1917. John Bradshaw was killed 4 October 1917 while at Broodseinde Ridge, Mrs Martha Surman was advised of her friend's death, his effects consisted of 2 Wallets, Photographs, Cards and a Bible. Initially it appears that John did have a grave as Mrs Surman received photos of his cross marking his burial. Today there does not appear to be any grave instead John is remembered on the Ypres (Menin Gate) Memorial in Belgium.

When Base Records wrote to Mrs Surman asking for any next of kin, she stated that he had no relatives at all. This does not appear to be the truth as when she filled out Where the Australians Rest it was stated that he was the son of John and Ellen Bradshaw. There is no marriage record for John and Ellen and it is thought that Ellen is Ellen Surman, the daughter of Martha Surman. Martha, in 1902 and again in 1904 charged John Bradshaw Snr with child desertion, he was never found.[17]

John's Service Record, at times, show Martha Surman as his grandmother however, this is crossed out and Foster Mother was noted in place of grandmother. John Bradshaw would have been 16 years of age when he enlisted, his mother Ellen Surman was still living with her mother when John left to become a soldier. Just days after her mother's death Ellen Surman at the age of 54 years married Walter Windle 12 January 1929, he was 66 years old.[18] John Bradshaw has clearly been forgotten.

The 37th Battalion also suffered many losses on the 4 October, one soldier by the name of **William Love [1868]** died that day. William enlisted 29 June 1916 at Yarrawonga, Victoria stating that he had been born in Melbourne about 1892 although there are no records to support his birth. William stood 6 feet and ½ inch tall, had a ruddy complexion, blue eyes and light brown hair, he named a friend Thomas Jones as next of kin.[19]

William left Melbourne onboard the troopship *Orontes* 16 August 1916 along with the rest of the 2nd reinforcements of the 37th Battalion. After arriving in England, he joined the 8th Training Battalion. He then spent some time in hospital with VD from 20 October to 27 November 1916. Once back at his training battalion William decided to break out of camp which earnt him 14 days detention. The beginning of February he left for France and was taken on strength to his battalion 7 February 1917. Back in hospital 11 April 1917 with a sore left foot he then contracted Bronchial Pneumonia resulting in a lengthy stay. Discharged to Base Depot 3 June 1917 rejoining his unit 10 days later only to go back to hospital with Influenza 23 July 1917.

William rejoined the 37th Battalion 8 August 1917 for more training in preparation for the Third Battle of Ypres. William was acting as a stretcher bearer 4 October 1917 when he took a direct hit from a shell killing him instantly.[20] Base Records wrote to Thomas Jones in 1921 requesting information on any blood relations of William. Thomas Jones replied stating William was deserted as an infant by both parents, he did not know who his father or mother was, as a result his file was marked Untraceable. William had written a will naming as a beneficiary Mrs Alice Fallen who received his effects which were a Souvenir Epaulette and Letters. Mrs Fallen also filled out the Circular for William stating that she was his foster mother and forwarded a personal inscription for his tombstone, *A Thoughtful Boy Loving & A Kind Beautiful Memory Left Behind*. William Love is buried in the Tyne Cot Cemetery in Belgium.

John Robert Davidson AWM H05712

A veteran from Gallipoli was killed 4 October, he was **John Robert Davidson [389]** from the 8th Battalion. John had enlisted shortly after war was declared 19 August 1914 at Warrnambool, Victoria aged 19 years and 9 months. He had been born at Creswick, Victoria naming an aunt Mrs Reg Selby as his next of kin. John stood 5 feet 11 ¾ inches tall, with fair complexion, grey eyes and fair hair, occupation Carpenter.[21] His parents were John and Elizabeth Davidson, there are no records for his parents' marriage or for his birth. His mother Elizabeth (Bessie) died 6 December 1906,[22] his father had previously died so his mother's sister, Sarah Selby adopted him.

John was allocated to the 8th Battalion leaving Melbourne 19 October 1914 onboard the troopship *Benella*. As he had previous military experience with the 71st Infantry before he enlisted John was promoted to Sergeant before leaving. The 8th Battalion took part in the landing on 25 April as part of the second wave. The 8th as part of the 2nd Brigade was transferred to Cape Helles in May to help in the attack on the village of Krithia. This attack was very costly for the Brigade losing almost a third of its strength. John suffered a gunshot wound to his shoulder 14 May and did not rejoin his unit until 24 August 1915, sickness saw him back on Lemnos 17 October then back to his unit 26 November 1915.

After the withdrawal from Gallipoli and the return to Egypt John was again promoted, this time to 2nd Lieutenant 20 February 1916 staying with his 8th Battalion. Moving to Marseille on 31 March 1916 with his battalion John took leave from 26 May to 4 June 1916. Shortly after his return he was promoted to Lieutenant 27 July 1916. John showed great promise as a soldier when he was sent to the 2nd Army School of Instruction 15 October 1916 rejoining the battalion 16 November 1916.

The winter of 1916/1917 in France was harsh, especially for the troops manning the trenches who suffered severely. John found himself back in hospital 16 April 1917 but rejoined his unit 29 April 1917. More training for the 8th Battalion took place over the next couple of months in readiness for the Battle of Menin Road which took place 20 September. During this battle John was again promoted, this time to Captain. Shortly after the start of the battle at Broodseinde Ridge, Captain John Robert Davidson was killed by a shell at the assembly point. He was buried approximately 800 yards south of Zonnebeke, Belgium, sadly after the war his grave could not be located. Captain John Robert Davidson is remembered on the Menin Gate Memorial in Ypres.

A capable young soldier also died 4 October, his name **Walter Liscombe Rowling [981],** a Sergeant from the 38th Battalion who in a short time proved his value in the AIF. Born in 1896 at Balranald, New South Wales, Walter was the only child born to Walter Elder and Rosaline Rowling. In 1902 Rosaline divorced her husband for desertion raising her son by herself.[23] Water enlisted at Melbourne 13 March 1916, he stood 5 feet 8 ¼ inches tall with dark complexion, brown eyes and dark brown hair. He was still serving with the 29th Australian Light Horse when he enlisted, as a result he was promoted to Corporal, allocated to 'C' Company of the newly created 38th Battalion.[24] Walter left Melbourne on board the troopship *Runic* 20 June 1916 arriving at Plymouth, England 10 August 1916.

Walter was only in England for six days when he came down with a bout of Measles resulting in a stay in the Fulham Military Hospital, Hammersmith until 1 September 1916 rejoining the 38th at Larkhill the next day. After more training in England, Walter's battalion arrived in France November 1916. Late in February 1917, 400 men from the 38th along with the same number from the 37th Battalion carried out a raiding party. It is believed that Walter took part in the exercise as a note on his Service Record states that on 4 June 1917, he was mentioned in dispatches for gallant conduct during a raiding party. Walter received another promotion after the raiding party, this time to Sergeant 3 March 1917.

The 38th Battalion fought its first major battle at Messines, Belgium 7 to 9 June 1917, Walter survived until 4 October 1917 when he was shot in the head and killed instantly. He was buried and the location duly marked however after the war the place of his burial was lost. Rosaline wrote many times to Base Records but she had to accept that her son had no grave. There were also no personal effects that could be returned to Rosaline, as Walter was her only support, she was granted a pension. Walter Liscombe Rowling is remembered on the Ypres (Menin Gate) Memorial.

As the Third Battle of Ypres continued so did the rain which turned the battlefield into a muddy mess. The Australian Field Artillery Brigades at times were unable to move their guns, ammunition had to be cleaned from mud before the guns could be used. A driver from the 11th Field Artillery Brigade was killed 11 October 1917, he was **William Isles [741].** William enlisted 9 November 1914 at Melbourne, Victoria stating that he was 23 and 6 months old, his birth place given as Warracknabeal, Victoria. When he signed the Attestation paper, he clearly signed his name as Islis, a note, placed on file, states that his correct name was Isles even though he kept signing his name as Islis.

There is no record of his birth and it is believed he enlisted under an assumed name, the next of kin was his father, Henry Islis, 165 Clarendon Street, South Melbourne, again there is no record of Henry Islis or Isles. William was allocated to the 3rd reinforcements of the 8th Light Horse Regiment with the Service Number of 691. He stood 5 feet 6 ½ inches tall with medium complexion, dark grey eyes and brown hair, occupation, Labourer.[25] William left Melbourne on the troopship *Pera* 8 February 1915 bound for Egypt. In May 1915 the 8th Light Horse Regiment was sent to Gallipoli leaving their horses behind. One Lieutenant and 30 other ranks were left behind to care for the horses. It is believed that William stayed in Egypt as he did not join his unit on Gallipoli until 25 October 1915.

At the end of December after the withdrawal from Gallipoli William, suffering from Jaundice, was admitted to hospital returning to duty 25 January 1916. William returned to Hospital 9 March 1916, after his discharge he was transferred to the 4th Division Artillery 1 April. The next day he was allocated to the

12th Field Artillery Brigade as a gunner with the 45th Field Artillery Battery and given the Service Number 741. William travelled to Marseilles with the 4th Division 7 June 1916 spending time in the nursery section near Armentieres. In August 1916 the 4th Division repulsed a major German counter-attack on the Pozieres Heights. During the rest of 1916 the 4th Division fought at Mouquet Farm, and Flers in October, then endured the dreadful winter of 1916/17.

William transferred to the 11th Field Artillery Brigade 5 January 1917 this time as a driver, all Field Artillery Brigades had 16 x 18 pounders. The gun and its 2-wheeled ammunition limber were towed by a team of six horses in pairs – lead pair, centre pair and limber pair, a driver rode the left horse of each pair.[26] The beginning of 1917 William saw action at Bullecourt then Messines and the battle of Polygon Wood. The War Diary for 11 October records the 11th Field Artillery Brigade firing from Broodesinde toward Passchendaele Ridge had 19 guns blown out with one ordinary rank was killed.[27] This was William Isles.

Base Records sent the usual notification to William's father Henry Isles however the mail was returned as he was unknown at that address. The usual steps were taken to locate any relation of William by advertising in all newspapers. There was never any reply and as a result William's file was marked Untraceable. There is no grave for William Isles, he is remembered on the Ypres (Menin Gate) Memorial, Belgium.

The next phase of the Third Battle of Ypres would be Passchendaele, at this point the battle had been in effect for two and half months. The 45th Battalion, part of the 12th Brigade of the 4th Division, was holding the front-line 20 October 1917 when **John Burnes [3116]** was wounded. Receiving a shrapnel wound to his back which penetrated into his chest, John died the next day (21 October) from his wound.

John Burnes enlisted at Cootamundra, New South Wales 8 November 1916 naming a friend, Mr William Holland, Post Office, Mangoplah, via Wagga Wagga as his next of kin. John had been born in 1883 at Woodend, Victoria, occupation Labourer, he stood 5 feet 4 inches tall with fair complexion, blue eyes and brown hair.[28] John was allocated to the 8th reinforcements 45th Battalion leaving Sydney onboard the troopship *Boltana* 25 November 1916 arriving in Devonport 29 January 1917. He attended the 12th Training Battalion before leaving for France 28 March 1917 where he was taken on strength to the 45th Battalion 1 April 1917.

John and his battalion were heavily engaged during the battle of Messines in June 1917 before moving into the Westhoekridge region at the beginning October where he received his fatal wound.[29] Base Records contacted his friend Mr William Holland to enquire if he had any blood relations. Mr Holland replied that both John's parents were dead and that he did not have anyone else, he had known John for many years. His file was marked Untraceable. John Burnes is buried at Lyssenthock Military Cemetery, Belgium.

A young soldier, a veteran of Gallipoli, died of wounds 31 October as the battle of Passchendaele was drawing to a close. **John Raymond Beckett [773],** the only surviving child of Cecilia Beckett was born in Sydney 1893.[30] John enlisted at Brisbane, Queensland 14 September 1914 naming his mother Mrs J Kelly Pambula, South Coast, New South Wales as next of kin. John stood 5 feet 9 inches, with fair complexion, brown eyes and light brown hair, occupation miner and his address at time of enlistment was St Elmo, Mount Morgan, Queensland.[31]

John was the eldest of two sons born to John and Cecilia Beckett at Redfern, his younger brother, Thomas Edward was born 1895, the family lived at 114 Eveleigh Street Redfern. Tragedy was to take place in the Beckett family when young Thomas, aged about four years on 30 September 1899 decided to climb onto the wheel of a timber cart near his home in Caroline Lane. The driver of the timber cart was unaware of Thomas standing on the wheel and when the horse moved Thomas was thrown under the wheel of the cart crushing his head. He was immediately taken to hospital but was dead on arrival.[32] Just one year later, in August 1900 John Beckett Snr died leaving only Cecilia and her seven-year-old son.[33]

When war was declared John was living and working at the Mt Morgan Mine as a Miner, his mother had remarried to John Kelly in 1904 in Bega New South Wales.[34] John, allocated to the 9th Battalion, left Brisbane 24 September 1914 onboard the troopship *Omrah*. The 9th Battalion was one of the first ashore at 4.30am on 25 April 1915. John stayed with his battalion until 21 October 1915 when he was admitted to hospital suffering from Dyspepsia, most likely from the extreme conditions that the Australian troops had to endure. He rejoined his unit at Tel-El-Kebir 13 January 1916. John and the 9th travelled to France 3 April 1916 where the battalion was deployed to the nursery sector around Armentieres but John was back in hospital 15 May 1916 suffering from Mumps.

The first major attack for the 9th Battalion was at Pozieres when John received a gunshot wound to his left hip which required him to return to England 28 July 1916. John rejoined his battalion 20 November 1916 where he endured one of the worst winters in France. John had another visit to hospital 16 June 1917 with a case of VD, rejoining his unit 19 August 1917. John must have displayed promise as a soldier as he attended Brigade School from 13 September to 15 October 1917, five days later he was promoted to Lance Corporal. John Raymond Becket died 31 October 1917, he is buried at Butts New British Cemetery, Polygon Wood.

The Service Record for John Raymond Beckett is only partly available as many pages from his file are missing. His mother, Cecilia, wrote an epitaph for his tombstone, *Oh for the touch of a vanished hand*, by then she had returned to Sydney. Cecilia had lost her whole family but tragedy was not finished with the Beckett family. On 17 March 1922 Cecilia attempted to board a tram in Oxford Street near Dowling Street from the opposite set of rails, she seemed to hesitate and as the tram started caught hold of one of the stanchions and was dragged along. A passenger in the tram tried to pull her into the car but she slipped from his grasp, and fell underneath the tram. The wheels passed over her feet, severing the right foot and crushing the left. A private car conveyed her to St Vincent's Hospital, where she died from shock.[35]

The Canadians were brought in 18 October to relieve the weary Australians, they eventually took the village of Passchendaele. The fighting in the wet conditions cost the Australian about 38,000 casualties. The last of the Australians had moved by 15 November 1917 to the comparative quiet area of the Messines front.

CHAPTER 8
VILLERS – BRETONNEUX 1918

From October 1917 until March 1918 was the longest period of rest for the Australian troops, which enabled the men to recuperate and bring the battalions up to fighting strength. During this period Russia had sued for peace following the October 1917 Revolution which meant the German Army could transfer about 30 divisions from the Eastern Front to the West. By early 1918 the German Army had 196 Divisions on the Western Front, which meant that the German Forces would greatly outnumber the entire Allied army, the German planned attack would be mid-March.

The German attack on the British front lines started 21 March, the sheer numbers of the Germans managed to surge through the British lines. The resistance of the British at times appeared strong however the Germans outflanked the British and decimated a large portion of the Allied front line. Meanwhile back at the Australian Corps Headquarters the news of the German advance had been received. The Commanding Officers of all five Australian Divisions have been told that they may well soon be called on to fight. General John Monash was on leave and could not be contacted although the message was sent to the Headquarters of the 3rd Division.

The German attack had been fierce, compelling the withdrawal of the British forces and now two Australian Divisions are called upon to help stem the advance of the Germans. The 3rd and 4th Divisions were ordered to defend the line from the Ancre River to south of the Somme. The battlegrounds that killed so many young men in 1916 and 1917 was falling back into enemy's hands as the German offensive outflanked and outfought the British.

The 10th Machine Gun Company from the 3rd Division established Headquarters at Heilly 27 March and immediately went into the line. Whilst moving into position the company had five casualties, two killed and three wounded.[1] **Sergeant Leslie Davis Cairns [1176]** was named in the War Diary as one of the killed in action. Leslie enlisted 21 January 1916 at Melbourne, Victoria stating he was 18 years old, naming his grandfather, the Rev John Thomas Kearns as next of kin as both parents were deceased. He stood 5 feet 10 inches tall with dark complexion, brown eyes and black hair, occupation clerk.[2] Leslie's parents were Frederick Cliff and Sarah Jane Kearns, for reasons unknown he changed his surname to Cairns when he enlisted. Leslie was born in 1898 at Midland Junction, Perth, Western Australia, he was the only surviving child to Frederick and Sarah.[3] There was another child, Edith May Kearns, born to Frederick and Sarah in 1892, sadly she died at the age of 6 months in1893.[4] Leslie's mother died in 1900, his father in 1908, after his mother's death Leslie was taken to Victoria at the age of 16 months to live with his grandparents.

Leslie was allocated to the 39th Battalion, 10th Brigade of the 3rd Division. A short time after enlisting Leslie was promoted to Corporal 6 March 1916. Two months later he was promoted again, this time to Sergeant, most likely because he had spent four years in the Senior Cadets. He left Melbourne onboard the troopship *Ascanius* 27 May 1916. After training in England Leslie sailed for France 23 November 1916, in time to spend a very cold winter in the trenches. He went back to England 17 May 1917 to the 10th Training Battalion then returned to France 5 December 1917 transferring to the 10th Machine Gun Company 9 December 1917. He further trained at the Division Bombing School rejoining his unit 24 February 1918, it was obvious that Leslie was an outstanding soldier.

During the move into his position Leslie was killed outright at 4.00pm 27 March 1918 by a shell which also killed another and wounded three others.⁵ Leslie Davis Cairns is buried in the Villers–Bretonneux Military Cemetery, the inscription on his tombstone reads *Loving Loyal and God-fearing*. His grandparents never received his personal effects as they were on the *SS Barunga* that was hit by a torpedo from a German submarine and sank 15 July 1918. Leslie's grandparents had already lost two sons killed in South Africa during the Boer War and one daughter to the Influenza Epidemic in 1919.⁶ When the Rev John Thomas Kearns filled out the Circular for the Roll of Honour, he stated that Leslie was studying to be an Accountant, he also said that Leslie was extremely intelligent and an above average student.

By early April 1918 things were getting desperate for the Allies, the Germans were still advancing in large numbers while the British were retreating. The 47th Battalion from the Australian 4th Division received orders 2 April to relieve the 45th Battalion in the Dernancourt region. On 4 April advice was received from 12th Brigade of an impending attack on the battalion's sector, which was at an important railway viaduct with heavy casualties that were inflicted upon the men by Machine Gun fire.⁷ A casualty from the 45th Battalion was **Charles Archer [1669]** killed in action 5 April 1918. Charles enlisted at Newcastle, New South Wales 11 August 1915, stating he was aged 23 years and 11 months old, birthplace was Liverpool, England occupation, Night Porter. Charles stood 5 feet 2 ¼ inches tall, with fair complexion, grey eyes and brown hair, next of kin was given as father, Charles Archer, Geraldton, Western Australia.⁸ There are no records in England that can confirm the birth of Charles also there are no records of him or his father coming to Australia.

Charles was initially assigned to the 30th Battalion leaving Australia onboard the troopship *Berrima* 17 December 1915 arriving Suez 23 January 1916. He was not long in Egypt before he fractured his Fibula 18 February requiring a hospital stay at Heliopolis, he was transferred to a convalescent hospital until 29 May 1916. Charles left Alexander 6 June 1916 for England having more training with the 8th Training Battalion. Shortly after it was determined that he was unfit for service and was posted to the No. 2 Command Depot at Weymouth. This depot was for men unfit for return to service within 6 months and therefore to be returned to Australia. He was reclassified 21 November 1916 as temporary unfit and re-examined 24 April 1917, then declared fit 24 May 1917. Charles left England for France arriving 19 June 1917 and was taken on strength to the 45th Battalion 9 July 1917. He was given leave back to England 27 February 1918 rejoining his unit 15 March 1918 dying three weeks later. Any correspondence sent to Charles Archer, Geraldton, Western Australia was returned with the stamp Not Known. After many unsuccessful attempts by Base Records to locate anyone who may have known Private Charles Archer his file was marked Untraceable. Charles does not have a grave however his name is listed on the Villers-Bretonneux Memorial.

One battalion from the 12th Brigade, the 47th was to face the strongest attack by any Australian battalion on 5 April, 1918. The 47th was hopelessly outnumbered by the Germans when they attacked the line of the Australians at Dernancourt. The War Diary for the 47th stated: *A day of heroic endeavour on the part of all ranks showed losses to be heavy. After spending four days in the line, they withstood the attack of over 2 enemy divisions and took part in a counter-attack.*[9] The losses for the 47th Battalion proved to be fatal for the survival of the battalion, what was left of the battalion was disbanded on 31 May 1918 and absorbed into other battalions.

An Irishman by the name of **Michael Joseph Delaney [3728]** was one that died that day, born at Roscrea, Kings County, Ireland. He enlisted 21 August 1915 at Brisbane, Queensland. Michael initially named his mother Mrs Delaney, c/- Miss J O'Mara, Ballingrawn, Kings County, Ireland as his next of kin however a note on his Service Records state that the whereabouts of his mother were unknown. Next of kin was changed to Miss J Clark, Geebeegimba, West Burleigh S C Line, Queensland. Michael stood 5 feet 3 ½ inches tall with fair complexion, blue eyes and brown hair, his occupation, Labourer, his age was given as 21 years and 2 months old.[10] There are no birth records for Michael due to the common nature of his name in Ireland, however it is believed that he left England 2 October 1914 onboard the ship *Rimutaka,* leaving the ship at Brisbane.[11]

Initially allocated to the 15th Battalion, he left Sydney onboard the troopship *Suffolk* 20 November 1915. After his arrival Michael was transferred to the 47th Battalion 7 March 1916 arriving in Marseilles 9 June 1916. Michael spent a great deal of time in and out of Hospital suffering from various illnesses throughout 1917, finally rejoining his unit 9 February 1918. Michael Joseph Delaney is buried in the Dernancourt Communal Cemetery, there is no epitaph on his tombstone. His next of kin was contacted in the hope some blood relation may be found for Michael. Miss Clark replied stating that she did not know of any although she did have the address of Miss G O'Mara in Ireland. There is no indication on Michael's file that Base Records was successful, no one filled out the Roll of Honour for him.

Another Irishman from the 47th Battalion also lost his life the same day as Michael Delaney, he was **James Fitzpatrick [2424]** born 1882 at Stradone, Ireland, Stradone is a small village located in County Cavan, Ireland. There are many Fitzpatrick's in and around the area and as a result it is very difficult to find the correct birth for James. James enlisted in Mackay, Queensland 15 April 1916 stating his was 34 years and 3 months old, he stood 5 feet 3 ¼ inches tall with medium complexion blue eyes and dark brown hair, occupation, Labourer. He named a brother Joseph Fitzpatrick as next of kin Joseph's address was Balough, Cavan County, Ireland.[12]

James was allocated to the 5th reinforcement of the 47th Battalion leaving Brisbane on the troopship *Seang Choon* 19 September 1916 arriving at Plymouth 9 December 1916, he was immediately sent to the 12th Training Battalion before being taken on strength at Etaples 6 February, 1917 to the 47th Battalion. James along with his battalion, during 1917, took part in the attack of Bullecourt, Messines and Passchendaele. His Service

Record stated that he was detached for duty to the 4th Canadian Tunnelling Company as a miner 11 January 1918. He rejoined his battalion 4 February 1918 and two days later was granted leave to England until 23 February 1918.

James Fitzpatrick disappeared 5 April 1918 and it was not until 27 June 1918 there was a query regarding his whereabouts. James was last paid in the field 13 March 1918, and a report from the 12th Brigade stated that he was not at present doing duty in the brigade and there was no trace of him in Germany as a prisoner of war.[13] A statement made 16 December 1918 by Private Sutchkoff 7339 stated; *I was captured by the Germans on 5 April 1918. I came across Private Fitzpatrick who was wounded in the legs arm and back, by shrapnel. I carried him to a German Clearing Station and here some other men assisted me to carry him to a hospital about 7 kms behind Albert.... I am certain of his name as he wrote his name and address and gave it to me. The Germans however took this from* me. A Court of Enquiry held 7 April 1919 found that James Fitzpatrick was taken prisoner by the enemy on or about 5 April 1918 and declared he was killed in action.

No one made any enquiries regarding the disappearance of James Fitzpatrick, no family or friend, it was only after the 47th Battalion was disbanded that the Authorities found he was missing. The medals etc were sent to London so that they could be forwarded to his brother, sadly his brother could not be traced, his medals were returned from London 6 August 1925. There is no grave for James, he is remembered on the Villers-Bretonneux Memorial.

The 49th Battalion from the 13th Brigade, 4th Division was held in reserve but was warned that their position would be shortly under attack on 5th April.[14] **Francis Jay Heathcote [4262]** a member of the 49th Battalion died on that day. Francis enlisted 19 August 1915 at Charleville, Queensland stating that he was 27 years and 7 months old giving his birth place as New York, America and that he had no next of kin. He stood 5 feet 7 inches tall with dark complexion, brown eyes and brown hair, his occupation was Labourer.[15]

Initially assigned to the 10th reinforcements 26th Battalion Francis left Brisbane 28 March 1916 onboard the troopship *Commonwealth* for England. Francis seemed to have some problems taking to a soldier's life as he was constantly committing various offences including AWL while at the 7th Training Battalion at Rollestone. Francis eventually sailed overseas to France 2 October 1916 and was taken on strength to the 49th Battalion where he appears to have settled down and kept out of trouble. Francis with the 49th Battalion took part in the battle at Messines 9 June1917, but was on leave in England when the battalion was involved in the taking of Polygon Wood, arriving back to his unit 28 September.

Base Records in Melbourne initially marked his Service Record as Untraceable, however a Mrs Lilian Maud Allison of 171 Gladstone Road, South Brisbane claimed that Francis was her adopted son. Base Records wrote back asking for more information, Mrs Allison replied providing a Statutory Declaration, dated 1 November 1923 stating that Francis Jay Heathcote was adopted by her when he was eleven years of age. An elderly gentleman, Mr James Hunter, who died at the Diamantina Hospital Brisbane about 1906 adopted Francis from unknown parents at sea and at his request before he died, she adopted the deceased soldier who always regard her as his mother. She did not know his parents and have never heard him mention anybody's name as relations in fact she did not think he had any. He lived with her from 1906 as her own boy.

Searches have failed to locate a James Hunter who died in Queensland about 1906, there is no record of Francis arriving into Australia by sea and attempts to find his birth in American records have failed. Mrs Allison did receive Francis' medals and filled out the Circular for the Roll of Honour. Francis has no grave; his name is on the Villers-Bretonneux Memorial.

The German Spring Offensive and the battle for Villers-Bretonneux killed many brave Australian soldiers, some were Gallipoli veterans that not only survived the Gallipoli campaign but also the bitter battles of 1916 and 1917. One such soldier was **Captain Frank Herbert Hancock** who was killed in action 24 April 1918. Frank enlisted 15 March 1915 at the 4th Military District of South Australia which included Broken Hill. Within 10 days Frank received his appointment as 2nd Lieutenant and was allocated to the 5th reinforcements of the 10th Battalion leaving Adelaide 20 April 1915 onboard the troopship *Hororata*.[16] Frank named his mother Emma as next of kin, he was aged 33 years at enlistment.

Frank joined the 10th Battalion at Gallipoli June 1915, sadly there are no war diaries available for the battalion from August 1915 to March 1916, his Service Record shows he was

Frank Herbert Hancock. AWM P091.072

promoted to Lieutenant 4 August 1915. While Frank was on Gallipoli, he was Mentioned in Despatches, this appeared in the Commonwealth Gazette No.44 6th April 1916. After the withdrawal from Gallipoli Frank was transferred to the 50th Battalion 27 February 1916 and was again promoted, this time to Captain 1 April 1916.

Frank with his battalion, moved to France June 1916, the battalion's first major battle was at Mouquet Farm. The battalion was to attack at 10.30pm 12 August 1916, during the attack Frank received a gunshot wound to his upper thigh, he had the wound dressed then returned to his Company.[17] Frank's wound was bad enough for him to return to England 13 August 1916 where he was admitted to the 1st London General Hospital, he was discharged 15 October rejoining his unit 29 October 1916. Frank's time back with his battalion was again cut short when he was posted for duty 25 January 1917 with the 13th Infantry Training Battalion at Rollestone, England.

Frank left England 10 August, returning to the 50th Battalion 20 August 1917 and into the front line at Ploegsteert Wood. Frank took part in the battle of Polygon Wood in September 1917 with a winter of trench routine following. Captain Frank Herbert Hancock was killed in action by machine gun fire the night of 24 April 1918 during an attack at Villers-Bretonneux. His devastated mother Emma Hancock was notified of his death, she wrote many letters to Base Records expressing her heartache at losing her only son and how proud she was that he had served.

Frank's father Robert, had died when Frank was only young leaving Emma to raise Frank and her daughter Laura who was five years older than Frank. Laura was a nurse working at the Broken Hill and District Hospital when she decided to also join, enlisting 9 June 1917. Laura served her time at an Army hospital near Salenika, in the northern Greek region of Macedonia. Laura returned to Australia 27 August 1918 after her brother was killed, then volunteered to nurse Influenza patients in Western Australia. She was finally demobilized 28 June 1919.

Frank's mother Emma waited for all of her son's personal effects to return to her, sadly they were all onboard *Barunga* which was torpedoed by a German submarine. Frank is buried at the Adelaide Cemetery, Villers-Bretonneux, his epitaph: *All The Waves And Storms Have Gone Over Me.* Laura Hancock never married dying in Victoria 22 January 1965.

A young man from the 51st Battalion was killed in action during the night of 24 April 1918, he was **John Michael Quinn [4578]**. John was born 20 November 1897 in Coolgardie, Western Australia, the name of his parents are not known. John, aged 13 years, entered the Roman Catholic Boys Orphanage at Subiaco on 8 April 1910. The decision to send John to the orphanage was on direction of the Special Magistrate of the Childrens Court at Coolgardie as his family conditions were described as neglected. The term of the Special Magistrate's Order was until John reached the age of 18 years. John left the orphanage 20 November 1911 aged 14 to work on a farm.[18]

As soon as John reached the age of 18, he enlisted into the AIF at Perth, Western Australia 7 December 1915 stating that both parents were deceased. John was 5 feet 4 inches tall with fresh complexion, blue eyes and brown hair, religion, Roman Catholic, occupation Farm Hand. He gave his address as C/- General Post Office, Perth, naming a cousin, Robert George Gray, Cue, Western Australia as next of kin.[19] He was initially allocated to the 14th reinforcements of 11th Battalion leaving Fremantle onboard the troopship *Miltiades* 12 February 1916.

After spending time with the 3rd Training Battalion, John was taken on strength to the 51st Battalion 19 April 1916 before travelling with his battalion to France 12 June 1916. John's battalion moved into the trenches of the Western Front within a fortnight of arriving in France. The battalion fought its first major battle at Mouquet Farm during August and September 1916 then spent the bleak and terrible winter of 1916/17 in the trenches.

Early in 1917 the battalion took part in the advance that followed the German retreat to the Hindenburg Line. The beginning of April the battalion attacked at Noreuil, then later the 51st Battalion moved to Belgium where it fought in the battle of Messines in June 1917. The next month the 51st Battalion was in the front-line when on 19 July, John Michael Quinn received a wound.

At about 3.30am John with five others were manning No 3 Post with 2 Lewis guns, the remainder of the garrison had about 15 minutes previously, withdrawn to the day position about 150 yards in rear of the post. One man on each gun was observing towards the front when they were attacked from the rear. The enemy must have seen the rest of the garrison withdrawing and attacked. The six men realized they were outnumbered and withdrew via their trench system; they were able to tell the garrison what had happened. A party was immediately sent out and re-gained the post, the Germans retreated taking the Lewis guns with them.[20]

John suffered a gun-shot wound to his arm, leg and foot which required a stay in hospital back in England. He was transferred to a Training Battalion at Perham Downs before returning to his unit 3 December 1917. The 51st Battalion in late March moved to defend positions around Dernancourt on the River Ancre. The battalion assisted in the repulse of a large German attack on 5 April 1918, launching a critical counter-attack late in the day.

Orders from the 13th Brigade for a counter attack on enemy positions near Villers-Bretonneux was received by the 51st. The attack was to start at 10.00pm on the 24 April 1918 in order to dislodge the enemy from Villers-Bretonneux which cost John Michael Quinn his life.[21] John was killed in action during the night of 24/25 April 1918, however his next of kin could not be located. All mail to Robert George Gray was returned, Base Records then placed many advertisements in all Australian newspapers asking for any relation to come forward.

The Rev. Brother Bodkin wrote to Base Records asking for the date of John's death as he wanted to place his name on the Orphanage Honour Roll. Later, in more correspondence Rev.

Bodkin stated that the only person he knew of was a Mr Gray who would often write to John when he was in the Orphanage. John had written a will leaving his entire estate to the Orphanage, however a Mrs M.M. Quinn from 31 Coogee Street, Randwick, Sydney wrote to Base Records. She stated that John had written to her in December 1917 leaving everything he owned to her and that he made an allotment for some of his pay to go to her. She claimed she could not produce any letters as they had been thrown away in the belief he would return.

Base Records replied asking what relation she was to John and even though she did not specify the relationship, Mrs Quinn stated that when they resided in Coolgardie, she wanted to adopt John, however his mother would not allow this. Mr Henry Martin Quinn and his wife Maud Margaret Quinn did live in Coolgardie for a while. Mr Quinn was a baker, they lived in Jenkin Street, Coolgardie 1906 to 1917 before moving to Sydney, there was also a Kate Quinn who lived in Ellis Street, Coolgardie.[22] This Kate Quinn may have been the mother of John, this cannot be proven. Mr and Mrs Quinn were living in Coolgardie when John was sent to the Orphanage however Rev. Bodkin did not know of them and after much research there is no family link between Kate Quinn, John Quinn and the Quinn family from Randwick. Henry Martin and Maud Margaret Quinn were originally residents of Young, New South Wales before moving to Western Australia.

John's medals were sent to Mrs Quinn, the rest of his estate was sent to Rev. Bodkin. Mrs Quinn never filled out the Circular for the Roll of Honour and nothing was sent to the Imperial War Grave for John. John Michael Quinn has no grave, he is remembered on the Villers-Bretonneux Memorial.

The 54th Battalion of the 14th Brigade had been in the trenches during the winter when they received notice to stand fast and wait for movement orders. The battalion arrived in Acheux late March then moved 5 April 1918 to Aubigny. At 3.45am 24 April, 1918 the 54th Battalion was subjected to a German bombardment which included high explosives and gas shells which ended the life of **Charles James Dillon [2642],** a 31-year-old Labourer from Portland, New South Wales. In the 1913 Electoral Roll, Charles was living in Portland with his brother, Francis William Dillon.

Charles was born 1887 in Oberon, New South Wales, his mother was Bridget Dillon, there is no mention of a father.[23] His brother Francis was born 1889, Bathurst New South Wales, again his mother was stated as Bridget Dillon with no name for a father.[24] The birth index states his name as Frank although he always went by the name of Francis. There is no birth record for Bridget however, it is thought that Bridget married a George Montgomery in Bathurst, 1890.[25] Bridget Montgomery died at Temora, New South Wales, 1906.[26] **Francis Dillon [195]** was the first to enlist at Liverpool, New South Wales 13 February 1915, naming his brother Charles as next of kin, Francis saw action at Gallipoli and was killed 28 August 1915.[27] After the death of Francis, Charles then enlisted 27 June 1916 at Bathurst, first he named Henry Cooper from Kelso as next of kin, this was then changed to Mrs McMenamin, Kelso, a step sister. Eliza Jane McMenamin was the daughter of George Montgomery and his first wife, Ellen.

Charles was a tall lad standing 6 feet high, his complexion was medium with grey eyes and dark hair. He left Sydney onboard the troopship *Ceramic* 7 October 1916. After arriving in England Charles attended the 14th Training Battalion at Folkestone before leaving for France. Arriving at Etaples Charles was taken on strength to the 54th Battalion 8 February 1917. Just a month later he attended the 14th Field Ambulance for eye treatment 2 March 1917 rejoining his unit 11 March. Charles received a gun-shot wound to his scalp 16 March 1917 which required his return to England and a stay at the Holborn Military Hospital until 24 March 1917. After a 2-week furlough Charles was posted to No.1 Command Depot at Perham Downs 28 April then transferred to the newly created 63rd Battalion at Windmill Hill 1 May 1917.

Charles travelled back to France 12 September but as the 63rd was disbanded Charles went back to the 54th Battalion 2 October

1917. After his death 24 April 1918 Base Records contacted his step sister, Eliza Jane who claimed the medals of Charles and his brother Francis. Sadly, Eliza Jane never filled out the Circular for the Roll of Honour for either brother and ignored the Imperial War Graves Commission. Francis is buried at the Embarkation Pier Cemetery Gallipoli, Charles is buried at the Aubigny British Cemetery, France.

The 52nd Battalion also took part in the battle for Villers-Bretonneux, at 10.00pm on 24 April, 1918 the 52nd made the advance from the south west of Villers-Bretonneux when one of its members **Henry Norman Taylor [1955]** was killed. Henry was born about 1895 at Surry Hills, New South Wales, his birth was never registered and as a result the name of his parents are unknown. Henry enlisted at Frasers Hill, Brisbane 9 August 1915 naming as his next of kin Mrs Beatrice Marcentelli, 3 Bennett Place, Surry Hills. Within his Service Record Henry named a brother, J Thomas, 8 Hutchinson Street, Surry Hills as next of kin, this was later changed back to Beatrice Marcentelli. Henry stood 5 feet 8 inches tall with fair complexion, blue eyes and fair hair, occupation, Horse Trainer.[28]

Henry was allocated to the 3rd reinforcements of the 26th Battalion arriving on Gallipoli 12 October 1915 while the battalion was at Russell's Top. He came down with Dysentery 4 November resulting in a short stay in hospital, rejoining his unit 12 November. Not long after he was back in hospital suffering from Rheumatism, after recovering Henry was transferred to Base Depot 17 December at Giza. While at Giza Henry found himself on the wrong side of Army regulations (the first of many) when 5 March 1916 Henry was acting as a lookout for some gamblers. For this indiscretion he was awarded 14 days Field Punishment No.2. Finally, Henry was taken on strength to the 52nd Battalion 2 April 1916.

The 52nd Battalion arrived in Marseilles 12 June1916 and did not take part in any major battle until early September when the battalion attacked Mouquet Farm. During the attack Henry suffered a gun-shot wound to his right thigh which required him to return to England to recover at 4th General Hospital. After recovering at Dartford Henry went AWL 11 November, 1916, he received 14 days confined to barracks. Henry just could not stay out of trouble, while stationed at Wareham he faced a Court Martial 14 March 1917 on two charges. The first; Conduct to the prejudice of good order and Military Discipline, in that he, at Wareham on 23 February 1917, was improperly in the Canteen at No. 4 Command Depot at 2.15pm or thereabouts, during prohibited hours. The second; Improperly took off Major Reilly's cap and put it on his own head. Pleaded not guilty to both, the finding of the Court was guilty, sentenced to undergo detention for nine months. In custody awaiting trial 21 days, total forfeiture 290 days and fined £74.

With numbers down on reinforcements Henry's remaining 175 days were remitted and he left for France 25 August 1917. While at Havre he went AWL again 9 September 1917 losing 2 days' pay. During the Third Battle of Ypres the 52nd Battalion at Westhoek Ridge was the target of enemy shelling. At 10.00pm 23 September 1917 Henry was with 6 companions next to the Lewis Gun Section when a shell landed, killing 5, wounding one and burying Henry. Luckly Henry was dug out but the experience left him suffering from Shell-Shock which required a return to Hospital, rejoining the battalion 9 December 1917. Henry just kept going AWL, this time it was 17 January 1918, his fine, 10 days' pay.

Henry was with his battalion at Villers-Bretonneux when he was killed 24 April 1918. When Base Records enquired the whereabouts of his blood relations Mrs Marcantelli replied stating that he was an ex-nuptial child to her sister. Henry's aunt informed Base Records that she raised Henry from 12 months and the whereabouts of his mother was unknown. Mrs Marcantelli received Henry's medals although she did not fill out the Circular for the Roll of Honour or for the Imperial War Graves Commission. Henry has no grave; he is remembered on the Villers-Bretonneux Memorial.

Many soldiers who enlisted into the AIF did so using assumed names, their next of kin contacts were also unknown, these soldiers died and today have been forgotten. One was **William John Hales [2628],** enlisting at Broadmeadow, Victoria 12 August 1915, William claimed he had been born 1889 at Hobart naming an uncle, William John Hales, as next of kin. William stood 5 feet 7 ½ inches tall, with medium complexion, grey brown eyes and dark brown hair. He gave his address as New Norfolk, Tasmania, the same address as his uncle.[29] Initially he was allocated to the 6th Battalion leaving Melbourne 26 August 1915 onboard *Anchises*. He joined the 6th Battalion at Lemnos 31 October 1915 then travelled with the battalion to Gallipoli arriving 16 November 1915.[30] After the withdrawal from Gallipoli William transferred to the newly created 58th Battalion 17 February 1916 at Tel-El-Keber, but one month later he was taken on strength to the 57th Battalion. William arrived at Marseilles 24 June 1916 where the 57th Battalion took a support role in the Battle of Fromelles.

William must have shown some leadership as he was appointed Lance Corporal 2 August 1916. The conditions in late 1916 were very unfavourable for the troops while manning the trenches with William taken to hospital suffering from Trench Feet 29 November 1916. After recovering he was transferred to the No. 4 Command Depot 18 January 1917 before rejoining his unit 18 February. The 57th Battalion was rotated in and out of the front line for the next few months until 6 August 1917, when William was granted furlough back to England.

William clearly did not wish to return to France as he appeared at a Court Martial held at Warwick Square, London 10 October 1917. Charge: When on Active Service absenting himself without leave, in that he in London at 6.15am 17 August 1917 failed to report to the R.T.O. at Victoria Station and remained absent until apprehended by the civil power in London 19 September 1917. He pleaded guilty and was found guilty, William was sentenced to undergo detention for 120 days and forfeiture was 174 day's pay. He was reverted back to private at the AIF Detention at Lewes.

Again, falling number of recruits for the AIF meant William's unexpired portion (41days) was remitted as from 27 December 1917. Travelling back to France he rejoined the 57th Battalion 1 January 1918. Receiving a gun-shot wound to his spine 25 April 1918 William was transferred to the 20th Casualty Clearing Station where he died the same day. After extensive advertisements in all local papers, Base Records was unable to locate William's uncle or anyone who knew him. William's file was marked Untraceable, he is buried at Vignacourt British Cemetery. The photo of William's grave is still within his Service Record.

The only surviving child of William George and Isabella Hughes was **George Albert Curnick Hughes [448]**, a member of the 59th Battalion who lost his life on the third anniversary of Anzac Day. George, the third son of Willian and Isabella was born 1891 in Kerang, Victoria, an older brother, **Arthur Wesley Hughes [936]** was born 1888 and the eldest son, George William Hughes, was born 1879, he died aged 4 months in 1880.[31] Arthur enlisted first 18 August 1914, allocated to the 5th Battalion, he was killed in action at Cape Helles sometime between 8 and 12 May 1915.

George soon followed his brother, enlisting 24 August 1914 at Ballarat, Victoria he was allocated to the 8th Battalion. George was 5 feet 5 ½ inches tall with dark complexion, brown eyes and dark hair, occupation Labourer, he named his father, William George Hughes as next of kin.[32] George left Melbourne 19 October 1914 onboard the troopship *Benalla,* arriving at Alexandria 8 December 1914 before moving to Ismailia where the battalion would train and camp in readiness for the landing at Anzac Cove.

George's 8th Battalion and Arthur's 5th Battalion were part of the second wave on 25 April 1915 with both battalions moving to Cape Helles 6 May for an attack on Krithia. George received a gun-shot wound to his left thigh 15 May 1915 and was transferred to St George Hospital on Malta 28 July 1915 to recover from his wound. Discharged from hospital 12 October 1915 rejoining his battalion at Gallipoli. By now he would have known of his brother's death.

Grave of William John Hales, National Archives of Australia

After the withdrawal from the Gallipoli Peninsula George was back in hospital at Alexandria 31 January 1916 suffering from an Enteric disease. George, with the 8th Battalion moved to France during March where for the next few months the battalion manned trenches in the nursery section. George transferred to the 59th Battalion 21 July 1916, the following September he attended the Grenade School of Instruction. He was granted leave in France from 7 to 24 December 1916 and was back with his battalion in time to spend a very cold and bitter winter rotating in and out of the front-line trenches. The 59th Battalion's first major battle was the second attack at Bullecourt May 1917, George survived but was sent to the 5th Army Rest Camp 24 June 1917 rejoining the battalion 9 July 1917. George's battalion also took part in the Third Battle of Ypres at Polygon Wood during September.

As George had been a member of the AIF since 1914, he was granted leave in England from 17 January to 3 February 1918. In early April 1918 George's battalion moved into the Villers-Bretonneux region in readiness to retake the village. 25 April 1918 William and Isabella Hughes lost their remaining son. George is buried at the Villers-Bretonneux Military Cemetery, his parents did not place an epitaph on his grave. Arthur has no grave, he is remembered at the Helles Memorial, Cape Helles, Gallipoli Peninsula. The Circulars for both sons were never filled out. George's effects which consisted of a Testament, Cigarette Case, Photos, Cards and Letters never reached the parents as the ship they were on was the SS *Barunga* which was sank by a German submarine 15 July 1918 on its way to Australia.

On 25 April 1918 the Australians re-captured the village of Villers-Bretonneux from the Germans who had taken the village only days before. Brigadier-General George Grogan of the 23rd British Brigade was to state: *Perhaps the greatest individual feat of the war – the successful counter-attack by night across unknown and difficult ground, at a few hours' notice, the Australian soldier.*[33]

CHAPTER 9
AMIENS TO MONT ST QUENTIN 1918

In the early morning hours of the 8 August 1918 a huge battle began in France, taking part with the Allies was the entire Australian Corps under the command of Lieutenant General John Monash. All five divisions were under strength with some brigades having only three battalions. Enlistments back in Australia had fallen to a trickle but the Australian troops were mainly battle hardened and eager to finish this war.

The day before the battle John Monash sent a message to all of his troops, in part he stated....... *For the first time in the history of this Corps, all five Australian Divisions will tomorrow engage in the largest and most important battle operation ever undertaken by the Corps.*

They will be supported by an exceptionally powerful Artillery, and by Tanks and Aeroplanes on a scale never previously attempted......I earnestly wish every soldier of the Corps the best of good fortune, and glorious and decisive victory, the story of which will echo throughout the world, and will live forever in the history of our homeland.[1]

The battle for Amiens began at 4.20am in thick fog and by morning it was clear that the Australian Corps were heading for a victory. The battle became the start of the Hundred Days' War which included the Hindenburg Line. The Australians, in company with the Canadians, spearhead the assault taking all of their objectives, the German front line had been overrun by morning. The total Allied casualties, including the British and French, amounted to 21,243 with one-quarter killed. German moral was already low which brought the German Commander Erick Ludendorff to famously describe the first day of the battle as *the black day of the German Army.*

One Australian soldier who died 8 August 1918 was an Irishman by the name of **William Butler [283]**, William was one of three children born to James and Marianne Butler in Waterford, Ireland. William's birth was about 1892, an older sister Bridget was born 1889 and a younger brother Patrick born 1896.[2] William enlisted at Nanango, Queensland 16 April 1915 naming his father James as his next of kin. His father at the time lived at Beau Street, Waterford, Ireland. William stood 5 feet 10 ½ inches tall with fair complexion brown eyes and red hair, occupation, Cordial Maker.[3]

From the records in Ireland, it has been difficult to locate when William arrived in Australia, and the Embarkment Roll does not state any address other than his father's. On 6 December 1916 William changed his next of kin to a wife, Mrs A Butler, her address 39 North Quay Sydney. William left Brisbane onboard the troopship *Ascanius* allocated to the 26th Battalion. Why William enlisted we will never know, as soon as he arrived in Egypt William was constantly AWL. He eventually arrived at Gallipoli 13 September 1915 then went AWL from Parade almost immediately.

Sickness became another problem for William when 12 October 1915 he was admitted to the hospital ship *Valvdivia* suffering from Epididymitis. Before he could rejoin his unit, William was sent back to England, this time suffering Tuberculosis 4 November 1915. He was AWL again from 30 to 31 December 1915, this was repeated again and again for the next six months. On 9 June 1916 William was back in hospital with VD and after recovering was sent to Perham Downs, as soon as he arrived AWL again. William eventually was sent to France 16 November 1916 to the 2nd Division Base at Etaples but 23 December 1916 faced a charge for out of bounds. By now William had forfeited most of his pay. William proceeded to his unit under escort 6 January 1917. He was back in hospital 2 March 1917 with Trench Feet and after his discharge went AWL repeatedly, finally rejoining his unit 24 April 1918.

On the day William rejoined the 26th Battalion he found himself in the front-line area, this must have worried him as throughout May and June he was charged with drunkenness and AWL, resulting in forfeiting more pay. On 14th July the 26th Battalion attacked the enemy which resulted in 8 killed and 52 wounded.[4] William for the first time saw action on the Western Front, deciding to make out his will 21 July 1918 naming his father James as beneficiary, not his wife. During the advance 8 August 1918 the 26th had 25 killed, William was one of them.[5]

When it came time to contact William's wife it was revealed that his wife's address did not exist, there was a Mrs Butler living at a similar address in Manly however in a letter to Base Records she did not know William Butler. Attempts were made to locate William's parents; it was believed that they were deceased. William's brother Patrick received his medals, sadly he did not fill out any paperwork for William. William Butler is buried in the Adelaide Cemetery, Villers-Bretonneux, there is no epitaph on his tombstone, his Roll of Honour Circular was filled out by Australian War Memorial Staff. It is believed that both Patrick and Bridget may have died unmarried.

Before the attack on 8 August the 4th Machine Gun Battalion moved to the Boves Wood area from 1 to 5 August in preparation for the operation. A member of the battalion **George Harris [634A]** was killed 8 August while manning his machine gun. George claimed he was born 1882 in Dubbo, New South Wales, there is no registration for his birth. George's height was 5 feet 6 inches, he had medium complexion, blue eyes and fair hair, occupation Gardener. George named a friend Miss Esther Bennett as his next of kin, Esther's address was 11 Pelican Street, Sydney. George enlisted 18 November 1916 at Brisbane, Queensland giving his address at time of enlisting as Peoples Place, Brisbane.[6]

George applied for home leave 1 December 1916 giving his home address 11 Pelican Street, Sydney to visit friends before he was sent overseas, this was granted. Initially George was allocated to the 13th Machine Gun Company leaving Melbourne onboard the troopship *Ascanius* 11 May 1917. After his arrival in England more training was undertaken at the 13th Training Battalion, Codford, Wiltshire. He spent time in hospital when he suffered a sprained ankle 25 September 1917, finally heading overseas to France 2 January 1918. After arriving in France George was allocated to the 24th Machine Gun Company 29 January 1918, this was when he had the letter A added to his number.

George was back in hospital 25 February 1918, this time suffering from Scabies, after he was discharged, he had more training before rejoining his unit 4 March 1918. George's unit took part in the Villers-Bretonneux attack, then 17 July 1918 he spent 9 days at the 4th Army Rest Camp rejoining his unit 26 July 1918. George was killed in action 8 August 1918; he is buried in the Cerisy-Gailly Military Cemetery.

George had written out a will before he left for overseas naming his friend Miss Esther Bennett as sole beneficiary. When it came time to dispose of his medals Base Records contacted Miss Bennett for information on any relation. Miss Bennett replied that he did not have any at all, Base Records marked his medals as Untraceable. Shortly after a Mrs Dinah Solomon contacted Base Records stating that George was her adopted son and nephew. To prove her claim she sent letters and cards that she had received from George during his time in the Army. These were returned to Mrs Solomon; Base Records then sent his medals etc. to her. The epitaph on his tombstone are the letters *R.I.P.* On the Roll of Honour circular Mrs Solomon claimed she did not know the place of his birth.

A member of the 48th Battalion also died 8 August 1918, his name was **Reginald Stow Kentish [2189],** a young man from the Laura district of South Australia. Reginald was one of two children born to Albert Stow and Edith Octavia Kentish. Reginald's birth was 27 February 1891, his sister Edith Idonia was born 6 September 1892.[7] Reginald enlisted 21 August 1915 at Adelaide naming his mother Edith Octavia Kentish as next of kin, he stood 5 feet 5 ¾ inches tall with fair complexion, blue eyes and fair hair, occupation Bank Clerk.[8]

Reginald spent time at the Depot Battalion before leaving Adelaide onboard the troopship *Ballarat* 12 August 1916 as 4th reinforcement to 48th Battalion. Prior to leaving his parents held a farewell for their only son which was reported in the paper. *Mr & Mrs A S Kentish, of Austral Terrace, Malvern, entertained their immediate relatives on Friday evening last at a farewell gathering to their only son, Pte. Reginald Stow Kentish, who will leave shortly for the front. A pleasant evening was spent in listening to musical items, recitations etc, by different members of the company and various games were indulged in. Pte Kentish was the recipient of various useful gifts from the guests, including a handsome wristlet watch from the whole of the company. The singing of the National Anthem concluded the proceedings.*[9]

On arrival to England Reginald was allocated to the 12th Training Battalion at Folkstone, arriving in France 29 December 1916, he was taken on strength to his unit 6 February 1917. The 48th Battalion took part in the battle of Bullecourt in April and then in October the capture of Passchendaele. Private Reginal Stow Kentish was killed in action 8 August 1918, originally he was buried in the Heath Military Cemetery however the actual position of his grave was lost.

Reginald's effects were sent back to his parents 14 May 1919, they consisted of 2 Discs, 1 Wallet, 1 YMCA Wallet, Letters, Photos and Cards. After receiving his son's belongings father Albert Stow Kentish wrote a letter dated 19 May 1919 back to Base Records stating: *The package came to hand intact to day. Thank you very much for all your kindest in the past, that is the end and nothing more can be done. Like the King of olden times, I would cry out my son my son, would that I had died for him. He was one of the best of sons full of promise and killed in his 28th year again thanking you.*[10] Edith Idonia, Reginald's sister died 6 September 1969, she never married.[11]

Reginald Stow Kentish. South Australian State Library

Over the following days the Allies pushed on towards the disorganized German lines capturing many prisoners although the Australians were still taking casualties. **William Charles Gibbs [6128]** was killed in action 10 August 1918. William was born 2 August 1885 at Hindmarsh South Australia to William Gibbs and Julia Yon. William was the older brother to his sisters, Julia

Emmaline born 16 September 1887 and Irene Doris born 15 August 1892.[12] William married Elsie Edith Payne 8 August 1912 in South Australia, they did not have any children.[13]

William Charles Gibbs enlisted 26 February 1916 at Adelaide South Australia naming his wife as next of kin. He was 5 feet 6 inches tall with medium complexion, blue eyes and dark hair, occupation Clerk.[14] William was attached to the 2nd Battalion Depot 13 March 1916 for approximately two months before attending Musketry School from 16 May 1916. William left Adelaide onboard the troopship *Ballart* 12 August 1916 attached to the 9th reinforcements of the 10th Battalion. On arrival in England, he spent time at the 3rd Training Battalion before heading overseas to France 23 October 1916 where he was allocated to 1st Anzac Headquarters. William found himself in hospital 12 April 1917 with a case of VD returning to Headquarters 15 June 1917 then finally joined the 10th Battalion 18 August 1917.

William obtained leave to England 28 November 1917 where he suffered an injury to his ankle. After his discharge from hospital, he left Southampton for France rejoining his unit 26 February 1918. William then received his first taste of war and the exhausting conditions of trench warfare. He came down with Influenza 19 June 1918 that required a stay in hospital, rejoining the battalion 7 July 1918 only to suffer another attack 25 July 1918. William rejoined his unit 2 August 1918 from hospital in time for the push onto the German lines where he was killed.

William's wife received her husband effects; Disc, Spectacles in Case, Pipe, Match Box Cover, Belt with Badges attached, Wallet, Religious Medallion, Photos, Letter and 2 Unit Colours. William is buried in Rosieres Communal Cemetery Extension, his wife Elsie filled out all of William's paperwork and received all of his medals. She never applied for a pension and appears to have disappeared from all records in Australia. William's sisters, Julia and Irene never married and lived together for the rest of their lives.

A young professional cyclist received a wound to his right knee when he was hit by an Allied shell 8 August 1918. Taken to the 5th Casualty Clearing Station for treatment he stated that this would be the end of his riding career.[15] The soldier's name was **Angus Livingstone [3840],** born in 1893 at Coraki, New South Wales, Angus was the only child to Miss Nellie Frances Baillie. Angus enlisted 14 September 1915 at Lismore naming his mother Nellie as next of kin. Angus stood 5 feet 7 inches tall with dark complexion, grey eyes and black hair, occupation Farmer.[16] The birth record for Angus is recorded as Angus Baillie, mother, Nellie F Ballie, father is not listed.[17] Angus sailed from Brisbane 31 January 1916 onboard the troopship *Wandilla,* after his arrival at Alexandria Angus was allocated to 2nd Australian Division Base Depot, then to the 1st Anzac Cyclist Battalion.

When he arrived in France Angus was transferred to 26th Battalion, joining his unit 30 August 1916. Not long after joining his unit, Angus 21 November 1916, was put in hospital suffering from sore feet requiring his removal to England. After his discharge Angus was sent to Perham Downs where he was re-allocated to the newly created 69th Battalion. When that battalion was disbanded Angus then went back to the 26th Battalion 9 December 1917 which was stationed in France. Angus with his battalion took part on the attack to turn back the German offensive in April 1918.

It was during the battle for Amiens on the 8 August 1918 that Angus received his wound. It took six days for him to die from the shell wound to his right knee. Angus is buried in the Crouy British Cemetery, CrouySur-Somme, his mother placed the epitaph on his headstone, *For God, King and Country His Life He Bravely Gave By His Mother.* When it came time to dispose of Angus' medals, Base Records wrote to Nellie asking after his father. Nellie replied: *The loss of Angus is more to me than all a medal can make up.* Base Records did send everything to Nellie when they realised that Angus was an ex-nuptial child. His effects from the field were also sent to his mother, they consisted of: 2 Discs, 2 Wallets, 2 YMCA Wallets, Letters, Photos, Cards, 1 Calendar, Nail Clippers, 1 Metal Ring and 1 Badge.

Angus Livingstone. Australia's Fighting Sons of the Empire

In November 1918 Nellie place a notice in the paper: *In sad and loving memory of my dear son, Pte. Angus Livingstone, No. 3840, 26th Battalion AIF, who died of wounds in France on August 14th, 1918. Age 25 years and 1 month. His heart was good, his spirit brave. His resting place a hero's grave. To have to love and then to part, is the saddest pain to a human heart. Inserted by his sorrowing mother, N F Baillie.*[18]

A young soldier died 16 August 1918, he was **William John Robertson Ingham [6039]** the only child born to Frederick and Annie Ingham, William was aged 2 years old when his mother Annie died in 1900 aged 26 years.[19] Frederick married again in 1904 to Henrietta Baker in Kalgoorlie, Western Australia when William was 6 years of age.[20] William enlisted at Blackboy Hill,

Western Australia 11 March 1916 aged 18, naming his father Frederick as next of kin. He stood 5 feet 5 ¼ inches tall with medium complexion, grey eyes and brown hair, occupation Dairyman.[21] William was allocated to the 19th reinforcements of the 16th Battalion leaving Fremantle 9 August 1916 onboard the troopship *Miltiadis*.

After his arrival in France 29 December 1916 William was taken on strength to the 16th Battalion and into the front-line trenches at Flers. On the night of 4/5 February 1917 the 16th sent about 50 men (with an Officer) to support the 13th Battalion who were attacking on their right. Casualties among this party were heavy.[22] During this attack William received a gunshot wound to his right foot, the wound was classed as serious which required his return to England for treatment 10 February 1917. After his discharge William was sent to the No.3 Command Depot 28 July 1917 where he was classified A3 (fit for general service). After spending time at Perham Downs William returned to France 24 October rejoining his battalion 2 November 1917 in time for another cold winter in the trenches.

In 1918 the 16th helped stop the German Spring offensive, then there was the success at Hamel where William took part. On 16 August 1918 the push for the Hindenburg Line was in the Harbonnieres region where it sustained heavy shelling by the enemy killing William John Robertson Ingham. Buried at Heath Cemetery, Harbonnieres William's father and step mother wrote on his tombstone *Thy will be done*.

Five months before William's death, Frederick and Henrietta had a son Kenneth Victor Ingram born 6 March 1918, a half-brother to William. Kenneth's father Frederick may have had doubts when his only surviving son joined the Royal Australian Air Force 21 June 1940. Kenneth trained to become a pilot, eventually a Squadron Leader, taking part in many areas of World War 2. Kenneth, while on an anti-submarine patrol off the East Coast of Ceylon 28 November 1944, with 9 others onboard the Sunderland never returned to base.[23] Kenneth had received a Distinguished Flying Cross and had been Mentioned in Dispatches, his name is on the Singapore Memorial. Frederick Ingham had lost both his sons to war.

By the 31 August 1918 the Allies started pushing the Germans back towards the Hindenburg Line although the Germans resisted causing many casualties, one Australian soldier to die that day was **Norman John Warren Hoffmeyer [2339]**. Norman was one of two children born to Olaf Ferdinand and Kate Hoffmeyer, they had married in 1892 at Bendigo, Victoria.[24] Mollie Magdalene was born in 1893, Norman was born the next year in 1894.[25] Olaf applied and was granted a Naturalisation Certificate on 3 February 1893 stating he was born 1868 at Copenhagen, Denmark.[26] It appears that by 1907 Olaf had left his young family as he was wanted in New South Wales for fraud. In the New South Wales Police Gazette on 18 December 1908 a notice was issued: *A warrant was issued for Olaf Ferdinand Hoffmeyer, charged with fraudulently misappropriating the sum of £7.10s, the property of the committee of the Howell Jockey Club. Offender is about 35 years of age, 6 foot 2 inches high, slender build, long arms, dark brown hair, dark moustache only; a Dane; a photographer. Last heard of at Newcastle on the 30th ultimo. May go to Western Australia.*[27] It is believed he travelled to Queensland, first to Charleville where he is located in the 1908 Electoral Roll working as a photographer. He then moved onto Rockhampton appearing in the 1913 Electoral Roll as a painter, this time there is a Marjory Hoffmeyer living with him, there is no marriage record for this couple.[28]

When Norman enlisted at Bendigo 20 September 1916, he named his father, Olaf Ferdinand Hoffmeyer 194 Barnard Street, Bendigo, as next of kin. Norman stood 6 feet 1 ½ inches tall, complexion was dark with grey eyes and dark brown hair, occupation Farmer. In support of his application to enlist, a letter dated 20 September 1916 was sent to Captain Dale, Recruiting Depot, Bendigo from the Town Clerk, City of Bendigo: *In reference to the enlistment of Norman John Warren Hoffmeyer I have no hesitation in certifying that he is the son of the most loyal and estimable Bendigo Citizens and should he be accepted as a soldier to fight for Great Britian and the Allies I am confident that the part allotted to him in any capacity will be worthily performed.*[29]

Norman was allocated to the 4th reinforcements of the 38th Battalion leaving Melbourne 20 October 1916 onboard the troopship *Port Lincoln*, for reasons unknown he was transferred to the *Willochra* at Sierra Leone 4 December arriving at Plymouth 29 December 1916. Norman undertook more training at the 10th Training Battalion at Larkhill before travelling to France to join his unit 2 April 1917. Norman's first major battle was at Messines between 7 and 8 June 1917 where he sustained a wound to his left eye which required a stay in hospital. Norman re-joined his unit 27 June 1917 surviving the battles at Broodsiende and Passchendaele in October 1917. Norman enjoyed some leave in England from 4 to 21 March 1918 rejoining the 38th in time for the Spring Offensive. Norman's war was over 31 August 1918.

Norman is buried in the Peronne Communal Cemetery Extension, his mother Kate wrote on his headstone, *His Last Message I Died Doing My Duty*. Kate also filled out his Roll of Honour Memorial Circular and received all of his medals. Kate and her daughter Mollie continued living at 194 Barnard Street, Bendigo. Mollie never married; it is possible that Norman's father changed his surname as after the 1913 Electoral Roll he disappeared from all Australian Official Records.

A capable young soldier was lost to Australia 2 September 1918, his name was **William James Gawith [6566],** one of three children born to Joseph and Henrietta Gawith. All three children were born in the Stanthorpe area of Queensland. The eldest, John Edwin was born 14 August 1888, William 29 September 1892 and Kate 22 April 1897.[30] William enlisted at Toowoomba, Queensland 9 January 1917 naming his mother Henrietta as next of kin.[31]

William stood 5 feet 7 ¼ inches tall with medium complexion, hazel eyes and dark brown hair, occupation Farmer. Allocated to the 19th reinforcements of the 25th Battalion William left Sydney onboard the troopship *Wilshire* 8 February 1917. After training for six months at Rollestone, England William arrived in France 17 October 1917. He joined the 25th Battalion 24 October 1917 in time to experience a cold and miserable winter in the tranches.

William James Gawith AWM P10736.002

The 25th was involved in the enemy's Spring Offensive and was actively involved in the battle of Morlancourt 10 June 1918, then the battalion had success in the battle of Hanel in July 1918.

Early on the morning of 2 September 1918 the 25th Battalion moved to the Jumping off Positions ready for Zero Hour which was 5.30am. The troops followed their orders advancing towards the enemy even though the enemy's machine gun fire was extremely hot. This caused the 25th to pause then all ranks showed great dash and initiative forging ahead causing many casualties to the Germans.[32] William was wounded about 6.00am, taken to a dressing station where he died later that day.[33] He was buried in an isolated grave in a shell hole near barbed wire just east of Mont St. Quentin and 1 ¼ miles north of Peronne.

His effects were returned to his mother Henrietta which consisted of 1 Devotional Book, Cards, Photos and Leather Case. Base Records later wrote to Henrietta explaining that her son's body was exhumed from his isolated grave and re-interred in the Peronne Communal Cemetery Extension. The family never placed an epitaph on his tombstone. Neither John Edwin or Kate ever married, John died 16 September 1963, Kate died 9 July 1995 (aged 98), they are both buried with their parents.[34]

The 2 September 1918 caused many dead and wounded among the Australian troops, they were fighting under extreme conditions as the battalions were totally undermanned from the fighting strength normally required for a battalion. Fight they did charging straight into machine-gun nests, by the end of the day gains were made, losses were again heavy. A young soldier, **Bert Shumack [3721]** received a gun-shot wound to the skull. Taken to the 37th Casualty Clearing Station Bert died 9 September 1918. The report from the Casualty Clearing Station stated that when he arrived his case was recognised as hopeless from the first. He seemed to be fairly comfortable and passed away in an unconscious condition.[35]

Bert was born to Elizabeth Shumack, an unmarried woman from Sunny Corner near Bathurst, New South Wales, there is no record of a father.³⁶ He enlisted at Bathurst, New South Wales 16 July 1917 naming an uncle Mr John Shumack as next of kin, this was later changed to another uncle, Mr Richard Shumack. As Bert was underage his uncle Richard Shumack gave Bert permission to enlist stating that both Bert's parents were deceased. Bert stood 5 feet 11 inches tall with dark complexion, brown eyes and black hair, occupation was Stockman. Allocated to the 10th reinforcements of the 56th Battalion Bert left Sydney onboard the troopship *Euripides* 31 October 1917 arriving in England 26 December 1917.³⁷

Bert went straight into the 14th Training Battalion where shortly after he came down with Influenza 3 February 1918 which required a stay in hospital at Codford. He returned to the Training Battalion then travelled to France 7 April 1918 and was taken on strength to the 56th Battalion. Bert's battalion spent time in the front-line trenches and when withdrawn more training took place. Bert was in the Peronne area when his battalion attacked the enemy and where he received his wound. Both John and Richard Shumack were advised of Bert's death, his effects were returned to Richard Shumack. They consisted of: Pocket Book, Metal Cigarette Case, Knife, 2 Diaries, Match Box Cover, Belt, 1 Pipe, 1 Fountain Pen, Photos, 1 Letter and 1 Card.

Base Records received a letter from Gladys Chiplin, Public School, Heddon, Greta, Via West Maitland asking after Bert. She explained that they were fond of one another and wanted to know more information on him. Base Records replied stating that he had been killed and his burial place Daours Communal Cemetery Extension. Richard Shumack received Bert's medals, he did fill in the Circular for the Roll of Honour however, there is no epitaph on his tombstone. Bert's mother Elizabeth had married in 1901 to George McLennan in Bathurst.³⁸ Just one year later Elizabeth McLennan died in 1902, there is no record for her death however she is buried in the Dark Corner General Cemetery, Lithgow, New South Wales.³⁹

The battle 8 August 1918 by the Australians did play a large part in ending the First World War later that year. At 4.20am the 46th Battalion, part of the 12th Brigade of the 4th Division, embarked on its biggest undertaking since landing in France. On that morning every infantry member of the 46th carried a heavy load into the attack. The load, consisting of rifle, equipment, 48 hours of rations, 2 water bottles, 220 rounds S.A.A., 1 pick or shovel, 5 sandbags, 2 No.36 Grenades and waterproof sheets.[40] The casualties were heavy with many wounded or killed, one who received serious wounds 8 August 1918 was **James Buller [1839A]** an Englishman, he was shot multiple times dying over a month later 14 September 1918.

James enlisted 13 July 1915 at Brisbane, Queensland stating he was born 1878 in Halifax, England. James stood 5 feet 2 inches tall, his complexion was dark with grey eyes and brown hair, occupation was Labourer. James named his cousin Mr E Garnet, Kingsholme, New Farm, Brisbane as next of kin. Embarking 29 December 1915 on board the troopship *Demosthenes*, arriving at Suez 31 January 1916 as part of the 2nd reinforcements of the 31st Battalion. Shortly after moving into camp at Tel-El-Kebir James was transferred to the 46th Battalion 6 March 1916 where the letter 'A' was added to his Service Number.[41]

The 46th Battalion moved to France 8 June 1916 where James took part in the battle of Pozieres and later at Bullecourt where the battalion suffered many casualties. The winter of 1916/17 was difficult for the troops manning the front-line trenches, James in particular as he was admitted to hospital 8 May 1917 suffering from Rheumatism. James then suffered from Trench Fever so back to England 18 June 1917 to recuperate. While in England James was granted leave 17 July to 31 July 1917 then sent to the Depot at Codford rejoining the 46th 6 October 1917 while the battalion was in the Ypres area. James was granted leave again back to England 19 March 1918 marrying Eliza Ann Fearnley 23 March 1918, James was aged 40 and Eliza 34 years old.[42]

James Butler. The Queensland 12 November 1915 page 26

After James died from his many wounds 14 September 1918 his effects were sent to his cousin Mr Garnet however after learning of James' marriage Mr Garnet was asked to return them so they could be passed onto Eliza Ann. His effects consisted of Letters, Cards, 1 Prayer Book and 1 Disc. His wife also received his medals and the Roll of Honour Circular which was filled out by Eliza. James was the only child of Albert and Charlotte Buller; he did have 2 younger sisters however they died as infants. Both parents died when James was still a young man, they are buried along with their baby girls at St Thomas Churchyard, West Yorkshire.[43] James Buller is buried in the Terlincthun British Cemetery, Winille, sadly there is no epitaph on his tombstone.

After four years of war, back in Australia the number of families grieving for their brave sons, husbands and brothers was growing steadily, particularly the family who lost their only son or sons. The brothers, who were only children, that never returned home left behind inconsolable parents. One parent was Ernest George Watts, a widower from Brisbane who lost both sons. The two sons of Ernest enlisted together at Brisbane, Queensland, **Frederick Watts [358]** and **George Ernest Watts [359]** 20 October 1914, both naming their father Ernest as next of kin. Frederick was born 4 August 1896, George Ernest the eldest was born 23 May 1893, both at Brisbane, their mother Margaret Oliver Watts had died 10 May 1911.[44]

Frederick stood 5 feet 5 ½ inches tall with fair complexion, brown eyes and light brown hair, occupation Groom. George stood 5 feet 3 ½ inches tall, fair complexion, blue eyes and light brown hair, he was also a Groom. Both allocated to the 15th Battalion they left Melbourne onboard the troopship *Ceramic* 22 December 1914.[45] After training at Mena Camp, the 15th Battalion landed at Gallipoli in the afternoon of 25 April 1915. The brothers were involved in an attack on Turkish trenches at Quinn's Post by the 15th during the night of 9/10 May. Initially the attack was successful but owing to a portion of the trench being held by the enemy, who could not be dislodged, it was necessary to withdraw the troops to their original position.[46] George Ernest was declared missing; his brother last saw him alive during the attack then lost sight of him. 1 July Frederick was admitted to the ship's hospital with a shrapnel wound to his left shoulder and a gun-shot wound to his back. Back in Cario Frederick was transferred to a convalescent hospital where he stayed for some time.

Frederick was attached to Garrison Headquarters 13 March then later in the year transferred to Headquarters Depot in England 25 August 1916. Meanwhile back in Australia Ernest, George's father was writing his many letters to Base Records asking after his son who was still listed as missing. Ernest did not understand why the Army could not tell him what happened to

George. Even though Ernest's letters showed his frustration with the Army, Base Records were always cordial in their reply. Ernest was getting so desperate he attempted to enlist himself, the Army turned him down because of his age and height requirements. In one of his letters, he suggested that the Army should have a battalion made up of short men, short men could still fight. He was finally accepted into the Australian Army Medical Corps allocated to the 13th Clearing Hospital at Enoggera, Brisbane where he served 2 years and 68 days before his discharge.

He wrote many letters in a bid to find his eldest son, even offered to enlist again so he could be sent overseas, again he was refused. The Army, after a Court of Enquiry found 15 May 1916 that Private George Ernest Watts was killed in action 9/10 May 1915. Ernest then wrote asking for his effects to be returned to him and where his son would be buried. He also told Base Records George had died on the anniversary of his wife's death. His letters told of his heartache at losing his eldest son and as his other son Frederick was still recovering from his wounds when would he be returned back to Australia. Frederick did not return instead he travelled to France 12 January rejoining his battalion 17 January, 1917. Frederick and his battalion took part in the battle at Bullecourt in April 1917 and the gains on the Hindenburg Line. Frederick was granted leave back to England 18 October returning to his unit 13 November 1917 for another winter in front-line trenches.

The German Spring Offensive in March and April 1918 saw Frederick and his battalion back in action. The next month Frederick earned a Military Medal, the recommendation stated: *Is recommended for conspicuous gallantry while in action near Villers-Bretonneux on 5/6 May 18. This man established a listening post within 30 yards of an enemy post, enemy machine guns were particularly active in the vicinity of this spot, but he pushed out with utter disregard for personal danger, and remained out there till about an hour before daylight, having obtained some very useable information regarding the enemy posts and definitely locating two enemy machine-guns which had been troubling our post. As a result of this information both the posts and machine-guns were engaged and silenced time after time with No.36 Grenades. His cheerfulness and gallantry throughout this tour of duty in the line greatly inspired all the men around him.*

Signed E.G. Sinclair Maclagan Maj. Gen. Commdg. 4th Division.[47]

Frederick became a Lance Corporal 20 July then a full Corporal 20 August and finally a Lance Sergeant 5 September 1918. Frederick's war was to end 18 September 1918 when he was wounded during an attack, he was taken to the 4th Australian Field Ambulance where he died that day. Ernest had lost his youngest son, now he was all alone. His letters became even sadder with the loss of Frederick. As Frederick had enlisted in 1914 and landed on Gallipoli, he may have had the chance to return home for leave, he didn't. When he received news that Frederick's Military Medal was on its way to him, he asked if the Prince of Wales could present it to him. This was not possible so instead he asked if he could have it presented to him publicly on Anzac Day at Albert Square, the medal arrived too late for this to happen.

Ernest continued to write to Base Records for some years after the Armistice, still asking for George's personal effects. He did receive Frederick's, they were 2 Discs, 1 Wallet, Private Papers, 1 Metal Cigarette Case, 3 Fountain Pens, 1 Pencil Holder, 1 Knife, Metal Wrist Watch, 1 Badge, Medal Ribbon, 1 Purse and Coins. Ernest filled out the Roll of Honour Circulars for his sons, for George he wrote that George was aged 22 years 11 months and 16 days old when he was killed. For Frederick he was 22 years and 46 days old. Frederick is buried Hancourt British Cemetery, his epitaph reads: *In memory of the dearly loved son of Mr E G Watts, of Brisbane.* George has no grave and is remembered on the Lone Pine Memorial.

In one of his last letters, he asked if he could travel to France to visit Frederick's grave, he said he had no money and inquired the price to travel to France, after all he said he lost his two sons. Base Records did reply saying that they did not know the price. Ernest

FALLEN NOW FORGOTTEN

Ernest George Watts with his two sons Frederick Watts and George Ernest Watts AWM P10794.001

missed his boys; he wrote that they remained the world to him and were the best sons a father could wish for. Ernest George Watts died in Brisbane alone 23 July 1944 73 years old, he is buried in an unmarked grave alongside his wife Margaret in Toowong Cemetery Brisbane.[48]

Just one week after Frederick was killed the 15th Battalion was withdrawn from the front line to Crouy 26 September 1918. Crouy was 16 kilometres north-west of Amiens on the west side of the River Somme, on the Amiens-Abbeville main road. The whole of the AIF was gradually sent to rest areas during October and did not take any further part in the war. The Armistice was signed 11 November 1918. Ernest George Watts and all the other families that lost their loved ones were left to mourn; their war would never be over.

Acknownledgements

The research for this book would not have been possible without the Australian War Memorial's Databases. There are 61,678 names within the First World War Roll of Honour which meant researching all names was not an option. By using the Memorial's collections, I was able to narrow down my workload and locate names and service numbers of soldiers that were killed in the major battles of the war. The National Archives of Australia was then used to locate the soldier's Service Record. Australia's record keeping of this country's soldiers are second to none, in other countries there are not the capabilities that are available here. War diaries and service records are readily available on-line along with Red Cross Society Wounded and Missing Files and Honours and Awards Databases, just to name a few plus the many photos that are on-line on the Australian War Memorial's website.

I must applaud the many authors that have written books over the years on Australia's involvement in World War 1. These books have been invaluable to me along with the works of Charles Bean *Official History of Australia in the War of 1914-1918.*

The support of my family has been the driving force in getting this book finished. My eldest daughter, Terry Ewan, who read and re-read my manuscript many times advising me of my grammar errors. My husband, John, who encouraged me to continue when I was faced with so many names to research and his expertise in restoring some of the photos from old newspapers. I could not have finished without his encouragement.

Endnotes

Chapter 1 Gallipoli 1915

1. Bean, *Official History of Australia in the War of 1914-1918*, Vol. 1. p. 125.
2. Denis Winter, *25 April 1915 The Inevitable Tragedy*, p.52
3. Bean, *Official History of Australia in the War of 1914-1918*, Vol. 1. ps. 223 & 224
4. Ibid, p.243
5. Denis Winter, *25 April 1915 The Inevitable Tragedy*, p.91
6. Ibid, p.93
7. Bean, *Official History of Australia in the War of 1914-1918*, Vol. 1, ps. 253 & 254.
8. Ibid, p.256
9. Trove Newspapers, The Mercury (Hobart Tas: 1869-1954) Saturday 3 July 1915 p.5 (assessed 26 January 2020)
10. Ancestry.com, Worcestershire, England, Church of England Deaths and Burials 1813-1997 – John Henry Adcock (assessed 28 January 2020)
11. Ancestry.com. UK & Ireland, Outward Passenger Lists 1890-1960 (assessed 28 January 2020)
12. NAA, Service Records, Frank Henry Burton Adcock 394 and Frederick Brenchley Adcock 1044
13. Trove Newspapers, Sunday Times (Perth, WA: 1902-1954, Sunday 31 October 1915, page 14
14. NAA, Service Records, George Willcox 39, George Willcox 39
15. Ancestry.com.au, Southwark, London, Surry, England, Poor Law and Board of Guardian Records assessed (2 February 2020)

16 NAA, Service Record, Charles Llewellyn William 554.
17 Ancestry.com, UK Royal Navy Registers of Seaman's Service 1848-1939, assessed (5 February 2020)
18 Trove Newspapers, Weekly Times, Sat 14 April 1883, p7, (assessed 6 February 2020)
19 NAA, Service Record Boer War, Joshua David Sussex Service No. 501
20 Victoria Police Gazette, April 1902
21 New South Wales Police Gazettes July, August & December 1907.
22 NAA, Service Records, Charles Sussex 310 & Joshua Sussex 996
23 Australian Red Cross Society Wounded and Missing Enquiry Bureau files 1914-1918 War 1DRL/0428
24 Harvey Broadbent, *Defending Gallipoli, The Turkish Story*, p.121
25 Victorian BDM Indexes Birth Index Reg. No. 11010/1893
26 prov.vic.gov/au/search Ward Registers VPRS 4527/P2 item Vol.15, record page 6, Reg. No. 19019, (assessed 8 February 2020)
27 Ibid
28 NAA, Service Record, Alexander Henry Osborne 159.
29 Ibid, Service Record, Charles Percy Pennells 83
30 Ancestry.com.au, 1881 England Census (assessed 15 February 2020)
31 Ibid, 1901 England Census
32 Ibid, 1911 England Census
33 Freemantle, Western Australia, Passenger Lists, 1897-1963, Reel 034: June 1911.
34 NAA, Service Record, Charles Percy Pennells, 83
35 Harvey Broadbent, *Defending Gallipoli, The Turkish Story*, p. 121
36 New South Wales BDM Indexes, Births Reg. No. 37440/1894.
37 NAA, Service Record, Sydney Thomas Smith 786
38 Roland Perry, *Monash, The Outsider Who Won a War*, p.190

39 Ibid, ps.191-192
40 Ibid, 192
41 NAA, Service Record, Alfred Mayne 67.
42 Ibid, John George Robb 908
43 Peter Fitzsimons, *Gallipoli*, p. 360
44 Ibid, p. 372
45 Ibid, p. 373
46 NAA, Service Record, George Jones 757
47 Ancestry.com UK, Royal Navy Registers of Seamen's Services 1848-1939. (assessed 1 March 2020)
48 New South Wales Police Gazettes 19 April 1911, p. 50
49 NAA, Service Record, Arthur Frederick Kitson 116
50 AWM War Diary 1st Battalion – AWM4 Subclass 23/8 August 1914 to June 1915
51 Trove Newspapers – The Age, Melbourne, 24 November, 1915. (accessed 3 March 2020)
52 Ancestry.com.au, Victoria, Australia *Corner Inquest Deposition Files (1840-1925)*. (assessed 5 March 2020)
53 NAA, Service Record, Frederick Fergus 344.
54 Bean, *Official History of Australia in the War of 1914-1918*, Vol. II, p. 161.
55 New South Wales BDM Indexes, Births Reg. No. 19998/1895.
56 NAA, Service Record, Frederick Cecil Swain 201
57 AWM War Diary 1st Australian Light Horse Regiment War Diary, AWM410/6/1-May 1915.
58 NAA, Service Records, Alfred James Clark 638
59 Victorian BDM Indexes, John Charles Marsh, Birth Reg: 35211/1891, Death Reg: 325/1907.
60 Trove Newspapers, The Argus Tuesday 14 September 1915 p. 5 (assessed 6 March 2020)
61 NAA, Service Records, Cyril Godfrey Marsh 187.
62 Ibid, Frank Bardon 166.
63 Ibid, James Field 1752
64 Trove Newspapers, Goulburn Evening Penny Post, Thursday 3 April 1902, p. 2 (assessed 8 March 2020)

65 Ibid, Saturday 5 April 1902, p. 4
66 Ibid, Thursday 25 January 1906, p. 2
67 Ancestry.com State Archives NSW; Series: NRS 3902; Item: 8/1750; Roll: 2889 (assessed 10 March 2020)
68 Ibid
69 Trove Newspapers, Goulburn Evening Penny Post, Tuesday 26 June 1906, p. 2 (assessed 11 March 2020)
70 NAA, Service Record, 2nd/Lieutenant Cecil Claude Oliver
71 New South Wales Birth, Death & Marriage Index – Birth Reg. No. 21187/1890
72 Ibid, Marriage 2323/1888
73 Trove Newspapers, The Australian Star, Tuesday 1 September 1891, p. 5 (assessed 22 March 2020)
74 Australian War Memorial Roll of Honour Circular – Cecil Claude Oliver
75 www.westernsydney.edu.au_data>assests>pdf_file>EVERS (assessed 2 March 2020)
76 NAA, Service Records, Otto Lessing Evers 1544
77 www.awm.gov.au/articles/encyclopedia/gallipoli/periscope_rifle (assessed 2 March 2020)
78 Australian War Memorial - Roll of Honour Circular – Otto Lessing Evers 1544
79 New South Wales BDM Indexes – Death Reg. No. 8206/1952.

Chapter 2 Fromelles 1916

1 Bean, *Official History of Australian in the War 1914-1918* Vol. 111, ps. 48 & 49
2 AWM, War Diary 9th Battalion – AWM4 Subclass 23/26 April 1916
3 NAA, Service Record, William Wilson 1626
4 AWM, War Diary 11th Battalion – AWM4 Subclass 23/28 May 1916
5 Bean, *Official History of Australia in the War 1914-1918*, Vol. 111, p. 211
6 NAA, Service Record, Albert Owen Hart 440

7   Ancestry.com. *Australian Electoral Rolls, 1903-1980* (assessed 14 March 2020)
8   Les Carlyon, *The Great War*, p.29
9   Ibid, p. 51
10 NAA, Service Record, William O'Sullivan 3867
11 Ibid
12 Les Carlyon, *The Great War*, p. 62
13 Ibid p. 75
14 Ibid ps. 95 & 96
15 NAA, Service Record, Henry Wilson 421
16 Victorian BDM Indexes - Walter Arnold Smith Birth Reg. No. 22426/1888
17 Ibid Marriage Reg. No. 6283/1894
18 NAA, Service Record, Walter Smith Arnold 2329
19 Victorian BDM Indexes William Arnold Death Reg. No. 2813/1903 & William Watkin Arnold Death Reg. No. 2271/1915
20 NAA, Service Record, Walter Smith Arnold 2329, p.14
21 Ibid, Herbert Evan Jones 194
22 Victorian Birth, Death and Marriage Indexes – Death Reg. No. 10803/1896 and 8108/1898
23 AWM War Diary 6th Brigade – AWM4 Subclass 23/6/1 – August – September 1915
24 Ibid, 60th Battalion – AWM 23/77/6 – July 1916
25 NAA, Service Record, Maurice Theodore Jones 21753
26 AWM, Australia Red Cross Wounded and Missing File – Herbert Evan Jones, 194
27 Victorian BDM Indexes – Death Reg. No. 2363/1936 and 13013/1944
28 NAA, Service Record, William Barry 505
29 Queensland BDM Indexes – Marriage Reg. No. 1877/B/5639
30 Ibid – Birth Reg. No. 1879/004342
31 Ibid – Birth Reg. No. 1881/005212
32 AWM War Diary – 31st Battalion AWM4 Subclass – 23/48/12 – July 1916
33 NAA, Service Record, Philip Athol Fargher 2022

ENDNOTES

34 Victorian BDM Indexes – Birth Reg. No. 20948/1890 and Marriage Reg. No. 3565/1903
35 NAA, Service Record, Percy Collier 1057
36 Trove Newspapers, Argus, Monday 14 September 1914, p. 7 (assessed 17 March 2020)
37 Lieut Col H Sloan *The Purple and Gold, A History of the 30th Battalion AIF*, p. 3
38 Ibid, p. 8
39 AWM War Diary, 8th Brigade – AWM4 23/8/8 – July 1916 Appendix B
40 Victorian BDM Indexes, Death Reg. No. 1325/1907
41 NAA, Service Record, Thomas Walker Jones
42 AWM, Australian Red Cross Wounded and Missing Files, Thomas Walker Jones 891
43 Victorian BDM Indexes – Birth Ref: 25922/1897
44 NAA, Service Record, Albert Charles Jenkins 883
45 Victorian BDM Indexes – Birth Reg. No. 28066/1897
46 Ibid – Birth Reg. No. 11239/1883
47 https://www.findagrave.com/memorial/211199041/albert-charles-jenkins (assessed 12 May 2020)
48 Victorian BDM Indexes – Death Reg. No. 847/1898
49 AWM War Diary, AWM4 23/48/12 – July 1916 Appendix D p. 29
50 Ibid Australian Red Cross Wounded and Missing Files – Albert Charles Jenkins
51 Australian War Memorial, AWM/Memorial Articles/Encyclopedia/Battle of Fromelles assessed (12 May 2020)

Chapter 3 – Pozieres & Mouquet Farm 1916

1 Bean, *Official History of Australia in the War 1914-1918*, Vol. 111, p.468
2 AWM, War Diary, Formation Headquarters – AWM4 1/42/18 Part 2, July 1916
3 Meleah Hampton, *The Battle of Pozieres*, p. 141
4 NAA, Service Record, William Patrick Buchan 4147

5   Email, Jasmine Murphy, *MacKillop Family Services*, 6 October 2021
6   AWM, War Diary, 9th Battalion – AWM4 23/26/19 – July 1916.
7   Victorian Birth, Death & Marriages Indexes – Death Reg. No. 18080/1952
8   NAA, Service Records, Charles Henry James Davis 2660A
9   AWM – Australian Red Cross Society Wounded & Missing Enquiry Bureau files 1914-1918 War DRL/0428
10 NAA, Service Records, Cecil Raymond Heaton 493
11 Ancestry.com – *London, England Workhouse Admission and Discharge Records, 1764-1930* (assessed 1 March 2021)
12 NAA, Service Records, Cecil Raymond Heaton 493 Pgs. 105 & 107
13 AWM, War Diary, 9th Battalion – AWM4 23/26/7 – June 1915
14 Trove Newspapers The Register (Adelaide S A 1901-1929) Monday 11 October 1915 pg. 4 (assessed 30 March 2021)
15 NAA, Service Records, John Edward Kenyon 741
16 AWM, Honours and Awards, John Edward Kenyon AWM 28/2/46 Part 1
17 London Gazette No. 29251, Certificate No. 5038, John Edward Kenyon
18 AWMl, Honours and Awards, John Edward Kenyon AWM 28/1/3
19 Trove Newspapers, The Telegraph (Brisbane Qld 1872-1947) Friday 27 July 1917, p.6 (assessed 6 April, 2021)
20 NAA, Service Records, Frederick Howard Arnold Horsfall 177
21 AWM, Roll of Honour Database, Frederick Howard Arnold Horsfall 177
22 The National Archives; Kew, Surrey, England; *War Office: Soldiers' Documents*. Regimental No. 10110
23 New South Wales Australia Unassisted Immigrant Passenger List 1826-1922
24 AWM, Australian Red Cross Wounded and Missing Files, Frederick Horsfall 177

ENDNOTES

25 NAA, Service Record, Richard McDonald 5182
26 https://www.illawarramercury.com.au/story/3023181/tracker-who-went-to-war/ (assessed 19 March 2021)
27 Ibid
28 Trove – Kiama Independent, and Shoalhaven Advertiser, Saturday 26 August 1916, p. 2 (assessed 23 March 2021)
29 Ibid – Saturday 28 April 1917, p. 3
30 New South Wales, Birth, Death and Marriage Index – Death Reg. No. 12084/1949.
31 www.library.kiama.nsw.gov.au (assessed 24 March 2021)
32 AWM, War Diary, 5th Battalion – AWM4 23/22/17 – July 1915
33 Victorian Birth, Death and Marriages Index – Albert Roberts Birth Reg. No. 3929/1887
34 NAA, Service Record, Albert Roberts 1641
35 Bean, *Official History of Australia in the War 1914-1918*, Vol. 111, p. 588
36 New South Wales Births, Deaths & Marriages Indexes – Birth Reg. No. 1/1900
37 State Archives NSW, Index Goal Inmates/Prisoners Photos Index 1870-1930, Item No: [3/6067] Digital ID: IE140646/Series NRS2138/Page No:412 Photo No:8790 (assessed 3 April 2021)
38 Ibid NRS-13495-28-[13/12619]-5392, Divorce Paper Edward and Jessie Cawe (assessed 3 April 2021)
39 Ibid NRS-12922-1 [11/16579]-[415] – Railway Cards Edward Sydney Cawe (assessed 4 April 2021)
40 Queensland Births, Deaths & Marriages Indexes – Marriage Ref: 002591 p.4196
41 NAA, Service Record, Edward Sydney Cawe 2342
42 Ancestry. com au, *Sydney, Australia, Anglican Parish Registers, 1814-2011* (2 April 2021)
43 Trove Newspapers, Illawarra Mercury (Wollongong, NSW 1856-1950), Tuesday 15 February 1916, p. 2 assessed 19 April 2021)

44 Ibid, Friday 6 April 1917, p.8
45 NAA, Service Record, Charles Miller 1044
46 AWM, War Diary, 20th Battalion – AWM4 23/37/12 – July 1916
47 NAA, Service Record, Henry Edwards 538
48 Ibid, Ernest Hogan 2036B
49 AWM, War Diary, 18th Battalion – AWM4 23/35/12 – July 1916
50 NAA, Service Record, Frederick Fawkner 864
51 Ibid, Naturalization – 1914/24162, Peter Pedretti
52 Ibid, Service Record, Peter Pedretti 5404
53 Ibid, Frank McKinnon 3088
54 AWM, War Diary, 3rd Battalion – AWM4 23/20/18 – August 1916
55 NAA, Service Record, George Henry Walker 1645
56 New South Wales Archives – Entrance Books for the Vernon & the Sobraon 1867-1911 (assessed 20 April 2021)
57 AWM, War Diary, 9th Battalion – AWM4 23/26/20 – August 1916
58 NAA, Service Record, William Patrick Bradshaw 5051
59 Ibid, John Lynch 3401
60 Ibid, John Lynch 3401
61 Trove Newspapers, The Daily Telegraph (Sydney NSW: 1883–1930) Wednesday 1 March 1922 P:8 (assessed 2 June 2021)
62 NAA, Service Record, Patrick Walsh 5222
63 https://www.forces-war-records.co.uk/name search (assessed 14 July 2021)
64 NAA, Service Records Alexander Charles Traise 2253 and Jack Herbert Traise 354
65 Ibid, James Clark 3728

Chapter 4 – Flers 1916

1 Bean, *Official History of Australia in the War 1914-1918*, Vol. 111, p. 862
2 Les Carlyon, *The Great War*, p. 270

3   Ancestry.com.au, Australian Birth Indexes 1788 – 1922 (assessed 19 April 2022)
4   Email from School Archivist, St Peters College, Adelaide Thursday 13 October 2022
5   Trove Newspapers, Chronicle (Adelaide, SA : 1895-1954), Saturday 4 November 1916, p. 42 (assessed 2 November 2022)
6   www.angloboerwar.com Oz-Boer War Database Project (assessed 8 August 2022)
7   www.forces-war-records.co.uk/units/5303/ Imperial Light Horse. (assessed 20 August 2022)
8   www.virtualwarmemorialaustralia 5th South Australia Imperial Bushmen. (assessed 20 August 2022)
9   Trove Newspapers, Port Pirie Recorder and North Western Mail (SA : 1898 – 1918), Wednesday 14 May 1902, p. 3 (assessed 10 September 2022)
10 Trove Newspapers, Chronicle (Adelaide, SA : 1895-1954), Saturday 4 November 1916, p. 42 (assessed 10 September 2022)
11 Ancestry.com.uk – Devon, England, Church of England Marriages & Banns 1754-1920 (assessed 20 October 2022)
12 Ancestry.com.au – South Australian Incoming and Outgoing Passenger Lists 1845-1940 (assess 29 October 2022)
13 Ancestry.com.au – England and Wales, National Probate Calendar (Index of Wills and Administrations) 1858-1995 (assessed 1 November 2022)
14 AWM, War Diary, 56th Battalion AWM4 23/73/9 – October 1916
15 NAA, Service Record, William James Day 5361
16 Trove Newspapers, Sydney Morning Herald, Friday 22 December 1916, p.6 (assessed 15 November 2022)
17 NAA, Service Record, James Day 6551
18 New South Wales, Birth Death and Marriage Indexes – Death Reg. No. 856/1918 & 6167/1925
19 Ibid – 6097/1930
20 NAA, Service Record, Alfred John Hopkins 6869

21 Trove Newspapers, Chronicle (Adelaide, SA: (1895-1954), Saturday 25 November 1916, p. 41 (assessed 22 November 2022)
22 AWM, War Diary, 15th Field Ambulance AWM4 26/58/6 – October 1916
23 Trove Newspapers, Australian Christian Commonwealth (SA: 1901-1940), Friday 15 December 1016, p.15 (assessed 19 December 2022)
24 https://www.findagrave.com/memorial/151308937/edna-hopkins (assessed 30 December 2022)
25 NAA, Service Record, Harold Edgar Burton 379
26 AWM, War Diary, 29th Battalion AWM4 23/46/15 – October 1916
27 Ibid, Australian & Red Cross Wounded & Missing File, Enquiry Bureau files, 1914-1918 War 1DRL/0428
28 Victorian, Birth, Death and Marriage Indexes – Birth Reg. No. 10213/1891
29 Ibid Death Reg. No. 8745/1921
30 Bean, *Official History of Australia in the War 1914-1918*, Vol 111, p. 904
31 AWM, War Diary, 27th Battalion, AWM4 23/44/15 – November 1916
32 Ancestry.com.au – Australia, Birth Index, 1788-1922 (assessed 20 November 2022)
33 AWM, Red Cross Wounded and Missing Files, Arthur Hooper 833
34 Trove Newspapers, Chronicle (Adelaide, S.A. 1895-1954 Saturday 23 December 1916, p. 44 (assessed 21 November 2022)
35 NAA, Immigration and Naturalization Records, NAA: A1, 1915/12190
36 Ibid, Service Record, Charlies Alvin Akerlind 1611A
37 https://www/findagrave.com/memorial/56161314-william-charles_wagenknecht-bannister (assessed 22 November 2022)
38 Trove Newspapers, The Advertiser (Adelaide, SA: 1899-1931) Thursday 15 July 1897 p. 5 (assessed 29 November 2022)

39 New South Wales Birth, Death and Marriage Indexes – Death Reg. No. 838/1904
40 Trove Newspapers, The Barrier Miner (Broken Hill, NSW: 1888-1954 Friday 11 January 1907 p. 1 (assessed 9 September 2022)
41 NAA, Service Record, William Charles Bannister 131
42 AWM28 1/10 [Recommendation file for honours and awards. AIF. 1914-18 War] 1st Australian Division 28-8-16 to 3-9-16
43 Ibid War Diary, 3rd Field Ambulance AWM4 26/46/23 – November 1916
44 Trove Newspapers, Barrier Miner (Broken Hill, NSW: 1888-1954), Friday 24 November 1916, p. 2 (assessed 27 September 2022)
45 Victorian, Birth, Death and Marriage Indexes – Death Reg. No.11943/1923
46 NAA, Service Record, William Adam Kinross 3857
47 Ancestry.com.au – Australian Birth Index, 1788-1922 (assessed 30 September 2022)
48 https://aif.adfa.edu.au – Sydney Campbell (assessed 5 October 2022)
49 NAA, Service Record, Sydney Campbell 1111
50 AWM, War Diary, 11th Battalion, AWM4 23/28/1 – August – April 1915

Chapter 5 – Bapaume To Bullecourt 1917

1 Les Carlyon, *The Great War*, p. 298
2 Ibid
3 AWM, War Diary, 13th Battalion, AWM4 23/30/28 – February 1917
4 NAA, Service Record, Martin Hamann 1401
5 Ibid, Abdel Ganivahoff 1703
6 AWM, War Diary, 2nd Pioneer Battalion, AWM4 14/14/6 – August 1916
7 Ibid 19th Battalion, AWM4 23/36/13 – February 1917
8 Les Carlyon, *The Great War*, p. 310

9   AWM, War Diary, 10th Battalion, AWM4 23/27/18 April 1917
10 Ancestry.com.au – South Australian Destitute Asylum Ledgers and Admissions to Industrial and Reformatory Schools, 1849-1913, Register of Admissions to the Lying-in Home 1886-1896 (21 October 2022)
11 NAA, Service Record, Albert Butler 1907
12 AWM, Australian Red Cross Society Wounded and Missing Enquiry Bureau files, 1914-1918 War 1DRL/0428, Albert Butler
13 Victorian, Birth, Death and Marriage Indexes– Henry Stanley, Fredrick Gordon, Caroline and John Davis
14 NAA, Service Record, Captain Henry Stanley Davis
15 AWM, Collection Private Record, 2DRL/0547 – Davis, Henry Stanley Captain
16 Ibid AWM28 1/188 [Recommendation file for honours and awards, AIF, 1914-18 War] 4th Australian Division 7.11.1916 to 21.11.1916 date 19-1-17, Lieutenant Henry Stanley Davis
17 Ibid, War Diary, 46th Battalion, AWM4 23/63/15 April 1917
18 Ibid, Australian Red Cross Society Wounded and Missing Enquiry Bureau files, 1914-1918 War 1DRL/0428 Captain Henry Stanley Davis
19 Ibid, Collection Private Record, 2DRL/0547 – Davis, Henry Stanley Captain
20 Victorian, Birth, Death & Marriage Indexes, Births, Henry Leslie, Alice Maud & Charles Beeson
21 NAA, Service Record, Henry Leslie Beeson 18636
22 Ibid, Charles Beeson 3260A
23 AWM Australian Red Cross Wounded and Missing Enquiry Bureau files 1914-1918 War, 1DRL/0428, Gunner Henry Leslie Beeson 18636
24 Trove Newspapers, Sydney Morning Herald, Saturday 7 June 1919 p.16 (assessed 6 December 2022)
25 Ibid, 7 February 1920 p.14 (assessed 6 December 2022)
26 Ibid, 11 January 1930 p.14 (assessed 6 December 2022)

27 Ancentry.com.au – Australia Birth Index 1788-1922. (assessed 12 December 2022)
28 NAA, Service Record, Hurtle William Emery 2611A
29 Ibid, William John Ireland 1937
30 Ancestery.com.au – Australian Birth Index 1788-1922 (assessed 19 December 2022)
31 AWM, War Diary, 48th Battalion, AWM4 23/65/15 April 1917
32 Ibid, Australian Red Cross Wounded and Missing Enquiry Bureau Files 1914-1918 War, 1DRL/0428 William James Ireland 1937
33 Trove Newspapers, Chronicle (Adelaide SA: 1895 – 1954) Saturday p. 27 (assessed 11 November 2022)
34 NAA, Service Record, William Guest 2756
35 AWM, War Diary, 14th Battalion, AWM4 23/31/14 December 1915
36 Ibid, Australian Red Cross Society Wounded and Missing Enquiry Bureau files 1914-1918 War, 1DRL/0428, Private William Guest 2756
37 Ibid, War Diary, 14th Battalion, AWM4 23/31/30 April 1917
38 Ibid 19th Battalion, AWM 23/36/16 May 1917
39 New South Wales, Birth, Death & Marriage Indexes, Jessie and Ernest Callaway
40 https://www.cricketnsw.com.au/news/norm-callaway (assessed 22 December 2022)
41 NAA, Service Record, Norman Frank Callaway 5794
42 AWM, Australian Red Cross Society Wounded and Missing Enquiry Bureau files 1914-1918 War 1DRL/0428 Norman Callaway 5794
43 https://en.wikipedia.org/wiki/Norman_Callaway. (assessed 23 December 2022)
44 Ancestry.com, Northamptonshire, England, Church of England Baptisms, 1913-1912 (assessed 17 December 2022)
45 Ibid, UK and Ireland Outward Passenger Lists 1890-1960
46 Ibid
47 NAA, Service Record, John Pauling Sives 2228

48 AWM28 1/5 PART 1 – [Recommendation file for honours and awards. AIF. 1914-1918 War] 1st Australian Division 23 to 26.7.1916 Part 1
49 Ibid, AWM28 1/23 1st Division 14-4-17 to 25-4-17
50 Trove Newspapers, Sydney Morning Herald (NSW: 1842-1954) Wednesday 6 June 1917 p.10 (assessed 2 January 2023)
51 https://www.medalsofengland.com (assessed 5 January 2023
52 Victorian Births, Deaths & Marriages Indexes, McKinlay family.
53 NAA, Service Record, Peter McKinlay 2648
54 AWM Australian Red Cross Society Wounded and Missing Enquiry Bureau files 1914-1918 War 1DRL/0428 Peter McKinlay 2648
55 Trove Newspapers, The Age (Melbourne Vic: 1854-1954) Thursday 16 October 1947 p. 9 (assessed 20 December 2023
56 NAA, Service Record, Frederick Arthur Caddy 158
57 NAA, Service Record, Herbert Creagh 4758
58 AWM, War Diary, 54th Battalion, AWM4 23/71/16 May 17
59 Trove Newspapers, Sydney Morning Herald, (NSW: 1842-1954) Wednesday 25 September 1912. (assessed 7 January 2023)
60 New South Wales, Births, Deaths & Marriage Indexes, Creagh family
61 NAA, Service Record, James Kerr 2512
62 England and Wales Civil Registration Birth Index Vol 10B, Line 50
63 Ibid, Vol 10B p.57
64 AWM, War Diary 55th Battalion, AWM4 23/72/15 May 1917
65 Trove Newspapers, The Sun (Sydney NSW: 1910-1954) Thursday 31 March 1921 p. 7 (assessed 14 January 2023)
66 Ibid, The Sydney Morning Herald (NSW: 1842-1954 Wednesday 11 July 1945 p 16 (assessed 17 January 2023)
67 New South Wales, Births, Deaths and Marriages Indexes, Death Sara Kerr, Reg. No 16085/1959

ENDNOTES

Chapter Six – Messines

1 D C Lewis, *Plantation Dream*, https://openresearch-repository.anu.edu.au (assessed 25 January 2023)
2 NAA, Service Record, Frank Osborne 1900
3 Victorian Births, Deaths & Marriages Indexes, Deaths James & Nellie Osborne.
4 Bean, *Official History of Australia in the War 1914-1918*, Vol 1V, ps. 592-3
5 Sydney, Australia, Anglican Parish Registers 1814-2011
6 NAA, Service Record, Eric Burton Chapman 28
7 Roland Perry, Monash: The Outsider Who Won a War, p 271
8 Sydney, Australia, Anglican Parish Registers 1814-2011
9 NAA, Service Record, Edward Laurie Chapman Lieutenant
10 Ibid, Harry Wentworth 2755
11 AWM< Australian Red Cross Society Wounded and Missing Enquiry Bureau files, 1914-18 War 1DRL/0428, 2755 Private Harry Wentworth.
12 NAA, Service Record, James Emanuel Callard 1641
13 New South Wales Births, Deaths & Marriage Indexes – Callard Family
14 New South Wales Australian Registers of Coroners' Inquests, 1821-1937 – 6 May 1907
15 Trove Newspapers, Evening Journal (Adelaide SA: 1869-1912) Saturday 28 August 1901 P. 7 (assessed 30 January 2023)
16 Ibid, Western Grazier (Wilcannia, NSW: 1896-1951, Saturday 15 April 1916, page 2 (assessed 30 January 2023)
17 NAA, Service Record, Leslie Edward Lee
18 AWM, War Diary, 10th Australian Machine Gun Company, AWM4 Subclass 24/25 June 17
19 Victorian Births, Deaths and Marriages Indexes, Death George Lee Reg. No. 6467/1917
20 Ancestry.com.au, Australian Birth Index 1788-1922 p. 461 Vol No. 552 (assessed 1 February 2023)
21 Victorian Births, Deaths and Marriages Indexes, Marriage Isabella Barnes Reg. No. 8998/1910

22 AWM, War Diary, 43rd Battalion, AWM4 Subclass 23/60/1- June 1917
23 NAA, Service Record, John Edward Harold Norman St Claire 2261
24 Ancestry.com.au. Marriage Index 1788-1950 (assessed 3 February 2023)
25 https://www.medalsofengland.com/chinawarmedal (assessed 5 February 2023)
26 Trove Newspapers, Chronicle (Adelaide S A 1895-1954) Saturday 7 July 1917, p. 37 (assessed 15 February 2023)
27 Ancestry.com.au – Australian Electoral Rolls 1925 (assessed 15 February 2023)
28 Queensland Births, Deaths and Marriages Indexes – Ref: 1926/C/7
29 Ibid – Ref: 1959/C/1394
30 Ibid – Birth Ref: 1892/C/10302
31 Ibid – Birth Ref: 1890/C/10733, 1894/C/9765, 1897/C/9902 & 1899C/9834

Chapter Seven – Third Battle of Ypres

1 NAA, Service Record, Leslie Charles Edwin Beard 1717
2 AWM, War Diary, 8th Battalion, AWM4 Subclass 23/25/33 – September 1917
3 Ibid, Australian Red Cross Society Wounded and Missing Enquiry Bureau files, 1914-1918 War IDRL/0428 1717 Private Leslie Charles Edwin Beard.
4 NAA, Service Record, Arthur Noel Russell Blayney 2745
5 AWM, War Diary, 58th Battalion, AWM4 subclass 23/75/20 – September 1917
6 Ibid Australian Red Cross Society Wounded and Missing Enquiry Bureau files, 1914-1918 War IDRL/0428 2745 Private Arthur Noel Russel Blayney
7 Victorian Births, Deaths and Marriages Indexes – Birth & Death Nancy Mary Blayney – Birth Reg. No. 6465/1903 & Death Reg. Mo. 4054/1911

ENDNOTES

8   NAA, Service Record, Thomas Carlin 4013
9   AWM, War Diary, 29th Battalion, AWM4 Subclass 23/46/26 – September 1917
10 NAA, Service Record, Marten Peater Hansen 2917
11 AWM, War Diary, 49th Battalion AWM4 Subclass 23/66/16 – September 1917
12 NAA, Service Record, Albert James Handley 2215
13 AWM, Australian Red Cross Society Wounded and Missing Enquiry Bureau files, 1914-1918 War 1DRL/0428 2215 Private Albert James Handley
14 www.rsl.org/news/battle-for-broodseinde-ridge (assessed 29 March 2023)
15 New South Wales Birth, Death and Marriage Indexes – Birth Reg. No. 377/1899 – John Bradshaw
16 NAA, Service Record, John Bradshaw 3025
17 NSW Police Gazettes 1854-1930, John Bradshaw child desertion, 24 September 1902, p. 373 and 5 October 1904, p. 400 (assessed 22 March 2023)
18 New South Wales Birth, Death and Marriage Indexes, Marriage Surman and Windle Reg. No.190/1929
19 NAA, Service Record, William Love 1868
20 AWM, Australian Red Cross Society Wounded and Missing Enquiry Bureau files, 1914-1918 War 1DRL/0428, 1868 Private William Love
21 NAA, Service Record, John Robert Davidson 389
22 Trove Newspapers, The Age (Melbourne, Vic 1854-1954) Friday 7 December 1906, p. 1 (assessed 4 April 2023)
23 State Archives New South Wales – Divorce Records Index 1873-1923 Divorce No. 4488
24 NAA, Service Record, Walter Liscombe Rowling 981
25 Ibid, William Isles 741
26 https://en.wikpedia.org/wik iQF 18pounders_gun (assessed 12 April 2023)
27 AWM, War Diary, Headquarters 11 AFAB AWM4 Artillery 13/38/21 – October 1917

28 NAA, Service Record, John Burnes 3116
29 AWM, War Diary, 45th Battalion AWM4 23/62/20 – October 1917
30 New South Wales, Birth, Death & Marriages, Birth Indexes John R Beckett Reg. No. 31334/1893
31 NAA, Service Record John Raymond Beckett 773
32 State Archives New South Wales, Coroner's Inquest 1821-1937 2 October 1899
33 Trove Newspapers, Sydney Morning Herald (NSW: (1842-1954)/Wed 8 August 1900 p.2 (assessed 6 June 2023)
34 New South Wales, Birth, Death & Marriage Index Marriage Index Cecelia Beckett Reg. No. 8614/1904
35 Trove Newspapers, Sydney Morning Herald (NSW: 1842-1954) Thursday 30 March 1922, page 8 (assessed 14 June 2023)

Chapter Eight – Villers - Bretonneux 1918

1 AWM, War Diary, 10th Machine Gun Company AWM4 24/15/18 – March 1918
2 NAA, Service Record, Leslie Davis Cairns 1176
3 Western Australia Birth Death and Marriage Indexes, Birth Leslie Davis Kearns Ref: 4389
4 Victoria Birth Death and Mariage Indexes, Birth Edith May Kearns Reg. No. 33923/1892 – Death Edith Mary Kearns Reg. No. 6069/1893
5 AWM, Australian Red Cross Society Wounded and Missing Enquiry Bureau files, 1914-1918 War IDRL/0428 1176 Sergeant Leslie Davis Cairns.
6 https://www.findagrave.com.memorial (assessed 30 June 2023)
7 AWM, War Diary, 45th Battalion, AWM4 23/62/26 – April 1918
8 NAA, Service Record, Charles Archer 1669
9 AWM, War Diary, 47th Battalion, AWM4 23/64/23 – April 1918
10 NAA, Service Record, Michael Joseph Delaney 3728

ENDNOTES

11 UK and Ireland, Outward Passenger Lists 1890-1960
12 NAA, Service Record, James Fitzpatrick 2424
13 ibid
14 AWM, War Diary, 49th Battalion, AWM4 23/66/23 – April 1918
15 NAA, Service Record, Francis Jay Heathcote 4262
16 Ibid Frank Herbert Hancock (Captain)
17 AWM, War Diary, 50th Battalion, AWM4 23/67/2 – August 1916
18 Email received 23 October 2023 from General Manager, Heritage and Information Services – MacKillop Family Services.
19 NAA, Service Record, John Michael Quinn 4578
20 AWM, AWM4 23/68/17 War Diary, 51st Battalion – July 1917
21 Ibid, AWM4 23/68/26 – Ware Diary 51st Battalion – April 1918
22 Australia, Electoral Rolls 1903-1980
23 New South Wales, Birth, Death & Marriage Indexes, Births – Charles James Dillon Reg. No. 15556/1887
24 Ibid – Frank William Dillon Reg. No.15241/1189
25 Ibid Marriage – Bridget Dillon Reg. No.2288/1890
26 Ibid Death – Bridget Montgomery Reg. No. 10710/1906
27 NAA, Service Record, Francis William Dillon 195
28 Ibid, Henry Norman Taylor 1955
29 Ibid, William John Hales 2628
30 AWM, War Diary, 6th Battalion, AWM4 23/23/7 – November 1915
31 Victorian BDM Indexes, Birth George Albert Curnick Hughes Reg. No. 4376/1891 – Arthur Wesley Hughes Reg. No. 23690/1888 – Death Reg. No. 2920/1880
32 NAA, Service Record, George Albert Curnick Hughes 448
33 https://sjmc.gov.au/battle-villers-bretennoeux (assessed 11 October 2023)

Chapter Nine – Amiens to Mont St Quentin

1. Roland Perry *Monash: The Outsider Who Won a War*, ps. 372-374
2. https://www.census.nationalarchives.ie/pages/1901 (assessed 3rd December 2023)
3. NAA Service Record, William Butler 283
4. AWM, War Diary, 26th Battalion, AWM4 23/43/36 – July 1918
5. Ibid AWM4 23/4/37 – August 1918
6. NAA, Service Record, George Harris 634A
7. Australian Birth Indexes – Birth Reginald Stow Kentish Page No.415 Vol. No. 474, Birth Edith Idonia Kentish Page No. 326 Vol. No. 502
8. NAA Service Record, Reginald Stow Kentish 2189
9. Trove Newspapers, Mail (Adelaide, SA:1912-1954), Saturday 22 July 1916, page 8 (assessed 12 December 2023)
10. NAA Service Record, Reginald Stow Kentish 2189.
11. Australian Death Index, 1787–1985 Edith Idonia Kentish page 6430 Vol. 74a
12. Australian Birth Index, 1788-1922, William Charles Page No.337, Vol. No.357, Julia Emmaline Page No.455, Vol. No.402 and Irene Doris Page No.394 Vol. No.505
13. Ibid, Marriage Index, 1788-1950, Page No.343, Vol. No.252
14. NAA, Service Record, William Charles Gibbs 6128
15. Australian Red Cross Wounded and missing Files, 1914-1918 War, 1DRL/0428, Private Angus Livingstone 3480
16. NAA, Service Record, Angus Livingstone 3840
17. NSW, BDM, Angus Baillie, Birth Index Reg: No. 10472/1893
18. Trove Newspapers, Richmond River Hearld and Norther Districts Advertiser (NSW: 1886-1942), Friday 29 November 1918, page 5. (assessed 8 January 2024)
19. Australian Death Index, 1787-1985, Annie Ingham Reg. No. 1830

20 Ibid, Marriage Index, 1788-1959 Frederick Ingham & Henrietta Baker Reg. No. 471
21 NAA, Service Record, William John Robertson Ingham 6039
22 AWM, War Diary, 16th Battalion, AWM4 23/33/15 – February 1917
23 NAA, Series A9300, Service Record, Kenneth Victori Ingham 406456
24 Victorian BDM, Marriage Indexes, Olaf Ferdinand Hoffmeyer and Kate Warren, Ref. No. 5870/1892
25 Ibid, Birth Indexes, Mollie Magdaline Hoffmeyer, Ref. No. 28963/1893 & Norman John Warren Hoffmeyer, Ref: No. 26728/1894
26 Ancestry.com. Victorian, Australia, Index to Naturalization Certificate 1851-1928 (assess 12 January 2024)
27 Ibid, New South Police Gazette, 1854-1930
28 Ibid, Australian Electoral Rolls, 1903-1980
29 NAA, Service Record, Norman John Warren Hoffmeyer 2339
30 Queensland BDM, Birth Indexes, John Edwin Reg: No. 1888/C/10612, William James Reg: No. 1892/C/3141 and Kate Reg: No. 1897/C/10387
31 NAA, Service Record, William James Gawith 6566
32 AWM, War Diary, 25th Battalion, AWM4 223/42/37 – September 1918.
33 AWM, Red Cross Society Wounded and Missing Enquiry Bureau files 1914-18 War 1DRL/0428, William James Gawith 6566
34 Queensland Birth Death & Marriage Indexes, Death – John Edwin Gawith Reg: No. 1963/C/4478 and Kate Gawith Reg: No. 1995/55580
35 NAA, Service Record, Bert Shumack 3721
36 NSW BDM, Birth Index Bertie Shumack Reg: No. 7452/1898
37 NAA, Service Record, Bert Shumack 3721
38 NSW BDM, Marriage Index Elizabeth Ellen Shumack & George McLennan Ref: No. 3278/1901

39 https://www/finagrave.com/memorial/51204205/elizabeth-ellen-mclennan (assessed 16 January 2024)
40 AWM War Diary, 46th Battalion, AWM4 23/63/31- August 1918
41 NAA, Service Record, James Buller 1839A
42 West Yorkshire, England, Church of England Marriage and Banns 1813-1935 James Buller and Eliza Ann Fearnley
43 https://www.findagrave.com/memorial (assessed 17 January 2024)
44 Queensland BDM, Birth Indexes Frederick Watts Reg: No. 1896/B/58850 and George Ernest Watts Reg. No. 1893/B/52662 and Death Indexes Margaret Oliver Watts Reg: No. 1911/B/14054
45 NAA Service Record, Frederick Watts 358 and George Ernest Watts 359
46 AWM War Diary, 15th Battalion, AWM4 23/32/7 – April 1915
47 NAA Service Record, Frederick Watts 358
48 https://www.findagrave.com/memorial (assessed 19 January 2024)

BIBLIOGRAPHY

BOOKS

Adam-Smith Patsy, *The Anzacs*, Penguin Books, Melbourne 2011
Bean, Charles E. W., *Official History of Australia in the War of 1914-1918,* Vol 1, 11th Edition, 1941
------ *Official History of Australia in the War of 1914-1918,* Vol.11, 12th Edition, 1941
------ *Official History of Australia in the War of 1914-1918,* Vol.111, 12th Edition, 1941
------ *Official History of Australian in the War of 1914-1918,* Vol. 1V, 11th Edition, 1941
------ *Official History of Australia in the War of 1914-1918,* Vol. V, 8th Edition 1941
------ *Official History of Australia in the War of 1914-1918,* Vol., V1, 1st Edition, 1942
------ *Official History of Australia in the War of 1914-1918,* Vol. X, 10th Edition, 1941
Bennett, Scott, *Poziéres: The Anzac Story,* Melbourne 2013
Broadbent, Harvey. *Defending Gallipoli: The Turkish Story,* Melbourne University Press, Melbourne 2015
Burness, Peter, *Amiens to the Hindenburg Line,* Department of Veterans' Affairs, Canberra, 2008
Carlyon, Les, *Gallipoli,* Macmillan, Sydney, 2001
------ *The Great War,* Sydney, 2006
Corfield, Robin S., *Don't Forget Me, Cobber, The Battle of Fromelles,* The Miegunyah Press, Carlton, 2009
Coulthart, Ross, *Charles Bean,* HarperCollins Publishers, Sydney 2015

Hampton, Meleah, *The Battle of Pozieres*, Big Skey Publishing, Pty Ltd, Newport, NSW, 2018

FitzSimmons, Peter, *Gallipoli*, Penguin Random House, Sydney, 2015

------ *Fromelles & Pozieres, In the Tranches of Hell*, Penguin Random House, Sydney 2015

------ *Victory at Villers-Bretonneux, Why a French town will never Forget the Anzacs*, Penguin Random House, Sydney, 2016

------ *Monash's Masterpiece, The Battle of Le Hamel and the 93 Minutes that changed the world*, Hachette Australia, Sydney, 2018

Lindsay, Patrick, *Fromelles*, Hardie Grant Books, Prahram, Victoria, 2007

Perry, Roland, *Monash, The Outsider who won a War*, Random House, Sydney, 2004

Rankin, Adam, *The Hindenburg Line, 1918*, Big Sky Publishing, Pty Ltd, Newport, NSW, 2019

Sloan, H, Lieutenant Colonel, *The Purple and Gold, A History of the 30th Battalion (AIF)*, The Naval & Military Press Ltd, Uckfield, East Sussex, England.

Winter, Denis, *25 April 1915, The Inevitable Tragedy*, University of Queensland Press, St. Lucia, Queensland, 1994

ONLINE DATABASES, WEBSITES & DIGITAL MEDIA

Ancestry http://www.ancestry.com/search
- Worcestershire, England, Church of England Deaths & Burials
- UK & Ireland Outward Passenger Lists 1890-1960
- Southwark, London, Surry, England, Poor Law and Board of Guardian Records
- UK Royal Navey Registers of Seaman's Service 1848-1939
- England Census 1881, 1901 & 1911
- Victoria, Australia Corner Inquest Deposition Files 1840-1925
- State Archives NSW; Series: NRS 33902; Item 8/1750
- Australian Electoral Ross, 1903-1980

Sydney, Australia, Anglican Parish Registers 1814-2011
Australian Birth Indexes 1788-1922
Devon, England, Church of England Marriage & Banns 1754-1920
South Australian Incoming and Outgoing Passenger Lists 1845-1940
South Australian Destitute Asylum Ledgers and Admissions to Industrial and Reformatory Schools, 1849-1913
Northamptonshire, England, Church of England Baptisms, 1813-1912
England and Wales Civil Registration Birth Index Vol. 10B, Line 50
Australian Marriage Index 1788-1950
Australian Electoral Rolls 1925
UK and Ireland Outward Passenger Lists 1890-1960
Australian Death Index 1787-1985
Victorian, Australia, Index to Naturalization Certificate 1851-1928

Australian War Memorial, Canberra
AWM 4, Australian Imperial Force Unit War Diaries, 1914-1918
    Artillery - Headquaters
    1st Battalion
    1st Australian Light Horse Regiment
    2nd Pioneer Battalion
    3rd Battalion
    3rd Field Ambulance
    5th Battalion
    6th Battalion
    6th Brigade
    8th Brigade
    8th Battalion
    9th Battalion
    10th Battalion
    10th Machine Gun Company
    11th Battalion

13th Battalion
14th Battalion
15th Battalion
15th Field Ambulance
16th Battalion
18th Battalion
20th Battalion
25th Battalion
26th Battalion
27th Battalion
29th Battalion
31st Battalion
43rd Battalion
45th Battalion
46th Battalion
47th Battalion
48th Battalion
49th Battalion
50th Battalion
51st Battalion
54th Battalion
55th Battalion
56th Battalion
58th Battalion
60th Battalion

Australian War Memorial, Roll of Honour Database
------ Australian Red Cross Society Wounded and Missing Enquiry Bureau files 1914-1918 War DRL/0428
------ AWM/Memorial Articles/Encyclopedia/Battle of Fromelles
------ AWM Honours and Awards 28
------ AWM, Collection Private Records 2DRL/0547

National Archives of Australia – Records
------ Service Records, Series No. B4418 Boer War
------ Service Records, Series No. B2455 World War 1
------ Naturalization Records Series No. A1

National Library of Australia, Trove Newspapers
- Argus (Melbourne Vic: 1848-1957)
- Australian Christian Commonwealth (SA: 1901-1940)
- Chronicle (Adelaide SA: 1895-1954)
- Evening Journal (Adelaide SA: 1869-1912)
- Goulburn Evening Penny Post (NSW: 1881-1940)
- Illawarra Mercury (Wollongong, NSW: 1856-1950)
- Kiama Independent & Shoalhaven Advertiser, (NSW: 1863-1947)
- Mail (Adelaide SA: 1912-1954)
- Port Pirie Recorder & North Western Mail (SA: 1898-1918)
- Richmond River Hearld & Northern Districts Advertiser (NSW: 1886-1942)
- Sunday Times (Perth, WA: 1902-1954)
- Sydney Morning Herald (NSW: 1842-1954)
- The Advertiser (Adelaide SA: 1899-1931)
- The Age, (Melbourne Vic: 1854-1954)
- The Australian Star (Sydney NSW: 1887-1909)
- The Barrier Miner (Broken Hill, NSW: 1888-1954)
- The Daily Telegraph (Sydney NSW: 1883-1930)
- The Mercury (Hobart Tas: 1869-1954)
- The Sun (Sydney NSW: 1910-1954)
- The Register (Adelaide SA: 1901-1929)
- The Telegraph (Brisbane Qld: 1872-1947)
- Weekly Times (Melbourne Vic: 1869-1954)

New South Wales State Archives
- Entrance Books (Industrial Schools Branch) Series NRS 3902
- Index Goal Inmates/Prisoners Series NRS 2138
- Divorce Papers Series NRS 13495
- Railway Cards Series NRS 12922

New South Wales Birth, Death & Marriage Indexes
Queensland Birth, Death & Marriage Indexes
Public Records Office Victoria – Online Collections
Victorian Birth, Marriage & Death Indexes
Western Australian Birth, Death & Marriage Indexes

Index

1

13th Clearing Hospital, Enoggera 209
16th Bavarian Regiment 45
16th Queens Lancers 65
1st Australian Auxiliary Hospital at Harefield
1st Auxiliary Norfolk War Hospital 135
1st Battalion Scottish Horse 90
1st Imperial Light Horse 90
1st Southern General Hospital, Birmingham 111
1st South General Hospital, Birmingham 111

2

20th Casualty Clearing Station 188
26th General Hospital 88
2nd Australian General Hospital at Ghezirth Palace 41
2nd Imperial Light Horse 96

5

5th South Australian Imperial Contingent 96

A

Abbassia 37, 120
Ailly-le-Haut-Clocher 95
Aker, Lieutenant Colonel Sefik 3
Akerlind, Charlie Alvin 105
Albany 14
Albert 74, 103
Albert-Bapaume Road 61
Alexandria 1, 2, 14, 31, 36, 38, 50
Alexandria (Chatby) Military and War Memorial Cemetery 31
Allison, Mrs Lilian Maud 178
Amiens 191, 198
Ancre River 172
Anderson, Mrs Erica 105
Annie, Arnold 47
Anzac Cove 3, 18, 21, 29, 30, 36, 79, 81, 136, 188
Anzac Cove. 136, 188
Archer, Charles 174

245

Ari Burnu   *3*
Armentieres   41, 42, 44, *61*, 149
Armistice   i, *60*, 210
Arnold, Walter Smith   *47*
Arnold, William   *47*
Arnold, William Watkin   *49*
Aubers Ridge   43, *45*
Aubigny   *183*
Aubigny British Cemetery   *185*
Australian Red Cross   *58*

B

Bailey, William   111
Baillie, Miss Nellie Frances   *198*
Bannister, Helen   106
Bannister, William Charles   106
Bapaume   62, 116
Bapaume Road   *62*
Bardon, Frank   30
Barry, William   *51*
Bartlett, Annie   137
Base Records   i, 6, 8, 10, 12, 14, 46, 49, 52, 58, 67, *69*, 70, *75*, 76, 81, 82, 85, 86, 87, 99, 101, 109, 110, 112, 114, 118, 126, 135, 137, 146, 147, 151, 152, 157, 159, 161, 162, 163, 167, 168, 169, 175, 176, 178, 180, 182, 183, 185, 186, 188, 193, 194, 195, 198, 203, 205, 208, 209, 210
Base Records.   *49*
Bayonet, Trench   104

Beard, Elizabeth Lillian   155
Beard, Leslie Charles Edwin   155
Beckett, John Raymond   *169*
Beckett, Thomas Edward   *169*
Beech, Lance Corporal William   37
Beeson, Charles & Alice   122
Beeson, Henry Leslie   122
Belgium   126, 141, 143, 145, 147, 148, 149, 151, 152, 153, 156, 157, 158, 160, 161, 162, 163, 166, 168, 169, 182
Bendigo Lying-in Hospital   *58*
Bennett, Miss Esther   *193*
Bigambul and Kamilaroi people   18
Birdwood, General Sir William   2, 16, *49*
Blackboy Hill   133, 199
Blayney, Arthur Noel   156
Blayney, Oliver   156
Boar's Head   42
Bodkin, Rev. Brother   *182*
Boer War   10, *66*, 90, 96, *174*
Bolton's Ridge   *24*
Botha, General   96
Boursises   133
Boves Wood   *193*
Bradley, James   116
Bradshaw, John   161
Bradshaw, John & Ellen   161
Bradshaw, William Patrick   *88*
Brennan, Miss May   82
Broodseinde Ridge   161, 162, 166
Brown, Lieutenant Charles Dan   84
Buchan, William Patrick   63

Bullecourt   125, 126, 127, 128, 132, 133, 135, 136, 138, 139, 140, 148, 168, 176, 190, 195, 206, 209
Buller, Albert & Charlotte   207
Buller, James   *206*
Bulls Road Military Cemetery   103
Burnes, John   *168*
Burrell, J A   *76*
Burton, Harold Edgar   102
Bussus   102
Butler, Albert   116
Butler, James & Marianne   *192*
Butler, Jane   116
Butler, William   *192*
Butler, William Henry   116

C

Cabaret Rouge British Cemetery   128
Caddy, Frederick Arthur   136
Caddy, William   137
Cairns, Sergeant Leslie Davis   *173*
Cairo   1, 78
Callard, James Emanuel   148
Callard, James Emanuel & Mildred   148
Callard, Mildred   148
Callaway, Norman Frank   129
Callaway, Thomas & Emily   129
Campbell, Sydney   110
Cape Helles   18, 20, *76*, 136, 165, 188, 190
Cape Helles Memorial   19, 21
Cario   156, 208
Carlin, Thomas   157
Carter, Esther Eva   120
Carton, 2/Lieutenant S J J   128
Cawe, Edward Sydney   77
Cawe, Edward Sydney & Jessie Maria   77
Central Methodist Missions Children's Home "Dalmar"   79
Cerisy-Gailly Military Cemetery   *194*
Chapman, Edgar & Emily   143
Chapman, Eric Burton   143
Chapman, Lieutenant Colonel A E   30
Chapman, Lieuteneant Edward Laurie   143
Chapman, Lydill Edgar Elliott   143
China Boxer Rebellion   151
Chiplin, Gladys   *205*
Clark, Alfred James   26
Clark, Alice   27
Clarke, James   92
Clark, Miss J   *175*
Clontarf Orphanage, Victoria Park   111
Cobb, Maud   *70*
Cockroft, Private   157
Codford   147, 159, 161, 194, 205, 206
Collier, Percy   54
Collier, Sarah   54
Contalmaison   *73*
Cook, Gaston   *27*

Cooper, Edward Leslie Barnes   150
Cooper, Henry   *184*
Cooper, Sergeant Alf   90
Cottonera Military Hospital   136
Courcelette   94
Courcelette British Cemetery   92
Court of Enquiry   6, *8*, *10*, 11, *16*, *44*, 64, 81, 85, 125, 126, 157, 158, 177, 209
Creagh, Herbert   138
Creagh, John & Alice   138
Creagh, John (Jack) & Arthur Frederick   139
Croix de Guerre   120
Crouy British Cemetery   198

D

Dale J   83
Damakjelik Bair   30
Daours Communal Cemetery Extension   *205*
Davidson, John & Elizabeth   165
Davidson, John Robert   165
Davis, Captain Henry Stanley   119
Davis, Charles Henry James   *64*
Davis, Frederick Gordon   119
Day, Albert   99
Day, James Snr   98
Day, Margaret   98
Day, Miss Fanny   19
Day, William James   98
Deakin, Vera   126
Delaney, Michael Joseph   *175*

Delville Wood   142, 145, 156, 157, 180
Demicourt   133
Dernancourt   *174*, *175*, *176*, *182*
Dernancourt Communal Cemetery   109
de Wet, General Christiaan   96
Diamantina Hospital Brisbane   *178*
Dicker, Kathleen Mary   97
Dillon, Bridget   *184*
Dillon, Francis William   *184*
Dillpm. Charles James   *184*
Distinguished Conduct Medal   66, 69
Doignies   140
Dunn, Miss Lucy Elizabeth   67
Du Rieu, Miss H   110
Durrant, Lieutenant-Colonel   113
Dutton, Mrs   131

E

Eastern Transvaal   96
Ecoust Military Cemetery   123
Edward & Elizabeth Oliver   31
Edwards, Henry   81
Egypt   1, 5, 19, 26, 27, 36, 37, 42, 43, 50, 54, 63, *64*, 71, 78, 81, 82, 85, 87, 100, 102, 104, 108, 110, 115, 135, 136, 138, 148, 156, 165, 167, 174, 192
Egyptian State Railway Workshops   37
Elliott, Lieutenant-Colonel Harold Edward   45, *46*, 156

Emery, Hurtle William   123
Emery James & Mary   123
Etaples   *192*
Etaples Military Cemetery   88
Evers, Frederick & Emile   35
Evers, Otto Lessing   35

F

Fallen, Mrs Alice   163
Fargher, Philip Athol   52
Fearnley, Eliza Ann   206
Fergus, Frederick   21
Ferry Post   42, 43, *47*, *48*, 56, *59*, 138
Field, James   *31*
First Battle of Krithia   18
Fitzpatrick, James   *176*
Fitzpatrick, Joseph   *176*
Flers   94, 102, 103, 105, 107, 110, 142, 168, 200
Floyce/Floyd, Mrs Margaret   82
Folkstone   195
France   i, 6, 10, 38, 39, 40, 41, *47*, 48, 50, 51, 54, 60, 61, 64, 67, 70, 75, 76, 78, 81, 82, 85, 87, 90, 94, 97, 99, 101, 105, 106, 108, 110, 115, 116, 118, 125, 127, 128, 129, 130, 131, 132, 133, 135, 136, 139, 142, 145, 147, 148, 149, 151, 153, 157, 158, 159, 161, 162, 163, 165, 166, 169, 170, 173, 175, 178, 180, 181, 184, 186, 187, 188, 190, 191, 192, 194, 195, 197, 198, 199, 200, 202, 203, 205, 206, 209, 210
Fraser, Sergeant Simon   60
Frederick, Fawkner   82
Frew, Susannah   106
Fromelles   42, *46*, 47, *48*, 50, 56, *57*, *58*, *60*, 94, 138
Fulham Military Hospital, Hammersmith   166

G

Gaba Tepe   66
Gallipoli   i, 2, 6, *8*, *9*, 14, 18, 22, *26*, *27*, 31, 35, 36, 37, *38*, 39, 40, *51*, 54, *65*, 70, 71, 77, 81, 91, 102, 104, 107, 111, 118, 127, 132, 136, 152, 153, 155, 165, 167, 169, 178, 179, 184, 185, 187, 188, 190, 192, 208, 210
Garnet, Mr E   *206*
Gaston, Cook   27
Gawith, Joseph & Henrietta   *202*
Gawith, William James   *202*
Genivahoff, Abdul   115
Gibbs, Charles   *196*
Gibbs, William Charles   *196*
Gibbs, William & Julia   *196*
Gilbert, Mr Horace   131
Godley, General Alexander   16
Gough, General Sir Hubert   *61*, 119
Gray, Robert George   *181*
Green, Mr A W   25
Grevillers British Cemetery   131, 139
Grove Town Cemetery Meaulte   97

INDEX

Guest. Edward   127
Guest, George & Maria   127
Guest, William   127
Gueudecourt   94

H

Haig, General Sir Douglas   94, 113
Haking, Major-General Sir Richard   42, *43*
Hales, William John   *187*
Halstead, M E   *69*
Hamann, Annie   114
Hamann, Martin   114
Hamel   *200*
Hamilton, General Sir Ernest   *66*
Hamilton, General Sir Ian   2
Hancock, Captain Frank Herbert   *179*
Hancock, Emma   *180*
Hancock, Laura   *180*
Hancourt British Cemetery   210
Handley, Albert James   160
Handley, Thomas & Mary Ann   160
Hansen, Marten Peater   159
Hansen, Private Henry   147
Harbonnieres   *200*
Harding, Mr W J   *64*
Harris, George   *193*
Hart, Esther   40
Hart, Owen   40
Havre   157
Hayward, Mrs & Mrs   16
Heath Cemetery, Harbonnieres   *200*

Heathcote, Francis Jay   *177*
Heath Military Cemetery   195
Heaton, Cecil Raymond   *65*
Heilly Station Cemetery, Mericourt-L'Abbe   107
Heliopolis   142, 174
Hill 160   *61*
Hill 60   30
Hindenburg Line   128, 129, 136, 181, 191, 200, 201, 209
Hoffmeyer, Marjory   *201*
Hoffmeyer, Norman John Warren   *201*
Hoffmeyer, Olaf & Kate   *201*
Hogan, Ernest   81
Holborn Military Hospital   *184*
Holland, Mr William   *168*
Hooper, Alfred & Eliza   104
Hooper, Arthur Henry   104
Hopkins, Alfred John   100
Hopkins, Alfred Stanley & Clara   100
Horsfall, Frederick Howard Arnold   *71*
Horsfall, Frederick & Louise   *71*
Howson, Martha   102
Hughes, Albert Curnick   *188*
Hughes, William George & Isabella   *188*
Hunter, James   *178*
Hunter-Weston, General Aylmer   18
Hurdcott   158
Hutt, Emanuel   148

I

Ingham, Frederick & Annie *199*
Ingham, Henrietta *199*
Ingham, William John Robertson *199*
Ingram, Kenneth Victor *200*
Ingram, Private John *43*
Ireland, John & Florence *125*
Ireland, Thomas James *125*
Ireland, William John *125*
Isles/islis, Henry *167*
Isles/Islis, William *167*

J

James, Harry *147*
Jenkins, Albert Charles *58*
Jenkins, Elizabeth *58*
Jenkins, Mary *58*
Jenkins, William David *58*
Jones, Albert & Ellen *56*
Jones, Alice Maud (May) *50*
Jones, David & Clara *49*
Jones, George *18*
Jones, Herbert Evan *49*
Jones, Maurice Theodore *50*
Jones, Thomas *163*
Jones, Thomas Walker *56*

K

Kandahar Farm Cemetery *147*
Kastberg, Miss Ruby *47*
Kearns, Frederick & Sarah *173*
Kearns, Rev. John Thomas *173*
Kellie, Hugh & Annabel *132*
Kelly, Mrs Cecilia *169*
Kemal, Lieutenant-Colonel Mustafa *11*, 15
Kentish, Albert Stow & Edith *194*
Kentish, Edith Idonia *195*
Kentish, Reginald Stow *194*
Kenyon, John Edward *69*
Kerr, Franklin G *139*
Kerr, James *139*
Kilburn Sisters *24*, *25*
Kimberley Light Horse *90*
Kinross, William Adam *110*
Kinross, William & Annie *110*
Kirby, Geraldine, Walter Owen & Charles *153*
Kirby, Henry & Mary May *152*
Kirby, Ralph Oswald *152*
Kitson, Arthur Frederick *19*
Knulla, William *17*
Krithia *136*, *165*, *188*
Kroger, Private H H *103*

L

Langham Hotel *65*
Leane, Captain Raymond *126*
Lean, Major James ii, 12, 15, 21, 75, 81
Lee, George *149*
Lee, Leslie Edward *149*
Lemnos Island *135*
Le Transloy *95*, *97*
Lijssenthoek Military Cemetery *161*

INDEX

Livingstone, Angus *198*
Lodge Hill Cemetery,
  Birmingham 112
Lone Pine 7, 8, *11*, 13, 16, 17,
  18, 26, *27*, 132, 155, 210
Lone Pine Memorial 7, 8,
  11, 13, 16, 17, 18
Louverval 116
Love, William 163
Lowry, May Eveline 77
Ludendorff, Commander Erick *192*
Lynch, Bernard 89
Lynch, John 88
Lyssenthock Military Cemetery *169*

M

Maclagan, Major General,
  E G Sinclair 210
Madigan, John Thomas 104
Malt Trench 115
Marcentelli, Mrs Beatrice *185*
Marseilles 38, 42, *48*, *50*, *52*, *56*,
  63, *64*, 73, 78, 79, 81, 84, 89,
  91, 99, 100, 102, 118, 127,
  138, 168, 176, 185, 187
Marsh, John Charles 28
Marsh, John Garrett & Clara 28
Marsh, Second Lieutenant
  Cyril Godfrey 28
Matthews, Private 130
Maud, Maynard 43
Mayne, Alfred 17
McCann, Miss Ellen *63*

McCay, Major-General
  James 42, *45*, *60*, 98
McDonald, Alexander &
  Elizabeth 109
McDonald, Richard (Dick) *73*
McKenzie, Private A 135
McKinlay, Peter 133
McKinlay, Peter & Berthia 133
McKinley, Annie 110
McKinnon, Catherine 85
McKinnon, Elizabeth 85
McKinnon, Frank 85
McLean, Samuel *64*
McMenamin. Eliza Jane *184*
Mena Camp 208
Menin Gate Memorial 166
Menin Road 155, 165
Mentioned in Despatches *66*,
  69, 133, 180
Merville Communal Cemetery 40
Messines 141, 143, 145, 147,
  148, 152, 153, 155, 166, 168,
  169, 171, 176, 178, 182, 202
Messines Ridge 141, 143,
  145, 147, 153
Messines Ridge British
  Cemetery 147
Midgley, Sapper E 78
Miles, Private William *60*
Military Cemetery, Bugnicourt, 128
Military Cemetery Rue Petillon 41
Military Cemetery, Sailly-
  sur-la-Lys *44*

Military Hospital Bethnal Green   39
Military Medal   *70*, 132, 133, 153, 209, 210
Miller, Esther   79
Milne Bay,   141
Ming, Joseph   *8*
M'Kenzie, Major D   96
Moascar   42
Monaghan, Messrs R, J & M   148
Monash, Brigadier-General John   141, 145, *191*
Montgomery, George   *184*
Morgan, Lieutenant   *43*
Morrow, Miss A M   *75*
Mortimer, Captain Kenneth   *60*
Mouquet Farm   162, 168, 180, 181, 185
Mrs Mackey   39
Mudros   125, 127
Mudros Harbour   2
Murdoch, Major Alexander   *60*
Murphy, Private F J   79
Murphy, Reverend W G   *47*

N

Nek   28
Newman, Henry & Harriett   130
Newman, Miss Esme Theila Jean   67
Newman, William Allan   130
New South Wales Police Gazette   *10*
Nicholas, William   137
Nicholson, Mr Henry Donald   115
Nies, Peter Joseph   89

Noreuil   125, 127, 133, 140, 147, 182
Noreuil Australian Cemetery   140
North-West Afghanistan   *66*

O

Oliver, Second Lieutenant Cecil Claude   *31*
O'Malley, Mr   118
Orange River Colony   96
Osborne, Alexander Henry   12
Osborne, Amy   12
Osborne, Gunner Frank Robert Warlward   141
Osborne, James Robert & Nellie   141
O'Sullivan, William   *43*
O'Sullivan, William & Emily   43
Otago Battalion   18

P

Passchendaele   *168, 169, 171, 176, 195, 202*
Patent Periscopic Sight   37
Paterson, Miss Adeline Agnes   23
Paton, General   104
Payne, Elsie Edith   *197*
Pedretti, Michele (Mick)   84
Pedretti, Peter   84
Pennells, Charles   ii
Pennells, Charles Percy   13
Pennells, Harriett Selina   13

INDEX

Pennells, James & Mary   13
Perham Downs   162, 182, 184, 192, 198, 200
Peronne Communal Cemetery Extension.   *203*
Pike, Sergenant J G   122
Ploegsteert Wood   145, *180*
Polygon Wood   *157, 160, 168, 170, 178, 190*
Pope, Lieutenant Colonel Harold   14
Pope's Post   27
Port Moresby   25
Potter, A/Sgt. Allan   44
Pozieres   61, *62*, 63, *67*, 70, 73, *77*, 92, 107, 111, 127, 132, 168, 170, 206
Pozieres British Cemetery   67
Prince of Wales   210
Purnell, Captain   121

Q

Quinn. Henry & Maud   *183*
Quinn, John Michael   *181*
Quinn, Kate   *183*
Quinn's Post   24, 208

R

Rabaul   25, 36
Rayson, Captain Hugh   *44*
Robb, John George   17
Robert, Albert   *76*
Roberts, Albert & Totten   *76*
Roberts, Isabella Turner   149

Robertson, Brigade General J C   121
Robertson, Lieutenant-General Sir William   120
Robinson, Ellen   43
Roff, Thomas   *13*
Rollestone   178
Roman Catholic Boys Orphanage, Subiaco   *181*
Rosieres Communal Cemetery Extension   *197*
Rowling, Walter Elder & Rosaline   166
Rowling, Walter Liscombe   166
Royal Australian Artillery   *10*
Royal Australian Naval Reserve   54
Royal Navy   *19*
Royal West Sussex Hospital, Chichester   111
Rue-Petillon Military Cemetery   *52, 56*
Russell's Top   24, 81, *185*

S

Sailly   70
Sausage Valley   *62*, 79
Selby, Mrs Reg   165
Shearer, Charles & Ellen   *51*
Shell Green Cemetery   35
Shrapnel Gully   *26*
Shrapnel Valley Cemetery   15
Shumack, Elizabeth   *204*
Shumack, John & Richard   *204*
Simcock, Mrs Annie   151
Sir George White   66

Sir Power Palmer 66
Sives, 2nd Lieutenant John Pauling 132
Sives, Elizabeth 132
Smith-Dorrien, Major-General 96
Smith, Ellen 47
Smith, John & Alice 16
Smith, Sydney Thomas 15
Sobraon 34, 87
Solly, Arthur 47
Solomon, Mrs Dinah 194
Somme 42, 44, 61, 63, 94, 95, 100, 106, 107, 110, 111, 120, 172, 198
South Africa 17
South African Light Horse 10
South Midlands Field Ambulance 74
Southwark Hospital and Infirmary 8
Spriggins, Miss B 159
Staines, Miss Violet 65
State Children Relief Board 89
St Claire, John Edward Harold 151
Steenbecque 79
Steenvoorde 106
Steenwercke 67
Stent, Ellen Vannan 53
Stewart, Captain William Malcom 95
Stewart, Robert & Gertrude 95
St George's Union at Westminster 66
Stormy Trench 113
Strathie, Miss Sarah 88
Suez 47, 51, 56, 57, 73
Sugar Loaf 42

Sugar Loaf. 42
Sullivan, Ellen 87
Surman, Ellen 162
Surman, Mrs Martha 161
Sussex, Charles Joshua 10
Sussex, Joshua 10
Sussex, Joshua David 10
Sussex, Maria 10
Sutchkoff, Private 177
Swain, Eliza 24
Swain, Frederick Cecil 24
Sweetman, Alexander 12
Sydney Benevolent Asylum 89

T

Taylor, Henry Norman 185
Taylor, Miss Violet 87
Tel El Kebir 42
Tel-El-Kebir 16, 47, 48, 51, 78, 132, 153, 161, 170, 206
Terlincthun British Cemetery 207
Third Battle of Ypres 157, 167
Thursday Island 25, 36
Tirah Campaign 66
Toowong Cemetery Brisbane 210
Traise, Alexander Charles 90
Traise, Charles & Agnes 90
Traise, Jack Herbert 91
Tyne Cot Cemetery 163

U

USA Cavalry 151

INDEX

V

Valetta, Malta   22
Vaughan's Mansion, Roman Catholic Refuge   116
VC   *49*
VC Corner Australia Cemetery and Memorial   *54*
VC Corner Australian Cemetery and Memorial   *58*
VC Corner Cemetery and Memorial, Fromelles   47
Victorian Child Welfare   12
Victoria Police Gazette   *10*
Vignacourt British Cemetery   *188*
Villers-Bretonneux   *64, 65, 70, 73, 78, 81, 82, 83, 85, 87, 89, 90, 91, 99, 105, 110, 118, 121, 125, 130, 133, 136, 138, 153, 174, 175, 177, 178, 180, 181, 182, 183, 185, 186, 190, 193, 194, 209*
Villers-Bretonneux Memorial   *64, 65, 70, 73,* 125, 130, 133, 136, 138, 153, 175, 177, 178, 183, 186
Villers–Bretonneux Military Cemetery   *174*
Voges, Annie Teresa   137
Voges, Ernest Frederick   137

W

Wagenknecht, Otto & Mary   106
Walker, General Harold   *61*

Walker, George Henry   86
Walker, George Richard   87
Walker, Mrs N   86
Walkers Ridge   114
Walker, Thomas   87
Walsh, Patrick   89
Wandsworth Hospital   132
Ware, Jane   81
Warloy-Baillon Military Cemetery   *74*
Watts, Ernest George   208
Watts, Ernest George & Margaret   208
Watts, Frederick   208
Watts, George Ernest   208
Waverly Cemetery   23
Wentworth, Alice   147
Wentworth, Harry   147
Westhoekridge   *169*
Westhoek Ridge   *186*
Westhop Farm Cemetery   143
Whitburn, Mr   25
White, Lieutenant Colonel Alexander Henry   28
White, Sir Cyril Brudenell   37
Willcox, George   *7*
Williams, Arthur Frederick   20
Williams, Charles Llewellyn   *8*
Williams, James Francis   137
Williams, Mary Jane   136
Williams, Mr J   19
Wilson, Henry   *46*
Wilson, Nora   40
Wilson, William   39
Wingate, Sir Francis   66

Workhouse of the Guardians of the Poor   13
Wytschaete   143

Y

Young, Jean   151
Young, Miss Tess   82
Young, Mr J M   *12*
Ypres   103, 106

Ypres (Menin Gate) Memorial   145, 151, 152, 157, 158, 160, 162, 167, 168
Ypres Salient   94
Yungaburra Rifle Club   *25*

Z

Zonnebeke   166
Zululand   96

www.ingramcontent.com/pod-product-compliance
Lightning Source LLC
Chambersburg PA
CBHW040302170426
43194CB00021B/2867